VACHEL LINDSAY

Photograph by Roy N. Kirshburg.

Vachel Lindsay.

VACHEL LINDSAY

A POET IN AMERICA

By

Edgar Lee Masters

CHARLES SCRIBNER'S SONS
NEW YORK . . LONDON
1935

INTRODUCTION

WHEN the friends and admirers of Vachel Lindsay first suggested that I was the one to write his biography and appraise his work, I was reluctant to undertake the task, both because I had other work on hand, and of an absorbing kind, and because I did not at once perceive that anything more than a factual chronicle could be made of his life. His poems, accessible to every one, seemed his own revelation, and an all-sufficient record of what he had lived and felt. However, when Mrs. Vachel Lindsay asked me to write the life of her husband, and when her letters on the subject disclosed such a wealth of material bearing upon the art of poetry, and upon the period of American life in which Vachel Lindsay lived and wrought, the subject took on an aspect so appealing that I felt that I could not decline the responsibility, the duty as it came to look, of writing this biographical study. Moreover, at some time I should have been impelled to write something about the poet who was native to Illinois, as I am in reality, and who knew the same people and the same culture that I do, and who practised the art of poetry, as I have, in the same part of America, and under the same social and political conditions. The Illinois country which he knew I also know, and have known all my life, including his own town of Springfield; and the New Salem and Petersburg neighborhood is mine by nativity, and was his by a life-long devotion to Lincoln. Therefore I understood, perhaps, better than any one, the character of his environment, the quality of the people among whom he lived. I knew the man himself, and saw him frequently from the beginning of his fame in about 1914 to 1926. Our relationship was fostered and then strengthened by the friendship which existed between our mothers; and some few letters exchanged between us along the years kept our sympathies and interest in each other alive.

The death of Lindsay was a great shock to me, since when I saw him last in 1926 he seemed destined to many years of life, to which his known and reputed habits gave assurance. A correspondence with Mrs. Lindsay, initiated by a letter of condolence from me, soon began to contain reminiscence on my part of her late husband as well as remarks upon his work; and on her part biographical confidences which increased my interest in his life. Then when the idea of writing this book was still tentative her revelations of her late husband's intimate difficulties and the courage which he strove to summon for their solution made me feel that the life of Lindsay was an American story of the first importance.

It was not only her keen critical comment on the biographical value of his letters and papers, which existed in great abundance, but her desire to turn over to me the whole of this material, or whatever I wanted, that led me from my state of hesitation about writing Lindsay's biography to an enthusiastic determination to do the best I could in a study of his life and work. For here was an American who was a pure instance of the poet by profession, who had devoted all his life to the preparation and the practice of poetry. I say this in spite of the fact that he tried for ten years to be an artist, and never during his life gave up that ambition. But while he was doing this he was writing verse, and much that he studied of painting and drawing was adjutant to the art of poetry.

When Mrs. Lindsay sent me Lindsay's diaries from the time he was eight years old to the time of his death, besides great folders of letters and other documents, I saw by a preliminary survey of this material that significant use could be made of it by way of a cultural study, and an analysis of a very baffling nature, and both American through and through. Lindsay's ancestry, his education, his religion, his morals, his tastes were Middle West, they were American in that peculiar sense, they were rooted in that Anglo-Saxonism which was one of his devotions, and which is American as Virginia, Tennessee, and Kentucky are American, and as his part of Illinois and mine are American. In brief, after spending some weeks in a study of these papers I could not resist the attempt to present Lindsay to the students in the schools of America, to those interested in the culture of America, to lovers of poetry and to posterity as I summed him from these records which he left, and as I knew him face to face. I had the purpose then to portray him as he lived and thought, as he struggled and sang, as he grew and failed to grow, as he had strength and was weak, as he surmounted the American prejudices and the Philistine mockers who dogged his steps, and as he fell a prey to them, and in a measure was at last overcome by them.

Relying upon these diaries, and upon his letters and other papers I have shown year by year "the growth of the poet's mind," to use Wordsworth's words; not neglecting to report his acts and movements and outer life, and attending fully to his lineage, his environment, his reading, education, contacts, and whatever went to the making of the man he was at his best, and his worst.

This book therefore is both a study of his mind and art, his character and his psychology; and it is also objective history in the biographical sense, which parallels and antiphonically explains his reactions and his achievements and his failures. What is here presented could not have come to pass without the sympathetic assistance of Mrs. Lindsay who gathered and classified the material spoken of, and who wrote me keen analyses of doubtful subjects along the way, and without reserve placed at my disposal whatever I asked to know. Her intuitive understanding of biography as truth, and of its insignificance when it is fiction or glossing has been invaluable to me. Any reception given this book should not fail to remember her intelligent co-operation, for which I had instant admiration, and now express my thanks for thus publicly.

If I could write one sentence that would magnify the vision of readers to a clearer reading of Vachel Lindsay's art and its problems, it would be this: Not in England, and in a measure with leisure, as was the case with Tennyson; but in America and against poverty, and the fatigues of a life of lecturing, did Vachel Lindsay pour forth his wholly original songs, songs more numerous than those of Poe, and nearly equal to the bulk of Whitman's. Not working with a rather calm mind like Tennyson's, richly schooled, and in quiet hours, but with a mind of Swedenborgian visions, and perplexed perspectives, and strange tumultuous fires and dreams, did Lindsay create the "Santa Fé Trail," the "Chinese Nightingale," and the "John Brown Trilogy." Mrs. Lindsay summed the whole matter in these words: "Much of Vachel's suffering was conditioned by his own personal endowment and special problems. To me it is a miracle that out of it, and it was always pain and darkness at the root, and unhealed wounds that grew deeper with the years, came not only the magnificent songs, the noble and valiant statement of truth and beauty, the mystic's vision, but until time and physical weakness pulled him down with a sense of ultimate impending defeat, a gallantry and high spirits, a deep communion with ultimate primal joys, such as laughter, rhythm, the play spirit, the roots of the country in which he lived, its legend and meaning, the color and significance of the many streams which have gone to the making of it; and always the ability to pierce below the shoddy and the temporal into the underlying reality, and to make clear to thousands of people, who are for that stronger and more aware, who could understand his idom, his dramatizing of it for them, and be lifted a step beyond their own dull plane, without realizing what had happened to them. It was a deeply sacrificial life, and a glorious one, and it did not end in defeat. It will never end."

The life and work of Vachel Lindsay are therefore the precious possessions of America. It would be well for the country if the conviction could become prevalent that martial heroism is only one kind, and perhaps not the highest. It is a vision which cannot penetrate beyond externals, which fails to see as much will and courage in Leopardi as it sees in Wellington, for example, and which can dilate upon the singleness of purpose in Grant or Lee, and overlook the resolution and faith of Poe. Who will not see as much strength of character and high resolve in Vachel Lindsay as panegyrists attribute to Wilson? Both lived at the same time. Which one contributed more to the enlightenment, the splendor, and the culture of America? Let time answer this question, as it will.

Edgar Lee Masters.

ILLUSTRATIONS

VACHEL LINDSAY

CHAPTER I

SPRINGFIELD, Illinois, destined to be the birthplace of Vachel Lindsay, started in 1820 as a colony known as Newsonville, formed chiefly of a Kelly family from North Carolina; then by a curious irony, as history unfolded, it was platted in 1823 and named after John C. Calhoun. A few years later the town was incorporated as Springfield, and in 1837 became the place of residence of Lincoln, who led the War between the States in which the constitutional philosophy of Calhoun was crushed. History seemed to see to it that the man who after Lincoln became the most famous citizen of this spot of earth, and whose poems on Lincoln are the most memorable in our literature, should not be born and nurtured in a town called Calhoun. We shall see that the poet's work is an answer to the lamentation, uttered before his day, that America has been lacking in tradition and stories of wonder of which literature can be made. For this Illinois country, and Sangamon County, in which Springfield is located, is an old country, and is replete with material for songs to the discerning genius. It was to this land that La Salle came from France in 1682, and took possession of Illinois, dreaming of a passage down its rivers into the great Mississippi, and from thence to the South Seas by a new way to the riches of Japan and China. It was here, too, that Marquette roamed, converting the Indians to Christianity, and where forts were built and rivers explored, and the prairie tramped over from end to end. A hundred years and more after La Salle, George Rogers Clark seized by force of arms the Vincennes and Illinois country; and by 1779 by group effort and single-handed endeavor and courage the wilderness was beginning to be subdued.

Springfield is situated upon a beautiful prairie, with fields of corn and wheat coming to the very edges of the town; from which the level land stretches afar and around, diversified here and there by rims of forests and groves of oak trees on rises of ground, and by the grass-grown banks of small creeks. This Springfield prairie extends from the Sangamon River on the north, to the timber lands which are intersected by its tributaries on the south. To this rich soil in the early part of the nineteenth century flocked an admixture of many nations, characters, languages, conditions, and opinions. They came from many States of the Union; and there was a large colony of Portuguese who settled here in an early day. But Springfield itself was recruited largely from Kentucky. From that State came such men as Ninian W. Edwards, the first territorial governor of Illinois; and Benjamin S. Edwards, his son, and John M. Palmer, later a governor and senator of Illinois; and also Lincoln, who first settled near Decatur, some thirty miles from Springfield; and then toward 1830 got over to the New Salem village, and finally to Springfield when that town became the capital, in 1837. There was wonder in the building of Springfield from a log-cabin settlement to the brick and stone of a small capital city; and in the growth of Chicago nearly 200 miles north; and the poet fed upon the chronicles of the pioneers, and the achievements of their sons, from his earliest breath. It was something to make an imaginative child grow open-eyed with wonder to hear of the first log courthouse of 1821, of the frame courthouse of 1824; of the more substantial structure of brick in 1830; of the removal of the capital, when a new courthouse was put up costing nearly $10,000, and when the center of the square was surrendered for the new statehouse, a building of limestone, which grew stained with brown rust and venerable in appearance with the years. Before the poet's birth in 1879 the present statehouse had been constructed at fabulous expense for those days on an elevation west of the square, and not far from the house where he was born and where he died in 1931. He grew up on the stories of the days fifty years before his birth concerning the labors and the diversions of the first people there; of the activities and grocery-store wrangles of Lincoln and Douglas, who had come to a town called Winchester, Illinois, from far north Vermont, about 1833. There were men in plenty in the poet's youth who remembered the buffalo grass and the wild flowers, which spread over the prairie land, and who told of wolf hunts, and the menace of strolling Indians; and of the early religious revivals, and the preaching of that Peter Cartwright, a picturesque divine born in Virginia, who became notable enough in central Illinois to be known far and wide over America, and who was buried at Pleasant Plains in Cartwright Township, Sangamon County, when death came to him in advanced old age, not many years before the poet was born. The central Indiana country where the poet's mother was born and reared was not dissimilar from this spot of Illinois. Both localities abounded in tales of primitive weddings and festivals, of bee hunts and snake hunts, for the Illinois country was infested at first with the venomous rattlesnake. Distinctively of the Springfield territory there were reminiscences of the tornado at Sugar Creek, the cholera plague of the 'forties, the snow blockade of 1863, and the California emigrants when gold was discovered at Sutter's Mill. And as the Kentucky stocks predominated here there was much talk of Daniel Boone, and the log-cabin joys of that land, and of the fiddlers and the dancers, the race-horses and the hospitalities, the blue grass and the wooded hills, and the romance of the Ohio River in the days of flat-boats and of the beginning of steam. If the poet had no classical education, and no life in a household where the myths of Greece were dwelt upon as the substance of a youth's training; if he had no Lemprière, as Keats had, he was nevertheless blessed with the fresh and fragrant atmosphere of this rich localism. Other youths had been born into this primitive culture, and had learned of its beginnings, only to depart in a matter of fact way into business or some of the professions. With Vachel Lindsay this whole storehouse of Americanism entered passionately into his being and became the food of his imagination, his dreams, and his aspirations for his country and for magical Springfield. We can well imagine, considering the poet's later observations of flowers and the details of landscapes, that he acutely noted the characteristics of this Springfield country, probably on drives with his father, who, as the good physician there, set about night or day in his buggy visiting the sick. Though the buffalo grass was gone when the poet was a boy, there remained the white blossoms of the May-apple in the woods and the Indian turnips, the brown-eyed Susans and horse mint by the roadsides, and the beautiful stretches of green meadows under Illinois skies as blue and enchanting in the June days as any in the world.

The poet's father was Doctor Vachel Thomas Lindsay, who was born in Gallatin County, Kentucky, August 31, 1843. There is a suggestion by one genealogist that the Lindsays and Lincoln were related, taking as a supposition first that Nancy Hanks, the mother of Lincoln, was the daughter of Lucy Shipley Hanks. Three Shipley brothers came to America as early as 1680 and settled in Anne Arundel County, Maryland, near Baltimore. In 1754 there was a Shipley child who was named Vachel. The Shipley and Hanks families intermarried in Anne Arundel County. It is a coincidence, too, that Thomas Lincoln, the father of Lincoln, bought from George Lindsay the so-called Knob Creek farm in Kentucky. There is a record at Bourbon County, Kentucky, of the marriage of a Vachel Lindsay with Anna Cushenbury in 1792.

Doctor Lindsay's father was a large landowner in Kentucky before the Civil War. During that struggle his farm was devastated, his horses were stolen, and he and his family were reduced to poverty. These distressing consequences bore heavily upon the son Vachel Thomas Lindsay, at the time a young man of eighteen or so. As one studies the life of the poet, with its restless aspirations caught and trammelled by rather sparing means and the intermittent schooling which in part resulted from it, one speculates upon the extent to which his growth and success were retarded by the fateful strife of North and South a decade or more before he entered innocently upon the scene and the circumstances which had been made for him. This grandfather of the poet, as an indignant victim of a war which he hated, kept to the last his sympathies with the South; though like many Kentuckians, and many in Illinois as well who shared his opposition to the conquest of the South, he preferred that the Union should be preserved. Doctor Lindsay, according to the poet, was haunted to the last by a vision of this implacable and unregenerate old father in Kentucky, who lived in blindness in an old log cabin, lamenting the loss of his fine farm, which had been taken from him upon mortgages engineered by those buccaneers known as carpet-baggers, who, to punish the South for its great sin, proceeded to carry out the revenges of moralists by confiscating the property of vanquished men. He never gave up his wrath and his pride. To the last he carried a gold-headed cane, he wore a long-tailed coat, and an old-fashioned plug hat. A strange spectacle he presented, tapping ahead with his gold-headed cane to find the way, and venting his indignation at the captains and politicians, and their principles of Constitutional construction which had brought him to this pass in his declining years. Thus accoutered and tempered he was accustomed to urge his son, the doctor-to-be, to forge ahead to success, in spite of the War and its demoralizing consequences. The assertion of such a will characterized the pioneers, those who first crossed the Alleghanies; it can be noted in the lives of the men who made a garden of Illinois and Indiana; and in no generation of Americans is it more noticeable than in the spiritual life of the poet himself.

[5]

Doctor Lindsay as a child of the War had enough of difficulty to overcome to test the stoutest heart; and to the last he bore the effect of the wounds which had been dealt his father in those bloody days in Kentucky. He received no better than a common school education, such as his neighborhood in Kentucky afforded. Soon he was teaching school, and studying medicine at night after school hours and work on the farm. After a short time he went to Miami Medical College at Cincinnati, Ohio, but only for a year. And then at twenty-three years of age he came to Illinois, and took up his residence in Sangamon County, in the township called Cotton Hill, a few miles southeast of Springfield. Here he stayed for two years, then he returned to Miami Medical College, from which he was graduated in 1869; then he resumed his residence in Cotton Hill, where in 1875 he married a Miss Couch, who died the same year. With that ambition which mounted and fought in the breasts of poor youths in this time and place of America, he set forth, in this year of loss, for Vienna to perfect himself there, in the hospitals, for a larger field of professional work than that of Cotton Hill. On the boat over he met Esther Catharine Frazee of Rush County, Indiana, then twenty-seven years of age, who had saved enough money from teaching mathematics and painting at Glendale Female College, Indiana, and at Hocker College, Lexington, Kentucky, to travel through Europe, where she might see the great pictures, and perfect her artistic taste and practice. Miss Frazee became ill in Rome, where Doctor Lindsay attended her, assisted by Eudora Lindsay, the doctor's sister, who was Miss Frazee's companion on this trip. A romance which had started, before the journey was commenced, between Doctor Lindsay and Miss Frazee, resulted in their marriage later, on returning to America.

In some of the pictures of Doctor Lindsay facial characteristics emerge upon study which can be recognized in the face of the poet, though in only a few of them. For the most part the poet took the imprint of his mother's countenance. The heavy ridge which was over his eyes, selected by phrenologists as the seat of perception, required the combined beetling of both his father and mother to construct it; and his retreating forehead was inherited from neither parent. In earlier photographs Doctor Lindsay's forehead shot up with perpendicular ruggedness; in later photographs, those taken near the time of his death in 1918, a symmetrical fullness had smoothed out the temple of the brain. Perhaps all in all it may be said that the poet's brow more nearly resembled his mother's than his father's; but in truth only fleeting similarities to either parent can be caught in the poet's face. He did not measure up to his father in physical magnitude or vigor. The doctor was a large, strong, black-bearded man, impulsive and resolute, who for long years drove about the country of Springfield bringing children into the world and recommending the buggy whip as a treatment for delirium tremens. The doctor was a fanatical prohibitionist always and hated tobacco with a deadly hate. The old buggy which he kept to the last, even after the automobile had come into full use, was stuffed with bottles like a travelling apothecary; with surgical instruments, with all the paraphernalia which he had carried about with him in his rural practice at Cotton Hill in 1875. According to a report made by the poet the doctor charged two dollars a call for white people. He treated the colored people gratis. As Springfield was one-fifth made up of Negroes the doctor had enough professional work attending to them alone; but there was no source of income here to enable the poet to study and reflect upon art and life and poetry. The Civil War and the doctor's professional principles took their toll on the poet. The doctor could not or did not adjust himself to a new age, which rapidly came over him, just as it did over the lawyers who were born in the forties in this part of Illinois, and who suddenly saw new principles and prac-

[7]

tices, dictated by corporations and the concentration of wealth, taking hold of an old and well-beloved jurisprudence, that jurisprudence which grew out of Jeffersonism and the Constitutional Fathers of democratic blood. When Springfield became a small city of 60,000 or more, and in the middays of the World War, it was an exciting spectacle to see Doctor Lindsay driving a rattling old buggy, with a fifty-five-year-old buffalo robe dangling from the shafts. He was still the good and benevolent country physician, who knew his business no less in that intimate way which has been to a degree lost by the supremacy of specialists. Of moral qualities of an old-fashioned sort he had enough.

In 1931 the poet wrote a confession of what he owed this father. He was a Bible democrat, wrote the poet; a transplanted Kentuckian who retained his Southern ways and prejudices. He had less enthusiasm for Lincoln than the poet had, and less than the poet's mother had. In fact, the doctor never forgave Lincoln for invading the South and for freeing the slaves by a confiscation which impoverished so many Southern families. His other Bible was the oath of Hippocrates, which he had printed and framed, and kept hung on the wall of his waiting room. "The Sermon on the Mount harnessed the savage in him," declared the poet; "the oath of Hippocrates harnessed the citizen. He was not too much of a democrat. His Kentucky pride was stronger than any medicine he ever gave." This virile, conscientious, primitive man went on for more than forty years in Springfield attending industriously to his profession, devoting himself to the Campbellite Church, supporting his family, rearing his children in comfort, and sending them to college. He labored to get advantages in life for himself and family, and increasing knowledge for himself; and like the eager spirits of the American suburbs he wanted to see other lands. In 1904, 1906, 1908, and 1910 he and his wife travelled in Europe; and in 1914 they went to Japan and China. The

passion for restless wandering, which the poet manifested all
his life, was fairly inherited; and indeed from the time of
the first emigration over the Alleghanies, down to the days
of the California trek, and later to the hegira of Illinoisians
into Iowa and Kansas and Nebraska, a feature of the middle
eighties of the last century, something in the American blood
has led its sons away and afar.

The poet confessed that he looked back to his father, as
the father had looked back to his, the blind farmer in Kentucky, that is, as the "terrific foe of woe and weariness."
One concludes after an examination of the records of this
family, so far as they are commandable, that the poet's
mother lived spiritually alone, in spite of the fact that she
and her husband shared the same religious faith, and the
same creed of family and social life. Perhaps convictions
concerning the justice of the Civil War divided them
slightly. For not only the environment of the Lindsay home,
but the environment of Kentucky Springfield itself, divided
the poet's heart, who declared in his maturity that the Mason
and Dixon line went straight through his thinking and nature, setting on one side a love for the culture of the South,
of Virginia in particular; and on the other side an admiration for Lincoln as the great national hero. But whatever
Mrs. Lindsay's inner attitude was toward her husband, it is
clear enough that the poet from the first shrank from the
masculine vigor, the robustious tempo of this Doctor Lindsay. The poet was in search of the soul of the U. S. A. The
soul of the U. S. A. was his quest and his pearl; and with
this adventure the doctor was evidently out of sympathy as
something highly visionary, and as untoward to practical
economics and that respect for money which early poverty,
a hard life, and a determination to overcome the disadvan-
tages of youth had bred in him to the very bone.

The poet from the first adopted the wise artistic method
of portraying himself and his feelings, his family and bio-

graphical confidences by dramatic mediums. And here it may be said that his poetical work from the first is as free from sentimental romantic oblations as any poet of this or any other time. His love poems were always delicately interwoven with symbols or dramatic devices. Let poems of this sort be compared to the effusions of the pavement-bred poetasters of New York, and elsewhere in America, and it will be seen how Lindsay exercised a fine taste and artistry in these matters from the first. What is important here, however, is the cryptic manner in which Lindsay dealt with his father in the poem called "Doctor Mohawk"; and also in like manner with his mother in the poem called "The Hearth Eternal." The point in hand can be elucidated by mention of Cowper's poem on his mother, and by Bryant's express references to his father. Lindsay took the way of indirection, of figurative language and symbolical summations. It is true that the titles of the various strophes of this poem are explicit enough; we are concerned here with the poetical method. How then, according to this poem, did Lindsay as a small boy regard his father, the doctor? He thought he had an eye like a tommyhawk, that he was tough stock, and old stock, that he was a furious swashbuckler, a street brawler, and world breaker; that he was an American dragon, with a buffalo beard, all beast, yet human. One can see the little boy clinging to a tender and sympathetic mother when this dark, powerful figure comes into the room after a ride in that rattling buggy to the country. The poet called him in this poem sire of Saint Tammany; also he named him Joseph Smith and Brigham Young, an old son of the sun-fire, doctor and midwife; but he had given long claws to the poet, and breathed fire through him. Lindsay confessed that he wept with his mother when the old Mohawk cried, "shame to you, coward and mourner." Here is a curled darling of a boy, resisting the manly contacts of a strong father, and turning to an indulgent mother, who teaches him to sing and to play, and tells him of the Spanish ancestor who transmitted Castilian blood through the poet's mother to the imaginative veins of the budding poet. The father has come into the room and gone his way somewhere, and the boy weeps for a time, and then is consoled with songs and tales. Then Lindsay has a grown-up hour on the Gulf of Mexico, perhaps on the occasion when he felt exiled from Springfield, to which we shall come. And there he dived and brought up the pearl, that is the vision of the soul of the U. S. A. And in that moment, as he wrote, he was as far from the Mohawk as peace from murder, as far as from May to November, as far as love is from scorning, as far as snow is from fire. These are hard words enough. But then he takes another view in this poem of his father, who becomes in this hour of recollected boyhood a good reprover and corrector, a good medicine man, a wise friend speaking with fine scorning for the poet for hunting favors with rabbits or men. The fire of the Mohawk is felt burning through himself, and the long claws inherited from the Mohawk grow into favorable appreciation. Lindsay's filial experience is not lacking in similarity to that of Goethe, whose mother was of altogether genial character, and whose father a stern disciplinarian, kept the future creator of Faust hard at law and other studies. We may read happy words of Goethe's visits to his mother, and of long peaceful hours spent in affectionate and understanding converse with her. Whitman, too, paid many tributes to his fine and perfect mother, and often sat in leisurely gossip with her. This speaks well for a man, and augurs something sound and vital, magnetic and promising in him, as of things that come out of the creative earth of human life. It may be said in conclusion of Lindsay's father that he was a man with a strong sense of duty; and no one can read of his labors and struggles without believing that he did his best without ceasing or varying. He did not accumulate riches, and perhaps by that fact did not expose the poet to their perils; and he did not surround the poet with the poverty of Burns. Neither did he give him ease, but rather mountains to climb, endowing him with enough strength with which to make the ascent. In a word the poet was not entombed between a gold throne and a mountain, as Jean Paul phrased the life problem, in that place where so many giant spirits, as he wrote, lie crushed. It seems that it was his mother who gave him the spiritual fire by which he lighted himself and went on to the end. He was his mother's rather than his father's son. She was the more gifted of the parents of the poet, and to her we turn for a careful delineation.

The Frazee family has been a notable one of doctors and lawyers in Indiana and various parts of the South. Doctor Ephraim Frazee, the great-grandfather of the poet, was of Mason County, Kentucky, whose great-grandfather was Joseph Frazee born in England in the seventeenth century, and who died in America in 1713. Doctor Frazee married Susan Doniphan, who was a direct descendant of Don Alexander Iphan. His grandson, Mott Doniphan, married a daughter of Sir Walter Anderson; and their great-granddaughter, Susan Doniphan, became the wife of Doctor Frazee of Mason County, Kentucky. The Spanish blood in the poet came from this family of Doniphans, or Don Iphan, as it was at the start. Ephraim Samuel Frazee was a son of Doctor Frazee and Susan Doniphan. He was born in 1824 in Mayslick, Kentucky, and died in 1896, in Rush County, Indiana. And as the grandfather of the poet he needs especial notice, since the poet as a youth frequently paid visits to the grandfather in Indiana, and was accustomed to receive letters frequently from this affectionate and preceptoral ancestor.

Susan Doniphan Frazee was left a widow at an early time by the death of Doctor Frazee, and for many years of her widowhood she kept a store in Germantown, Kentucky, in partnership with her kinsman, Joseph Frazee. Her son, Ephraim Samuel Frazee, together with herself, had inherited from Doctor Frazee a farm of 640 acres in Rush County, Indiana; and after a time she left the store in Germantown and went to the Indiana farm. Later still, and when Ephraim Samuel Frazee was fourteen years old, he followed his mother to Rush County, riding the distance on horseback. The date of this journey was in 1838, just at about the time that Springfield had become important as the capital of Illinois. Reaching the little town of Laurel, Indiana, the youth lost his directions, and stopped at a house to inquire the way on and to get lodging for the night. The family appealed to could not accommodate him, but sent him on a short distance farther to the home of Deacon Austen. There he was taken in; and when the deacon learned that he was the son of Widow Frazee, every hospitality was shown him. The deacon had a daughter then twelve years old, Frances by name, who attracted the eyes of the youth. In eight years he married this Frances Austen, who thus became the maternal grandmother of the poet Lindsay.

There is something of the poet's protruding brow, something of the eager expression of the eyes, and the alert animation of the whole face in the face of Ephraim Samuel Frazee, who is entitled an honorable, and was known as a reverend, as we learn from the genealogical book entitled *Ancestral Lines of the Doniphan-Frazee-Hamilton Families*, by Frances Frazee Hamilton, issued in 1928. This book, full of pictures of various branches of these families taken in groups and on occasions, here and there in Indiana and Kentucky and Mississippi, shows blood of unmistakable American enterprise and respectability. But to return to the maternal grandparents of the poet, there is nothing discernible in the countenance of Frances Austen Frazee to connect her with her famous grandson. So it is that the look of eyes, the shapes of noses and mouths, and things more subtle than these get washed away in the mixture of blood.

Ephraim Samuel Frazee was a very different type of man in nature and conviction from blind Grandfather Lindsay in Kentucky, and certainly had a very dissimilar experience in life. By 1860 Ephraim had built himself an excellent house in Rush County, two stories in height, with an ornate porch around the front door, whose upper part was roofed by a triangular gable decorated with scallops pointed with trefoils. Immediately in this gable was a small window, and back under the ceiling of this projected architecture a door which opened on to the upper part of the porch, and admitted one to the upper rooms of the house. The house had blinds, and the yard was planted with evergreens, and provided with necessary walks. It was far from being an imitation of Southern houses; it was rather what was being built in the Victorian days, in the sixties and seventies of America, in villages, and at times upon the farms. It was an un-æsthetic departure from the log-cabin tradition, and failed ignorantly to perpetuate in Indiana colonial features such as ample porches and great chimneys for fireplaces, which here and there in Indiana and Illinois, too, were carried over from Virginia and Kentucky.

When the Civil War came on, Ephraim Samuel Frazee was thirty-seven years old. He then had seven children; but above all he was a minister of the gospel; and though his heart was with the North he did not go to battle. He had two elder brothers who were for the South. His mother was also in sympathy with that side, and was very bitter against the North. One glance at the face of this farmer-preacher, however, shows clearly that his stand on any subject would be hard to change, and that any cause which was carried on in the name of morality would likely have his zealous support. Therefore when Lee surrendered at Appomattox, Ephraim Samuel Frazee stood for three hours ringing the large dinner bell, which was used to call the men from the fields to their meals. He rejoiced exceedingly at what the old blind grandfather in Kentucky uttered dreadful imprecations in the expression of lasting hate.

We must consider as briefly as possible the activities of this enterprising and in many ways typical American, for what bearing they may have on his grandson, the poet. He soon became a leader in many things in the county of Rush. He was a preacher, a teacher, a politician, a breeder of registered cattle and of Percheron, Norman, and Clydesdale horses. Reading of what he did day by day shows clearly enough that the nervous activity of Esther Catharine Frazee, the poet's mother, was clearly inherited from this man whose motto seemed to be to work before the night comes, when no man can work. That was the rule of life of the more successful pioneers of Indiana and Illinois. He also manufactured tile for his own land, and tiled his land. He was the first farmer in the neighborhood to have a reaper, a buggy, a double plow, a wheat binder, screens for windows, a washing machine, a clothes wringer, and like contrivances of a labor-saving character. In 1875 he gave a show of short-horn cattle and won the prize, as later he won many prizes for fine stock. He organized the first live-stock association in America. He had a gravel road made from Fayetteville to Falmouth, Indiana; and from the latter place to Rushville. He maintained a home where there was no gossip, no idle talk, no intermeddling with the affairs of neighbors. There was daily worship and reading of the Bible. His preaching about the country required research in which his wife, of keen critical mind, as it is said in this genealogical book, took a helpful part. His principal preaching was at Orange, Indiana, where he was known during a ministry of forty years as a near-bishop. In 1846 he had received a diploma from Bethany College, Virginia, signed by Alexander Campbell, the president of the institution, and with his father Thomas Campbell the founder of the Disciples of Christ Church,

[15]

more generally known as the Campbellites. Never was the doctrine that to train a child in the way that he should go will ensure his adherence to it for life better exemplified than in the life of Lindsay, the poet. He had this grandfather for an exemplar; and he paid the old farmer-preacher pioneer a high tribute in the poem "The Proud Farmer," one of his earlier productions, recited with others in the West when he was expounding the gospel of beauty and begging his way across the continent. Lindsay celebrated his grandfather in this poem as a man who stood towering above the furtive souls around him, whose brow had no stain, whose fearless eye made folk wonder at a democrat who was also well-nigh a king; who read by night, and toiled by day, who was a statesman of the fields, who served a rigid Christ, who burned a lamp of family worth and clear integrity; whose story must be heard with reverence, and with feelings of kinship by those of the lion-eyed breed who wish to build the world.

Esther Catharine Frazee was the first child born of Ephraim Samuel Frazee and Frances Austen Frazee, and from the first showed a happy mingling of maternal and paternal inheritances. She carried on her father's spirit for leadership and executive ability, and her mother's quieter faculties of analysis and penetration. As the mother-to-be of the poet she must be as carefully appraised as possible, not only for what of mind and will she bequeathed to this son, who was that mysterious being known as a genius, but because she had so much to do with his training and environment. One reads of her as of one who from her first day of life was occupied busily with serious things, and who never rested except when weary nature compelled her to do so. There in the farmhouse of her preacher-farmer father she was not only the stay of her mother in all household duties, but she was using what time remained after these were done in studies and the reading of books. Her religious education was conducted from the first under a sort of benign attention and in an atmosphere where no doubt crept in, and no hostile speculation had a voice. Nor was she amenable to such influences. Her thinking and the expansion of her mind progressed without hindrance within the boundaries of the Bible and Christian literature; nor is it to be forgotten that born of such a father in that time and place in America she was intellectually content with the materials upon which her mind fed. It is impossible to think of Reverend Frazee, especially if one may at the same time look upon his photograph, without seeing that self-confidence and power of will abode in his nature. The daughter had these qualities of character too. At twelve years of age her energy and household activity carried her to the task of picking blackberries on a hot day in July. Those who know the Indiana country will recall at once what a hot day in July is in a latitude somewhat south of Indianapolis. And one can well imagine the eager industry with which the girl went ahead, oblivious of the heat and her own danger, in her ambition to have the task done. While so engaged she received a sunstroke, which was so severe that her nervous system suffered an affection which remained with her for life. How much of this sensitivity, to a degree pathological, she transmitted to the poet need not here be investigated. One may indulge the belief that something of fire strung the nerves of the poet, perhaps from this misadventure; for the poet as a wanderer, a singer, and a lover of the long road was in truth a child of the sun.

There was a seminary just across the highway from her father's home, where the daughter prepared herself for entrance to Glendale Female College, which she entered as a junior, and from which she was graduated in 1869 as valedictorian, and with the highest honors. On this occasion she wrote and delivered the class poem. It speaks for her nature to note that she stood perfect in her marks from the beginning to the end of her course. All of this is revelatory of that America when remote places of life, remote from cities and magical centers of culture spurred the aspiring young, determined to rise from inferior levels, to use every moment of time and to achieve excellence to the utmost. One wonders if that America has wholly passed away; and if so what shall take its place that is as good for the country. During these days this dutiful daughter was helping her mother with the work of the house, often ironing far into the night, the twenty or more shirts of young gentlemen guests, the kinfolk of the Frazees who came frequently to this hearth of great hospitality and abundance. She was also teaching school at home, though part of the time nearly blind as the result of the unfortunate sun-stroke.

After her graduation she taught mathematics at Glendale Female College, and there she took up the study of painting, as she did later at Hocker College, at Lexington, Kentucky, where she attained a certain proficiency in landscapes. At Glendale her instructor was a Miss Birdsall, who had studied abroad; and at Hocker College, Miss Frazee became one of the instructors in art. Thus we are on the way now to the ambition of Lindsay, who some thirty years later was to be consumed with a desire to be an artist, and who has left strange drawings of maps of the universe and Blake-like sketches, but who saw in time that poetry was his medium and turned to it with the same consecration and sincerity which distinguished all the activities of this ardent-minded and aspiring mother.

At Hocker College one of the associate teachers was Eudora Lindsay, a sister of the poet's father-to-be. Eudora was preparing to take a trip to Europe; and Miss Frazee had herself saved enough money from her salary as a teacher to go along. Doctor Lindsay, now of Cotton Hill, in Sangamon County, Illinois, had decided upon a course in Vienna, and had planned to accompany his sister Eudora. But the question arose in the Frazee household, particularly in the breast of Reverend Frazee, if it were a proper thing for Esther Catharine to be on the same boat to Europe with this incipient suitor, even though Eudora were present to act as chaperone. To settle this grave question Doctor Lindsay was invited to the Rush County home, where he received a careful consideration at the hands of Reverend Frazee; and being approved the party set forth. The sailing trip and the travels on land gave sufficient opportunity for wooing; but it was Miss Frazee's illness of Roman fever in Rome, with Doctor Lindsay as the efficient attendant, which doubtless rounded to the full the romantic interest.

On Thanksgiving Day, amid a profusion of bittersweet, cones of fir trees, and pods of various sorts from the flower garden, Doctor Lindsay and Miss Frazee were married in the Frazee house already described. The bride's dress had been made in Paris, the officiating clergyman was the president of Butler University, and the ceremony was as elaborate and ritualistic as possible, accompanied by prayers and heavenly blessings, and followed by a great country dinner with many Frazees present to rejoice in the festivities. The couple left for Springfield, Illinois, where the doctor had already established himself, and there at once they took up their residence at 603 South Fifth Street in a house once owned and occupied by a sister of Mrs. Abraham Lincoln. This was their abode for life. The poet was born and died at last in this house. America needs more of this sort of constancy to the one hearth. It is one of the cures of the restless wandering which has come over to Americans from the emigrations of the pioneers. We shall see that the poet was not able to call this house his home throughout his life; but it is gratifying that he passionately wanted that he might have done so.

Doctor Lindsay was devout, and his wife was equally so. In consequence the couple started at once to take an active part in the Disciples Church of Springfield. Mrs. Lindsay showed her talent and her desire for leadership from the beginning in her new home. Oratory ran in her blood, as it did in the blood of Americans at that time. The gift was nurtured at colleges; the oratorical prizes were much handsomer than those for essays; while prizes for poems were rare, if heard of at all. Poetry was not taught in those days, or looked upon with nurturing favor. In consequence Mrs. Lindsay began to be a speaker on occasions and upon civic subjects. She was an organizer too, and brought into being such societies as the Woman's Missionary Social Union, the Via Christi Study Class, which was accustomed to meet in her home every other Monday with an attendance of about forty persons. Along the way of her life Mrs. Lindsay wrote several booklets; she contributed to *The Missionary Tidings, The Christian Century*, and *The Christian Evangelist*. She made more formal and elaborate addresses at conventions of Campbellites. She was a delegate to the Ecumenical Congress of the World held in Edinburgh in 1910, one of the years in which she and her husband toured Europe. All the while her house in Springfield was a place of bounteous hospitality; she was rearing her children, and the doctor might conceivably have been more prosperous. Despite his rugged appearance he was not always in perfect health; and as he neared sixty he showed signs of breaking under the strain of professional work and domestic care.

One would think that such strenuous activities as these would have fully engaged Mrs. Lindsay's energies; but there were many others, of which some mention may be made. The poet, in the preface to his *Collected Poems*, refers with some humor to her staging miracle plays and what she called colloquys, to take off the curse of a stage designation. In the Kentucky College she had adventured into this field together with painting and oratory. And so, later in Springfield, she produced in the church a dramatic composition entitled "Olympus." In this play of "Olympus" the characters ranged from Mercury to Father Time, with Uncle John Lindsay taking the part of Neptune, as his long red beard and tall stature well fitted him for this impersonation. The Sunday-school superintendent, draped in artificial grapes, took the part of Bacchus. The poet, at this time a curled darling, a sort of Little Lord Fauntleroy, as one gathers from the report, much adored by his mother, and already filled full with the idea of becoming an artist, was made into a dramatic figure of Cupid. The poet wondered to the last how his mother circumvented the rigorous asceticism of the Disciples Church to the extent of producing this pagan spectacle; but he observed in a preface that she was then a "riot," and with never-resting energy was accomplishing many wonders, including that of having the elders of the church approve this heathen colloquy. It flushed her with a sense of victory to have achieved this miracle; and at the time she was full of pride over the success of a paper which she read before the Illinois Art Association on the subject of the Italian Madonnas. Before the time of this colloquy the blind Grandfather Lindsay, who hated all effeminacy, had made Mrs. Lindsay cut off the golden curls which adorned the head of the poet-to-be; but at the time that it was given the curls had grown again, and Mrs. Lindsay's tears were well dried after having obeyed the thundering commands of the old rebel walking about with his gold-headed cane, in his high hat, and cursing Lincoln. The night before the colloquy was given the boy's hair had to be put up in papers by his mother, and so he came on the pulpit platform with the locks of an infant Apollo, dressed in a pink slip with dove's wings sewed to the back, and carrying a silver pasteboard bow and a quiver of arrows. Thus dressed, the boy Vachel Lindsay climbed into the pulpit with his Sunday-school teacher, who was taking the part of Venus, carrying a golden apple in her hand. Often this

Sunday-school teacher had told the boy of the virtuous adventures of Joseph, of the wisdom and courage of Moses, and of the sufferings of the Jews under Pharaoh. Now she was to let her beauty speak for her, together with lines composed for the occasion by Mrs. Lindsay in which Venus was made to speak in the language of the Song of Songs, put forth as the love song of Christ for the Church.

There was still another colloquy in which nations, not pagan gods, were made to speak, given on Washington's Birthday, first in the church, later in the Y. M. C. A. Hall. This colloquy, the poet confessed, contained the germ idea of his subsequent "Litany of the Heroes." All her life this eager, ambitious woman went on writing oracles and making speeches, organizing societies, urging civic reforms, reading religious books, studying about Egypt, and Confucius, and other religious heroes, standing strong for an Americanism, believing in social perfectibility, fighting the saloon, and the wicked diversions of the Springfield godless and idlers, opposing corruption in government and its ministrants, standing for a democracy in which God's law controlled, and in which human beings became equals as high-minded, devout, temperate, chaste, and clean citizens. We shall see in this catalogue of activities of the poet's mother the origins of all that the poet became, of all the themes that he treated, of all the aspirations that he cultivated, of the sincerity and consecration with which he tried to be an artist, of the thoroughly-bred and authentic power with which he became an American poet, speaking for that Americanism which was the dream of the founders of the country and to which the poet tried to call his country again. These characteristics of Mrs. Lindsay define an Americanism as distinctive as that of Jefferson, or that of the Virginia gentry; and it has features which any kind of Americanism however worthy would do well to adopt. It runs back perhaps to the savage sincerity of Michael Wiggleworth and Jonathan Edwards, and to the latter religiosity of Thomas Campbell and Alexander his son, who in a passionate kind of zealotry could found a sect on a manner of baptism, and make its observance a prerequisite of salvation.

These spirits are themselves engines of great power; but the comic muse is likely to make their descendants proficient practitioners of subtle politics and ingenious logics, as in the case of Jonathan Edwards's grandson, Aaron Burr. The principal point is that they have intellects not to be despised, though they are exercised upon spheres of interest which are indeed below the concern of first-rate minds. In Mrs. Lindsay's case one feels that she was a tender vine somewhat held down and covered from the sunlight by planks or bricks, which she in the process of growth naturally tried to elude and rise above, at the same time that she held to these obstructions as the very substances of truth. The fight between beauty and holiness is an old story in Christian annals, and those of other lands and religions. Even with the Greeks the Orphic cult with Pythagoras for a philosopher priest held aloof from the worship of Apollo; and in the case of Lindsay his chief concerns were holiness, truth, and beauty, with many speculations in all places and at all times as to their proper reconciliation. As different as he was from the Reverend Frazee, or high as his poetry is above the homiletic oratory of the Indian preacher, Vachel Lindsay was in truth his grandson.

As Lindsay portrayed his father in the poem entitled "Doctor Mohawk," so in "The Hearth Eternal" he has left us his portrait of his mother. Here as in the father poem he dramatized the subject, and began it by speaking of a widow learned and devout. He may have meant by this that she was not really mated to Doctor Lindsay, as we have before hinted. But however this may be, he made the home of this devout widow a place where sturdy beggars came for faggots, who gradually stole the walls and the floor, leaving at last a naked stone, which nevertheless blazed. Men left their churches to crumble in the sun, and came to the soft hill where the house of the widow stood, and there made of themselves one brotherhood. In other words her faith and her genius for life were to be a church, and of loftier principles than the sectarian spire. So it was according to this poem that the widow conquered half the earth, though living all alone, keeping her house as a place of magic, and making the town of her residence a throne for angels. This was the dream of Magical Springfield taking form and life from this mother's hopes and dreams, and from the vision of the poet himself who without knowing Plato to any extent preached the City of the Perfect in poems and in prose all his years of singing.

It will not be amiss to let foreign eyes give us their glimpse of this remarkable woman. In 1922 *The Liverpool Post and Mercury*, remembering her visit with her son to England in 1920, spoke in this manner of her, on the occasion of her death: "She had that precision and composure of mind that one finds in certain elements of American fiction. There was in fact an orderliness in her manner which contrasted most piquantly with the flamboyance and ebullience of her son. Her conversation had this orderliness in marked degree. She talked with singular ease and power."

By no means, however, can we say that she was in every sense a good influence and guide for her son. Revelations to follow will make this matter clearer.

CHAPTER II

NICHOLAS VACHEL LINDSAY, Vachel Lindsay as he came to be known, was born November 10, 1879, in the Springfield house already mentioned, under the very shadow of the capitol building, the product of much malversation and bad taste. A few blocks away stood the old residence of Lincoln, then or soon to become a museum, in charge of that Oldroyd who devoted much of his life there and in Washington to the collection of Lincoln souvenirs. The Gilded Age was commencing, the age of stock gambling, and railroad wrecking, of a new kind of swelldom, of centralization of money and governmental power. The republic of Jefferson, of Jackson, even of Buchanan, was deader than the Athenian democracy. People pretended to believe that the Civil War had made no change in the political system, that with the Union stuck through and held together with swords, it was saved, that with the emancipation of the Negroes liberty had been asserted and had taken up its march to greater triumphs. This was the oratory of moralist and politician, of such men in Illinois as Richard Oglesby, a governor, of John A. Logan, a senator, called "Black Jack" Logan, a strident swashbuckling commander of Republican forces, who having almost turned to the so-called Copperhead side of the War, being then in fact a Southern sympathizer, was able to appreciate the full villainy of that state of mind and that course; and with the psychology of Saint Paul went about persecuting and denouncing his former democratic fellows.

Springfield at this time swarmed with politicians and with lawyers; for the local courts were full of litigants, and the supreme court of the State sat there. Railroads were still being started in Illinois, city councils and legislators were being bribed; and labor disturbances, which had sprouted in this new soil of America long before the War, were multiplying. Two years before the poet's birth there had been a terrifying condition in Illinois on account of rebellious coal miners; and the troops had been called out. All this, and the prairie was not yet fully subdued, save as it had been reclaimed from complete wilderness. Log cabins were still plentiful; spinning wheels, hand looms, carpet looms, domestic candle-making were in use; and bad roads abounded over the State. There was no telephone, save the toy variety; and the tentacles of the metropolis were sheathed or ungrown. Looking upon this scene with his first seeing eyes, and contemplating it later and along his years Lindsay hoped to transform it into the Magical City of Springfield, and to fish up from the deep muck of corruption and blood the pearl of the U. S. A. with or without the assistance of Doctor Mohawk.

A daughter had been born to the Lindsays two years before the birth of the poet, who later became the wife of a medical missionary to China, sent out by the Foreign Board of the Christian Church. He had been graduated from the Christian College of Hiram, where the poet was later to go; and we shall not turn amid these annals of the Lindsays without finding evidence of the hand of Alexander Campbell, and the zeal which it propagated for social and spiritual betterment. Esther Catharine Lindsay, so full of ardent hope, so restless in her aspirations and imaginations, saw strange signs on the birth of this son. He came into the world long and thin and old looking, and with what is called a prophet's veil over his face. It is deemed lucky to be born with the caul over the face; it is a sure preservative against drowning. And according to Chrysostom the old midwives frequently sold such a caul for magic uses. Symbols might be indulged, too, to say that as the caul over the face would prevent the objective use of the eyes, the inner vision might be sharpened, making such a child a dreamer of dreams, but not an understander of the outer world. Lindsay all his life was at a disadvantage in perceiving the exact nature and position of the facts about anything, while passionately seeking the truth, and endeavoring to extract it from the facts. He was a visionary from the start like Blake or Jakob Boehme; yet with a kind of logic at times like Swedenborg; while we feel that he performed a work of sowing similar to that of his favorite Johnny Appleseed, his seed being dreams and ideas of and for his city and his country.

The name Nicholas Vachel Lindsay is made up from his father's name Vachel, which was also the name of his paternal great-grandfather; while Nicholas was derived from that old man of Kentucky of the gold-headed cane and plug hat. In maturity Lindsay seemed a robust well-set-up man, whose careful habits maintained the vitality which was going into his ceaseless travelling and lecturing, and which was filling his powerful poems with voluminous rhythms. In fact, his abstention from tobacco and drink did not compensate, perhaps, for his indulgence in confections and sweets; and he had inherited from his mother a nervous activity which kept his mind always stirred with thought and dreams, and his body alien to composure. In physical power and endurance he did not much resemble his father. As a baby the future poet was frail, so much so that for a year his mother carried him about on a pillow; and in after years did not let him forget this tender ministration.

Added to all this a serious illness in infancy lowered his vitality for years. It was in consequence of this that he was not sent to school for some years. His mother gave him first lessons in reading, bringing him to *Grimm's Fairy Tales,* those altogether charming creations out of folklore, so rich in the portraiture of strange witches and good princes, of speaking horses and frogs, of humor, human nature and imagery, of eccentricity of character in a setting of magical mediævalism. It was not long before the boy was reading these stories over and over again. No book has done more for the imaginative youth of the world, or given it such delight as this collection of tales by the German philologists of Göttingen. Also there was Dante's *Divine Comedy*, as illustrated by Doré, and the *Paradise Lost*, large books, which the boy laid upon the floor in order more easily to pore over them. Dante, it seems, never took much hold of the poet; but Milton became his lifelong study, we think from the fact of its Biblical theme. He read it at eight years of age, and fell in love with Eve, dreaming about her day and night. In the last year of his life Lindsay made a critical reading of *Paradise Lost*, filling a notebook with analyses and observations upon the poem.

Doctor Mohawk was a good father, we make no doubt at all; but somehow we surmise that the boy's brightness and eagerness, if not precocity, and what a fond mother made of them, rather startled and at times almost bewildered the man who was hurrying in and out of the house to his meals, and setting forth in his old buggy to bring children into the world and to quiet the nerves of inebriates. He may have wished that the boy was not so much coddled by the mother, that his curls were not so golden and so fine, that he failed to show a Tom Sawyer tendency to get out and around with the boys of the neighborhood. On the other hand Springfield was by no means an Athens in these days of the eighties, and there were bad boys about, and drunken men on the streets. Sharp-eyed politicians and flashily dressed men of cards loitered about the hotels. It was easy for a boy to imbibe evil ideas of life, and to see things that would not profit him. Mrs. Lindsay from the first, full of pride for this her only son, started at once to prepare him for a career in which goodness, purity, faith and holiness

The house in Springfield, Illinois, in which Vachel Lindsay was born, and where he died.

should be the dominant inspirations, and inform a Christian expression. And whatever Doctor Mohawk wished, whether it was that the boy should be a boy among boys, or later that he should become a physician like himself, the mother's way prevailed, both from her instructions, and by the nature of the youth himself. Yet these early days were not without their hours of normal playtime.

A few blocks away from the Lindsay home, in a house next to the Lincoln house, lived Johnson Lindsay, the uncle of the poet, whose daughter Ruby Lindsay became a favorite playmate. One of the games of these two was turning the lilac bush in the yard into a Christmas tree, which was maintained as such the year round. The custodian of the Lincoln home liked children and he allowed Vachel and Ruby to play in the historic rooms and to look at the cartoons and pictures which covered the walls, depicting events North and South before the War. On these occasions G. A. R. veterans frequently would be passing from picture to picture, talking over the events of the War, and what Lincoln and his generals had done, or had failed to do, and of the successes and misadventures of famous battles. The poet was eight or nine years old when he was listening to such things; so that he grew up on Lincoln. All the while there was his father's lukewarm feeling for the Lincoln cult; and there was the old blind man in Kentucky, whose bitterness against the author of his misfortunes was known to the boy as early as he knew anything about his people and their lives. Despite the fact that Lindsay from his first days at school was taught with Ruby to sing "The Battle Hymn of the Republic," and "John Brown's Body," and "Shouting the Battle Cry of Freedom," he had no illusions of the sort usually indulged in, especially at this time, respecting Lincoln. In a preface to his *Collected Poems* he wrote that at this time of boyhood he knew that Lincoln was a profound volcano, who produced controversy and infinite debate. Perhaps he

aligned Lincoln, somehow, with Alexander Campbell, who
held great debates with Presbyterians, and who stirred eris-
tical fury, as Lincoln did, whether meaning of purpose to do
so or not. In all this there was enough to make Lindsay
see that Lincoln was not a steel engraving, with fashionably
trimmed whiskers; nor was he that grave and formal figure
which was on the back of the dollar bill. Lindsay had a
deep division in his heart occasioned by the democratic
faith of his household, which was perpetually affronted by
a statehouse infested with the cohorts of John A. Logan. A
sinister cultivation of the G. A. R. was carried on in those
days of democratic dishonor. Lindsay, again relying upon
the preface to his *Collected Poems*, remained a Southerner,
due to the influence of the Lindsay kin, all of whom had been
Breckenridge democrats and who came up frequently from
Kentucky to pay visits to the Springfield family, where
asseverations of the heresies which had produced a schism in
the party and wrecked the excellent chances for the presidency of the Little Giant were still adhered to, though they
were traceable to the philosophy of John C. Calhoun, for
whom the poet never had any admiration. Of this his poems
on Jackson are proofs enough. These political faiths and
the reasons advanced for them carry people here and there
without consistency; and it cannot be expected that his
imaginative mind, inclined at times to intellectual caprices,
would logically find the way through the mazes twined
around Mason and Dixon's line. But when he said that it
ran straight through his heart, as well as through the heart
of his cousin Ruby, we must believe that in the case of himself he was speaking in terms of poetry. Nowhere has he
revealed himself in a favorable way to the doctrines of
Breckenridge. His admiration for the Little Giant was
based on that statesman's adherence to the Union cause when
the War began, and his own career was ended even though
he did so, and perhaps his personal security menaced if he

did not do so. But the poet imbibed a staunch democracy in these days, and his devotion was paid through life to Jefferson, later to President Wilson, and to Cleveland until the Bryan breach, and to Bryan as a gigantic troubadour, prairie avenger and speaker of siege-gun power.

The Republicans in those days were holding torchlight processions, both to save the country from those who had tried to break the Union, the perfidious Democrats, but to get the opulent offices for themselves, and to clothe their party with the powers of sovereignty, and to give its followers the grafts and the governmental privileges that went with this political business. In resenting imitation of these spectacles the poet and his cousin held parades for the democracy; and when Cleveland came along Doctor Lindsay and his brother Johnson rode in the parade which celebrated Cleveland's presidential victory, while these two children rejoiced at the joyous tumult and stood in admiration of the gaudy sashes and the high hats in which their elders were clothed. The next day at school the two young enthusiasts were mocked as rebels, and told that they were unwelcome wanderers from Confederate Kentucky, who had no place with the children of a loyal and heroic North. Lindsay heard enough from his own relatives, from the blind grandfather in Kentucky to have implanted in him the seeds of dislike of Lincoln, which might have grown into definite convictions on the subject of the War; particularly might he have looked with disfavoring eyes upon Lincoln in his general abhorrence of war, and his lasting admiration for characters like Tolstoy, and as a result of his devotion to the Christ of peace. But this did not happen; for always at the hearth was his mother; and back in Indiana was the grandfather who had rung the dinner bell for three hours when the work of Lincoln was brought to victory by the surrender of Lee. Then it was well nigh impossible for a boy to be reared in the seat of the growing chronicles concerning Lincoln,

[31]

where the veterans of his war repaired on Decoration Days, and memorial occasions were celebrated without filling his being with a species of worship so thoroughly interfused in his mind, that any thinking whatever would yield to the power of a culture so profound, and so surrounding him from the beginning.

At home with his mother Lindsay heard her version of the War, and the part that Harriet Beecher Stowe had played in it, and about Uncle Tom and the terrible Simon Legree. The mother was full of stories such as Peter Cartwright set down in his picturesque autobiography, stories of Daniel Boone, who was taught how to read by one of the pioneer grandfathers of Mrs. Lindsay. Peter Cartwright was a Methodist, and often was a guest for the night at the Masters homestead, eight miles north of New Salem, where he received warm hospitality from that Methodist household to the day of his death in 1872. A very different type of man was he from Alexander Campbell; a fact that Lindsay noted in one of his prefaces. For the Methodists under Peter Cartwright associated religious conviction with mysterious ecstasies; while the Campbellites "breathed fire and taught in granite." They had Scotch heads, being indeed offshoots of the Calvinistic Presbyterians; but their blood was "red Indian and Kentucky."

In such a home, presided over by a mother who had known but Kentucky and Indiana, even these re-visioned through the eyes of one European trip; and a father whose democratic blood knew Kentucky and Kentuckians, both in that State and in Springfield, it was not likely that Lindsay would hear much of the East, of New England, as in fact he heard nothing. These parts of America which have dominated the whole country for so long in finance and by their magazines, their literary critics, and their Boston and New York schools of letters would be surprised, rather would have been surprised to know how little this West of Illinois and of

Springfield knew about them, or cared about them. Some sort of a union, or centralization has brought them closer together, to no good end yet, since the West has been made in this amalgamation nothing better than an imitation of the East, and a payer of tribute to its banks and its academicians. It was not understood to be so in the boyhood of Lindsay; and there was no social consciousness of anything but a financial dictatorship twenty years before his day. This West had its own absorbing interests, its own language and tastes, its own standards of life, its own heroes, who obscured such faraway figures as Paul Revere, Perry of the Lakes, and others. Lindsay was reared in an atmosphere that made him a spokesman well informed to sing of his own locality, of an Americanism that is distinctive, if there be any such at all.

As the East has always been, in nearly all the departments of life, a province of Europe, of England in chief, transforming those foreign influences with the falsities of imitation, it was well that Lindsay heard of Europe every day over the head of the East, and directly in terms of history written there and in England, concerning the religious wars which had divided men and fortified sects, and sent into America Methodists and the Presbyterians, from whom the Campbellites sprang.

Lindsay recorded that there were a great many books brought by the Lindsays from Kentucky, among which was a small volume of the poems of Poe, which enthralled the imagination of the sensitive boy from the first. There were farther places than England to be interested in. The Bible lands and Egypt excited the wonder of Lindsay above all other places. When he was very young his father presented him with Rawlinson's *History of Egypt*, made the more attractive to the boy by illustrations; and this was one of the first books that he took thoroughly into his mind. As far as this delineation has proceeded now we are able to see

[33]

the genesis of his mature poems on Samson, Solomon, Amenophis; his fascination for hieroglyphics, his wonder about Kentcky, his own people, his own part of America. If ever an American poet was nurtured to sing of his land and for it in words and images deriving from nowhere except from the soil which bore him, it was Vachel Lindsay. We have here no Greek, and there will be little Latin, no study of English poets as models, as there never was; none of the conventional, classical courses against which Whitman warned the American poets-to-be. At the same time we shall find little in Lindsay to make him even a collateral relative of Whitman, but rather in many ways a mere spiritual brother who independently and in his own original way carried out some of the instructions on which Whitman was insistent all his life.

One would not expect Kentucky or Indiana to commence at once to make watches and clocks, to build churches of any richly original style of architecture, but rather from trees hewed down in the wilderness; to construct stone aqueducts, especially if not needed, to set up picturesque windmills, when there were rivers with falls, unlike Holland; to do anything in brief not adapted to the country, nor required by the necessities of its people. Yet the first peoples of these States and of Illinois saw no obstacle of an unseasonable sort in the way of painting and poetry. Springfield had poets forty years before Vachel Lindsay was born; and Esther Catharine Frazee applied herself to painting at the two country colleges mentioned, and all her life was reading papers on art subjects before the local societies of Springfield. There were conditions to prevent the rise of any Correggio or Rembrandt in those days, against which Mrs. Lindsay as a young woman strove in vain. Besides she was frail; and then motherhood and household cares put her ambition far out of reach. It seems clear enough that having suffered defeat in her own life in a cherished dream, she transferred her ardent hopes to the future of her son, by which she might achieve vicarious distinction and vindication for herself, desiring to live in him what she had failed to live in herself. In the remote infancy of Lindsay his mother destined him to be an artist, wrote the poet. So it was that before she had anything except the traits of a child to judge by, magnified by maternal enthusiasm, she was dreaming of his life as a creative painter. How far she was justified when he became a schoolboy, and later when he went to art school we shall see. It might have been better if he had devoted all his years to poetry, instead of so much time to drawing and to the theories of the plastic arts; for though Browning dabbled in painting, and to a degree in music, not to mention men of versatile gifts like Morris and Rossetti, Lindsay derived little from his art studies, except on the score of general culture. His poetry never concerned itself with painting; and it is not distinguished above other poets in those qualities which are determined by an education of the eye to color and form and description. It is difficult to say whether the mother was a fortunate or unfortunate influence in filling her son's "skin full," as the poet later expressed it, of an ambition to be an artist; and to do this at a time when he had no judgment of his own, or the possibility of any as to the wisdom of entertaining such aspirations.

Mrs. Lindsay had every reason to believe, however, that her son had talent of some sort, and a mind much above that of the average boy. Just as some boys will show an aptitude at once for a given game, for running or tumbling, or contriving playthings of an ingenious sort, so Lindsay showed from the first a disposition to make records of daily things, to write down what was happening, to scrawl pictures of what he saw, or imagined. When he was eight or nine years old his father took him to Trinidad, Colorado, there to pay a visit to Grandmother Lindsay; and the boy recorded in a notebook all the marvels of that journey. From that diary written in a boyish hand we take some extracts to show how his mind worked, and upon what subjects it exercised itself.

"Morning looks hilly for a while," he began; "level all the way the rest of the way to Kansas City, good deal like Illinois. Missouri is awful muddy, good deal of swamp along the road. Corn looks well, wheat is all reaped, more corn than anything else. Just come across an unreaped field of wheat, pretty hills in far distance. For about a mile the track has a long belt of yellow daisies . . . cars very easy, best I have ever travelled on . . . hills covered with trees . . . no trees on plains . . . another drove of cattle . . . cattle grazing is one of the chief industries . . . Missouri covered with red mud."

The diary at this point takes a turn to people: "Had fun in depot; family there that thought they were aristocratic, were very interesting; acted like a couple of toads . . . very interesting family indeed. Their little girl, about 17 was dressed in a dress of black up to her knees, fastened together with pins. They were very sentimental."

Missouri being past and the family left behind he turns to descriptions of the country: "Eastern part of Kansas is a good deal like Missouri, only more trees. Train stopped for dinner at Topeka . . . beautiful hills . . . largest drove of cattle I have seen. . . . Arrived at La Junta, stay three hours . . . very pretty little town. Papa and I took a walk on the prairie, got me two wild flowers that look like large red morning glories, but have an entirely different leaf. Found a beautiful lump of swartz, very large clear crystal, too big to carry; found piece of yellow quartz . . . Italian with big loaf of rye bread in his pocket . . . old woman smoking pipe . . . accident this morning, three persons killed, about 20 hurt . . . broken whisky bottles principal feature of washout. . . . Arrived at Trinidad Friday, started for Pueblo the 27th . . . have got a small collection of rocks. . . . Arrived at Pueblo . . . nothing special on the road. . . . Went to see the largest smelter, mostly lead is smelted. We had no guide . . . first room had the ores, in which the ores were measured and mixed ready for smelting in the second room . . . in the second room they were making lead pigs . . . after the lead had been taken out of the smelter they put it in very large brick bowls which were heated by means of a furnace, and these refined, after which it was put in a very large business, something of the shape of a keg with the head knocked out it was carried by means of pipes at the end of which were placed the pig moulds it ran out of." Here Lindsay inserted a drawing of a pig mould, shaped something like a bathtub, and not badly done. After this he proceeds to describe the smelting furnace, and the process of getting rid of the slag; he then drew a picture of the wheelbarrow in which the slag was hauled away.

"I was sick most of the time," the diary continues, "and so did not interest myself very much. There was a man in the room who was determining how much silver there was to the ton. He would take a piece of metal composed of silver with lead and some other metals and put them in little clay cups into the furnace where the heat carries the lead and other metals off in vapor leaving the pure silver . . . went to the opera house in the evening . . . at 9 A.M. went to the Grand Canon a most beautiful place . . . stopped in the gorge where a small stream flowed out of the mountain . . . had a most enjoyable time . . . got back to Pueblo at 4 P.M. . . . raining very hard . . . started for Manitou . . . had to change cars at Colorado Springs . . . missed train . . . had to wait walked to hotel mile in the rain. Don't feel very well. Next morning we went to Pikes pk. Depot ticket agent said it was clearing off. Papa decided to go 4 hrs ride . . . a stream flows by the railroad for some distance . . . is very pretty about ⅔s up. . . . It was raining or rather drizzling . . . covered the windows with steam . . . could not see out so that when we got out and looked around what a sight met our eyes . . . upon one hand the sublime sight of a jet black porter picturesquely banging upon a piece of dazzling bright tin pan with a clothes pin that had seen cleaner days, and upon the other peer where I may see nothing but white Glorious white! Yes! . . . Oh what emotion filled my breast as my eyes beheld piercing the gloom beheld the star spangled Banner, and placed beside the flagpole the time honored sign Keep off The Grass. . . . I got several pretty flowers on pikes Pk . . . in the afternoon we went to an azteck show. It was a collection of specimens from the houses of some cliff dwellers in Southern Utah 8 miles from civilization . . . the guide showed us some specimens of pottery most of the vessels had designs on them all angles . . . here are some specimens." (The diary here has reproductions of the geometrical borders which the Indians use on their pottery.) "Next morning walked along a beautiful path to the falls . . . went to depot . . . got an accident policy for 24 hours . . . found on train that it would not be allowed to children under 16."

Such is the boy's diary, quoted here as he wrote it, as he spelled and capitalized the words, and as he failed to punctuate his sentences. The leaders inserted are not his, and not intended to indicate breaks in the text, but to separate running matter where he did not place periods or other marks to indicate parts of sentences.

Writers are presided over at birth by the Muse of memory under whose direction they set down from their earliest years what comes to their eyes or ears; and then they put these records away as annals of growth and sources of recollection. All of this was very much so with Lindsay. He wrote from the time that he could make the letters; and from the amount of papers he accumulated and preserved one would think that he lost nothing along the way. He thus preserved for those who are interested to see what he could do with verses a number of experiments when he was about eighteen years of age. They are not very promising; and show no precocity, when one considers that Shelley wrote "Queen Mab" and Bryant wrote "Thanatopsis" at that age. But when Lindsay was about eleven years old, and at about the time that he joined the Disciples Church, he composed some verses entitled "Come," which may be incorporated here to show his manner and especially to manifest the beginning of that religious feeling which animated all his years. Whitman frequently declared that poetry must have religion to back it. In this respect Lindsay became a son of Whitman, perhaps at times with a vengeance; but at all times with a sincerity which makes his devotions incapable of disrespect. "Superstition," said Goethe, "is the poetry of life; hence the poet suffers no harm from being superstitious." The criticasters who have mocked Lindsay's religious attitude and utterances as the wild eloquence of the revivalist would do well to take note of these words. So for the purposes mentioned, the youthful poem of Lindsay is now inserted here, as it was spelled and punctuated:

> "He that is weary come, refreshed,
> He that is thirsty come and drink,
> 'I,' says the savior, 'I am he
> I am that fountain clear and free.
>
> Come sinner, Come, Why longer delay?
> Hear what the Master has to say;
> I have been crucified for thee.
> Why not come? now come to me.
>
> You may not live through the coming night,
> Why do you waver this battle to fight?
> The Master calls you with pitying voice
> You'll choose Heaven, or Hell, which is your choice?

[39]

If you obey his voice and follow him to day,
Then with a joyfull heart he will say;
Come blessed servant, come to me,
Inherit the kingdom prepared for thee."
(VACHEL, July 31, 1890.)

By this time, or shortly after he was in the Stuart Grammar School of Springfield, to which some particular attention must be paid. His first days at school were rendered unhappy by the attitude of the other boys toward him. His mother insisted on keeping him in curls and white piqué past the usual limits for such things; and thus he became an object of derision on the part of rowdy Huckleberry Finns of the hit-and-run variety, against whom the delicate boy was powerless to protect himself. It was only when he found champions in some lusty Irish boys that he was relieved of this tormenting persecution, which was similar to that experienced by Shelley at Eton. Eccentricities of dress or manner will always invite teasing; and as Lindsay between six and nine years of age was brilliantly precocious, and a startling conversationalist, it is no wonder that both envy and juvenile sense of the ridiculous preyed upon him.

In his early boyhood something happened which perhaps kept him in awe of his father for life. With a vagrant boy while playing with matches the poet set fire to some barns; and Doctor Lindsay in great wrath flogged the hapless son with great severity. Those who knew Lindsay most intimately, and talked with him most familiarly about the events of his life, give their word that this flogging had a lasting and unhappy effect upon the poet. His heart remained divided toward his father to the last. He admired the doctor's masculinity, and longed to please him; yet he had the old hurt in his heart, and was constantly shocked by the father's character, which was energetic if not tainted with ruthlessness. It was certainly limited in point of sympathy.

[40]

CHAPTER III

LINDSAY entered the Stuart Grammar School of Springfield in September of 1890, then being almost eleven years of age. With his light hair, the beetling prominence of his brow, and the intensity of his gray eyes he had something of seraphic intensity in his expression. His teachers reported that "he shows earnestness in whatever he does." True to that genius of memory in him his report cards have been preserved, and the reflect of his mind in these years of beginning can be given. Through nine months of this school year his marks in drawing ranged from 89 to 94; in writing from 89 to 91; in reading from 87 to 93; in spelling from 90 to 96; in composition from 92 to 98; in arithmetic from 89 to 98; in geography from 88 to 97; in grammar from 92 to 99. The standard being very good at 90, the boy was excelling from the first. The next year, 1891-2, he made an average for the months of the school year of 78 in writing, 84 in drawing, 92 in reading, 88 in spelling, 90 in composition, 85 in arithmetic, 79 in geography, 91 in history, 92 in physiology, and 74 in music. We surmise that the technical theories of music baffled him to some extent. As a mature poet he confessed to understanding very little of the technique of rhythm. In his first year in the grammar school he won a medal given as a prize for the best essay on the subject of "Labor and Learning." In his second year he won the same medal for an essay on the subject "Advantages of Farm and City Life." On this occasion the insignia of excellence was presented to him at the County Fair with great ceremony. He graduated from the Stuart School in 1893, and recited "The School Master's Guests" at the ceremonies.

Lindsay entered the High School of Springfield in the

fall of 1893, where he came under the instruction of Susan E. Wilcox, to whom he was attached for life, calling her his best and most understanding friend. Here he took a passionate interest in drawing, using his talent in the classes in botany and physiology, of which more will be said later. His standing in English was excellent; and in addition to his school work he read Carlyle's *French Revolution* in his sophomore year, then being fifteen years of age; and while absorbed in it was wont to come to Miss Wilcox's desk to invite her to share in his enthusiasm for the work. In his senior year he was showing some of his verses to Miss Wilcox. They were marked somewhat with the influence of Poe, according to the report of Miss Wilcox. One of them later became a poem called "The Battle," his "first picture drawn in words." For several years after his high school days he wrote verses as commentaries upon pictures, and inspired by his visual imagination. Just before his graduation Miss Wilcox asked him what his plans were for the future. His reply was, "If I were an orphan I should be an artist, but I'm not, so I'm going to college and be a doctor." These items are taken from an article written by Miss Wilcox, and published in *The Elementary English Review* of Detroit, in the May number, 1932. She made one comment which spoke for the independence of Lindsay's character in those days when school was over and he was trying to make his way somehow in this world so difficult to all without the business mind. She wrote of his dislike to be dependent upon his parents, and that in consequence of this he went none too presentably clothed, a misfortune which kept him out of contacts which would have encouraged him to write in days when his mind was most active and his imagination most vivid and luxuriant. At this time before he had found himself as a lecturer, when he was imprisoned, so to speak, in Springfield, he often came to Miss Wilcox's door saying that he had no money but that there was a good movie in town, and if she had the money they would go together. The teacher often responded to these appeals, and then Lindsay repaid the compliment whenever he managed to scrape the admission fee together.

We are able also to present his marks while in high school. In his first year his grade in Latin ranged from 50 to 68, 68 being bad, below passing, and 50 very bad. In algebra his marks ranged from 58 to 90, with an average for the nine months of the school year of 72+. In history he ranged from 75 to 90, with an average for the nine months of 82+; in English his lowest score was 88, and his highest 93, with an average for the year of 91+. The next year, 1894, he took botany for four months with marks from 70 to 92, and an average of 86. He had five months in zoölogy with marks from 87 to 91, and an average of 88. He had the whole nine months in English, with marks from 70 to 95, and an average of 86; in geometry, marks for 76 to 84, with an average of 81; in Latin, marks from 50 to 80, with an average of 66. He had five months of drawing this year, with marks from 90 to 95.

The next year, 1895, he had the following studies for the nine months' school year: physics, with an average mark of 88; physical geography, with an average mark of 88; modern history, with an average mark of 92; arithmetic, with an average mark of 87; English, with an average mark of 91; civil government, with an average mark of 88; and political economy, with an average mark of 92. In his senior year, 1896–7, his average in English was 90; 89 in chemistry; 78 in algebra and solid geometry; 72 in Latin; 92 in United States history; and 89 in geology.

Lindsay was graduated from the Springfield High School on June 10, 1897; and a few days after as a part of the commencement celebrations debated publicly with another graduate on the subject, "That the Latter Times Are Better Than the Former," in which Lindsay upheld the negative.

No memorandum seems to give the result of the debate. He probably lost it, as he had the unpopular side, and his efforts at debating later at Hiram College were not of the first order by any means.

We are dealing beyond question with a human being of tireless energy, at least of ceaseless mental activity and aspiration. During these high school years Lindsay wrote many essays, in 1894 one on the "Character of Brutus"; in 1895 one on the "Grand Jury System," which received a mark of 91. In 1895 a cornerstone was laid for a new high school in Springfield. Lindsay was selected to deliver the oration on this occasion. On the manuscript of this production Lindsay later noted that it was influenced by the orations of Webster, which he was then studying. In 1895 as a part of his school work he wrote an essay on Lowell, in which he declared that Lowell was a great genius, not of the mad sort like Poe and De Quincey, but the genius of a broad mind symmetrically developed. Speaking of Lowell's patriotism, he used these words: "it is a thing of tinsel and pasteboard. It seldom does harm, often does good, but no more deserves a place among the high virtues with which it has been classed than the oyster a place among vertebrates." Miss Wilcox did not like this tone, according to Lindsay's bequeathed notation on the manuscript, and refused to give the essay a mark. He then re-wrote the essay, but in a 4th of July style, and thus made it satisfactory.

In 1895 he produced an essay wholly devoted to the subject of patriotism. We may quote a few of its lines to get the point of view of the boy of sixteen. "There was a time," he said, "when this prejudice, this partiality for one's own environment was the only thing that upheld states, and kept anarchy from reigning supreme. . . . But in these days of civilization one has no right to oppress one nation for the benefit of another. Is it justice, is it true government that one citizen of the world shall have more privileges than another, simply because he was born in another state? Discrimination is a greater crime between nations than between individuals, in that it affects a greater number of our fellow men." He concluded, therefore, that patriotism cannot be a love of country, but that it was only a subservience to duty, an advancing of personal ambitions.

In this same year he handed in an essay on "True Charity," which was marked excellent, and such it is, considering the writer's age. We shall see later that Lindsay strove with all the sense of aristry which he possessed to become the master of a clear, terse prose style. It can scarcely be said that he ever achieved this ambition. The promises of these youthful productions in prose were not to any marked degree fulfilled.

Among Lindsay papers were preserved many folders of his drawings in high school in his classes in botany and zoölogy. Some of these are excellent, all things considered, and very unmistakably show the direction of whatever deftness as a draughtsman he was ever to possess, as well as the field of his imaginative interest. Among these is a sketch of a spider which is well done, and of a spider's foot so enlarged as to give its form and construction greater visibility. There are drawings here, too, of sow-bugs, and grasshoppers, and the wings of grasshoppers. There is one of a clam shell, not so good as those of the insects; one of a snail which is very good; one of a sea urchin which is very life-like; also of sand-dollars. A most faithful drawing of the foot of a pigeon is in one of these folders, and one of a squash bug. He drew the circulatory system of a fish, in red and black ink; and also the lateral view of a smelt with the body wall removed. His final essay in zoölogy won the verdict of very well done. His drawings in botany were successful when dealing with filaments, tendrils, and delicately arranged buds or blossoms. Already we see that his life-long interest in butterflies, crickets and snails, in ferns and airily blown leaves and vines sprang from an æsthetic with which he was gifted at birth.

During his life in high school, and in his fourteenth year, Lindsay was taken by Doctor Mohawk to see the World's Fair at Chicago. True to a habit begun at nine years of age he kept a notebook of this trip, though it is sketchily written, and in places scarcely legible. We may refer to enough of it to determine what took his eye on this occasion of wonder and cultural advantage. Evidently he was captivated with such things as the lions he saw, the strange people that crossed his vision, among them a Turk in a fez. There are boyish drawings of these objects in this notebook. He went to the Fisheries' Building, and there saw the aquarium, and was particularly interested in the boats and fishing apparatus, the tackle and nets, and the like. This he records in a hand much worse than that of his most youthful writing. He saw the boat of Grace Darling and a humpbacked whale forty-seven and one-half feet long, and at the Kentucky Building the desk of George Washington. Such things he noted in this diary. He was greatly interested in the Puck Building, where lithographing and printing, such as featured that celebrated comic journal, were carried on as an exhibition of such crafts. He watched the production of a cartoon and noted that the black lines were first printed, and then that the colors were separately added. He called the process very interesting. He walked about studying the cartoons on the walls, some of which looked like water colors to him. Whether his ambition to become a cartoonist began here or not, none can say. That profession was surely as alien to his hand as that of medicine; and we shall see him struggling in vain to become a cartoonist in the years soon to follow when he was trying to place himself economically in a hard and well filled world of ambition and business. He went to the horticultural building, and into the buildings of artistic work. It is evident that he made the rounds of all the buildings. A strange omission in this book is the lack of anything by way of comment on the wonderful exhibit of pictures brought from every gallery in the world, and housed against fire and theft in the Greek structure, which was one of the architectural marvels of the Fair. Here the young Lindsay could have seen Raphael, Rembrandt, and all the great masters—Spanish, Dutch, Italian, and English—as well as objects of ancient art from the museums of Rome and Naples and Athens. He must have toured this building more than once, as later he walked the corridors of the Metropolitan Museum for days at a time. We are denied, however, any observations on these works set down in this diary.

In these school years Lindsay was keeping up a steady correspondence with his Grandfather and Grandmother Frazee at Orange, Indiana. The grandfather's letters were written on his official stationery as a farmer, which contained the picture of a fine short-horn cow, with the sentence printed under it, "Stock for Sale." At the top of these letterheads were the words "E. S. Frazee & Sons, Breeders of Short-Horn Cattle and Draft Horses." In a letter to the grandson dated in 1886 the grandfather congratulated the boy upon the excellence of his letters. The old gentleman was reading a life of Lincoln and expressed surprise that the Sangamon River had once been declared navigable. He hoped some day to come out to see the river upon which Abraham Lincoln had helped under Captain Bogue to man the *Talisman,* the little steamer which they met at Beardstown, carrying axes with which to cut the overhanging boughs along the Sangamon as the boat proceeded. He remarked that Mr. Lincoln piloted the boat to the landing opposite Springfield. "The event was celebrated in poetry and prose," wrote the grandfather. This was a way of ringing the dinner bell as he had actually done twenty years before, thus to call the youth to a historic rejoicing in the career of the man who had made Springfield a shrine for all loyal souls.

[47]

Grandmother Frazee was also writing the future poet, and in an excellent chirography. Two of her letters may be noted as samples of her correspondence. There is one dated in April of 1890, in which she praised the boy for his fine letters. "I do really think they are extra nice for a ten-year-old boy." She gave him the neighborhood news and the news about various relatives. A new preacher had come to the neighborhood, who evidently was showing his inexperience and did not look at all like his father. The maple sugar product had failed, had stopped short like the old clock, and none can be sent to Springfield. Even for their own use there in Indiana ordinary sugar would have to be melted down to make molasses for cakes. There were ominous words in this letter. "Your grandpa's eye does not improve or change much." Already the farmer-preacher had developed a cancer which ended his days in 1896. We may refer to another of her letters written in 1893. Lindsay had sent her one of his essays, perhaps one of those to which reference has already been made. The grandmother wrote, "We all thought your essay a very good one, and would have been a credit to an older person. We are also glad to know of the advancement you are making in all your studies." If in these years Lindsay had a vision of himself as fulfilling some kind of a great career, it was natural enough for him to have had it, considering the tender appreciation with which he was clothed by his mother, and these words from fond grandparents, watching his life unfold.

Those late grammar school years, and the high school years were filled with dramatic stir in the country at large. No period in American history, when Mars was not stalking the land, have been more picturesque, or have had more color, more human noise of an arresting sort, whether of debate, complaint, or angry protest. For in these years one of those economic stresses struck the country, such as America had seen before; only now it was denounced more vehemently than ever before, perhaps more so than in the days of the Biddle bank and Andrew Jackson, when the country was saved for good and all from the money power, as it was then hoped. Lindsay saw a good deal of this storm with comprehending eyes, and later learned what awoke it, and what it did of harm, and who tried to protect the people against its devastations. He saw and heard Bryan, who sprang up as a leonine protest against the demonetization of silver, against the oppressions of monopolies, against banks who had gone into the "governing business" when the government should control both itself and the banks; against "government by injunction," and the use of the Federal army in local disturbances; against the tariff, of course; against everything in short which was robbing the poor man and making the rich man richer. The election of Cleveland in 1892 had brought no relief to the people, not even on the tariff, which was the paramount issue of that year, resolved by direction at the polls to lower it. It had not been lowered; but the banks had held to their privileges, and there had been bond issues to raise gold for the treasury with which to protect the gold reserve. There were questions here which Lindsay at that age could not understand, because no one of any age understood them. But no matter for that; people were suffering and something had to be done. The wails of Kansas had been heard all over the land; and strange characters like Peffer and Mary Ellen Leese had come from there. Coxey's army had marched to Washington asking for relief. There in Springfield was John P. Altgeld, elected governor of Illinois, a mild blue-eyed man, with a sad pallor over his thoughtful face who, in the late eighties and a little before, had been writing for the press on economic questions, on taxation and prisons, on juvenile offenders, and on police brutality. He had pardoned the Chicago anarchists and had brought down upon himself the execration of the metropolitan press from coast to coast.

He had protested against the sending of Federal troops to Chicago during the Debs strike of 1894, and he had been excoriated for that. But when the Democratic convention of 1896 convened he had his revenge. He and the radicals in that convention, the protestants of some years against the steady descent of the country into the hands of monopolists and imperialists, bounced Cleveland "in a glorious hour," as Lindsay in 1919 wrote in the poem "Bryan, Bryan, Bryan, Bryan." Lindsay lived close enough to the Executive Mansion in Springfield to see the stooped figure of Governor Altgeld shuffling along, bearing his ignominies with a pathetic patience. Here was another Lincoln, perhaps. Lindsay evidently thought so; but the two characters had little in common. Altgeld was radically reckless; Lincoln was astute and cautious. On political issues and questions, the very same that were alive in Lincoln's day, the two men were at the antipodes of each other. Altgeld never shirked a disagreeable task, or ran from a danger, or stood back when a desperate cause was failing and needed help. Lincoln played a careful course from beginning to end. One believes that Doctor Mohawk admired Altgeld profoundly and never deserted him. As to Mrs. Lindsay her general temperament was not so reassuring upon this subject. But however that may be, and whatever Lindsay heard at home, if anything, derogatory to Altgeld, he maintained an admiration for him and celebrated him in "The Eagle That Is Forgotten," verses that will keep Altgeld's name alive longer than anything Altgeld said himself. Everything that Altgeld stood for, and as it turned out died for, has become as dead as the issues between the Houses of York and Lancaster. But the spirit of the man, poured upon what engrossed his moral nature, deserves to live, and Lindsay has made it live.

It was a part of Lindsay's education, a part of the growth of his mind as a poet to live through these years of economic war and tumult. It was immensely to his advantage as a poet to get the color and drama of this humanitarian struggle; and his nature made him a sensitive plate to its impressions. In these years he gathered material for poems of inestimable value from the standpoint of an American poetry, and he made telling use of it in poems, later to be noticed. When he stood with his best girl at sixteen years of age on the occasion when Bryan in that whirlwind campaign of 1896 visited Springfield, he took into his poetical storehouse the spirit and the substance of poems the like of which no other American has written, as even none of his contemporaries was cognizant of what he saw, or could give it the same sympathetic treatment. That is, Lindsay had a certain rearing and environment, he was out of a definite American breed of people, and this campaign and its dramatic figures meant to him more nearly what they were in fact as American expressions than they did to poets of the East who were educated to believe that the West was raw and uninformed and that its cries of distress were comic articulations rather than ordered and sensible formulations of anything genuinely true, not to say were authentic arguments based upon any sane view of finance and economics. For that matter the East does not deserve to bear all the blame of this division of the country's mind and heart. The West then was and still is more East than South. It was the East and New York that peopled Illinois, Wisconsin, Indiana, Iowa, and the West, including Kansas, where the New England emigration societies more than held their own against the settlers from the South in the fifties of the last century. Illinois was Kentucky and Virginia from Springfield to Cairo, but it was also Whig in the old days; while the northern part of the State was New England and New York. These together, like a stalwart father and his sons, turned on the South which they never liked, and subdued the poet's beloved Virginia for money's sake, and under the guise of a regenerating theodicy. They also in the West and the East vanquished "boy Bryan," and made Kansas take some other remedy than free silver for her maladies, or continue to suffer.

The "Bryan, Bryan, Bryan, Bryan" will be discussed later in its place. Now it is sufficient to consider its biographical import. He wrote that he stood by his best girl as the Bryan parade passed. "We were fairy democrats." Her "gold chums" had cut her; but this was surely the day for two such young radicals unafraid to assert their faith. Was this the girl, one wonders, who scribbled back to Lindsay in school formal thanks for Lindsay's note, who felt "inspired to say some sweet things," these words being the only evidence among all these voluminous papers preserved for more than forty years, that Lindsay in school was romantically stirred, and like his brother poets in all ages had yielded to some girl's winsome smile, and believed himself in love? Whoever she may have been she was called his best girl in the Bryan poem; and they stood together in jubilation, while the earth rocked, and the bands played tunes of victory for the immediate destruction of all artificers in brass and their instructors, with Tubal Cain thrown in. They stood while Bryan was introduced, while Altgeld gave him greeting. They saw the prairie avenger lift his hand to quiet the multitude. They heard Bryan utter one of the epigrams for which he grew famous in that summer of 1896: "the people have a right to make their own mistakes"; they have a right to have whatever government they wish; they have a right to save themselves. If they do not do so who will save them? In this hour Lindsay was facing the path that Bryan was to follow to defeat. He, too, was to undertake the reform of conditions about him, and to shoulder the great task of making his city and his country freer and more beautiful. He was to make these attempts, however, not as a statesman, but in the spirit of Plato who dreamed of the City of the Perfect; of Matthew Arnold who arraigned the

materialism of Philistines as the source of England's deg-
radation, and especially of Ruskin who in his social work
sought to restore an expropriated earth to the children of
men, to the poor and dispossessed, and to those spirits "that
ordain and reward with conscious felicity all that is decent
and orderly, beautiful and pure." There will be no doubt
when this study is finished, and all the indisputable history
of Lindsay's life is laid before the reader, that he had the
moral fervor, the high seriousness from his first day, which
must always exist as the blood and flesh of a great poet. It
may have been his voice which was too ill-formed to carry
the utterance of his passion and his hope, which is a sop
thrown here to those who think Lindsay's work awkward,
and even out of taste; but none can deny his consecration to
his country, and to the art which he believed had corrective
powers. In these respects he was of the stature of Shelley
and Tolstoy. Like the former, dying not in youth, but in
middle life, he lived to learn that weak human nature, loath
to postpone the lesser things of today for the better things
of tomorrow, can be fooled with games and bread, with
movies and ice cream, and will not shoulder the battle of
having all these things, but under conditions of greater
freedom and beauty. Life breaks down just at this point,
and always does so. Where shall the rescuer work to prevent
this catastrophe? Shall he be a satirist, and say that there
is no hope, and the best thing to do is to laugh? Or shall
he sacrifice himself, and love that which will destroy not only
him, but itself? Lindsay chose the Promethean path. He
took upon himself the burden of poverty, hating the commercial materialism of his land, as Arnold and Ruskin hated
the machine civilization of England. The happy day of
Bryan's reception in Springfield turned into the bitter night
of "boy Bryan's" defeat. The merchant philosophy that
there is nothing to life but to get what you want and to get
it quick, and by any means, triumphed. What is all talk

about justice, and beauty, and the equal rights of all? It is pure twaddle, say these sons of Tubal Cain. Give people jobs enough to keep them quiet and deceived. The earth belongs to those who can seize it; and they are ideologues, disturbers, anarchists and fools, and on occasion what is called poets, who are trying to turn life into other channels from those where it seeps along ditches for the watering of favorite preserves and stolen gardens. Let us control these sources of food and profit, and we shall feed the people as much as they deserve, and as they deserve, say these tumorous giants grown on the doctrine of *laissez faire*. For the most part they have their way, against angels with ineffectual wings, against colossal power like that of Tolstoy, against the scholarly irony of Arnold. They put down Bryan without difficulty. And Lindsay, who stood there that day believing that he saw a hero sweeping on to conquest, was himself to die with his social dreams unrealized, leaving poems which grew from his spiritual consecration, as the only evidence of his life's passion and work.

CHAPTER IV

LINDSAY entered Hiram College as a full freshman in September of 1897. This school is located at Hiram, Ohio, and was founded in 1850 as a Campbellite institution. One of its distinguished graduates was the President, James A. Garfield, who after a course at Williams College returned to his alma mater to be a professor there, and afterwards to assume the presidency of the school. Lindsay was sent there, doubtless, because it was a Campbellite school, but the then president, Mr. Zollars, was an old and dear friend of Doctor Lindsay.

Lindsay recorded that he enjoyed his first year at Hiram immensely. He was recruited by the junior class to illustrate their annual. He worked very hard at his writing, on preparing chapel orations, and orations for the Delphic Society. He was supposed to study medicine, however, but according to his own admission could not remember a single lesson. Doctor Page, under whom he took his medical course, such as it was, donated him a few credits. Except for these his medical studies were a complete failure. In mathematics he was unable to fathom the meaning of a logarithm. On the other hand he got a credit in hermeneutics, but at the hands of a benevolent professor, who was won over because Lindsay had read Henry Ward Beecher's sermons. His work in Latin was most indifferent. He was tutored in Cæsar by a Miss Marcia Henry, whom he admired as much as he disliked Cæsar's Commentaries. All the while he was having a very good time. He spent endless hours at the home of Professor Wakefield, and we shall see from his diaries how active his mind was, and what plans he was forming for the future, under the happy auspices of school life at this country college. In his second year at Hiram he illustrated the college annual, and worked hard for a place in the oratorical contest.

His mother's addiction to public speaking and the pulpit eloquence of Grandfather Frazee were inspiring factors in this ambition. But also he was writing a good deal of poetry, most of which became lost, as he later declared, except as it may have been preserved in copies by Hiram students. In high school in 1896 he had written "How a Little Girl Sang," "The Foolish Queen of Fairyland," and "The Battle," already mentioned. In his second year at Hiram he wrote "The Song of the Garden Toad;" and in 1899 he had produced one version of "The Last Song of Lucifer." We shall see later, more in detail, how Lindsay as a boy set down poems which he afterward added to and revised, and made at last fit productions for his first published books. It was so with Poe, who wrote some of his best poems at twenty or before, such as "Israfel," first published in 1831 in an imperfect form, and then later given out in its present perfection. "The Litany of Heroes," for example, was changed and added to from Lindsay's early years until it became what it is in his *Collected Poems*.

The standards in oratory at Hiram were high, according to Lindsay's estimation. He came out last in such contests. In athletics he was indifferent, being beaten in every event. Once playing football he received a scar on his chin which he retained for life. He hated trigonometry, astronomy, anatomy, French, Latin, chemistry, physics, and materia medica. How make a doctor of such a mind? He loved speaking, in which he won no honors, writing and drawing. All the while he was reading omnivorously, and making endless notes in diaries, to which we shall come. He quit Hiram in the spring of 1900, but with credit about sufficient to have made him a full sophomore. In this last year of school he scarcely went to a class, but stayed at the house of Professor Mc-Diarmid, where he read Kipling over and over, from cover to cover; and explored the art history of Japan, and the works of Ruskin to the full.

In June of 1931 he returned to Hiram to receive an honorary degree. Continuous travelling over America since 1912, and observation made of every one of its universities, where he also spoke, had not dimmed his love for Hiram. It was still to him the largest of all schools, and the deepest in his affection. He thought that some magic word spoken by him for Hiram might make it an eternal creative force. Some Dante might be required to speak this word for Hiram at the parting of the ways, where it might turn one way and become an imitation of schools of the same size in duller regions, or become the only school on American soil true to its unique and beautiful hill. He thought that in twenty years it would be a place of pilgrimage for all eager creative artists of the world, or merely a hill with a mellow tradition. These prophecies he set down in the *Spider Web* for 1932, the manual which he illustrated in his first year. He may have meant by this extravagant language that Hiram would be a place of pilgrimage on account of his association with it, or because it would become more and more an American institution such as he dreamed; or he may have been dreaming as he did when he vaticinated about Magical Springfield. However, he was speaking in earnest when he asked for Hiram a literary course which would make creative writers such as Harriet Beecher Stowe and Willa Cather; and when he said that there should be a course in drama which would educate dramatists as surprising as Ibsen, and that the college did not need athletes, but should have aviators like Lindbergh and explorers like Byrd. After these years his loves and ideals had not changed. He despised the bond salesman as a man not needed in America. What was wanted was more Johnny Appleseeds, more Poes.

These would be worth more to the world than all the English departments ever imagined! He wanted Hiram to produce beautiful verse, since it was a superb example of unspoiled Americanism. "He who expresses Hiram will be an American artist." Did Whitman ever grow more rapturous upon similar American expectations? Lindsay thought the trees about Hiram suggested an American architecture. The outdoors quality of the place, the delight to be rural there, the religious tradition, and the desire to be devout, all these things made a place where creative artists should be born. Hiram should be not a liberal arts school, but an art school that was liberal for the production of unconventional drama, unharnessed singing, unmeasured mysticism, unhampered philosophy, unspoiled manners, unprisoned health and laughter, undefiled athletics, undraped sculpture, unbroken youth, unacademic lecture halls. All this and some more. The word of Dante was surely spoken among this list of hopes. His studies and reading at Hiram, his meditations there given full report in his diaries can be traced into these words of 1931. He did not change, but he grew. His radicalism was as pronounced as Whitman's, but it was not derived from Whitman. It took its source in a nature as original as Whitman's, which had nourished itself upon studies and examples of its own native choice. But no less the mystic was the essential Lindsay; and in "The Ezekiel Chant," which he wrote for the occasion when Hiram conferred a degree upon him, we have lines both mystical and radical; we have wings and wheels out of the Ezekiel vision, and matter of fact references to the mobs and towers of New York, remote from which the Ezekiel wings should soar strongly over Hiram hill. This poem written in quatrains of iambic tetrameter is among the most finished verses that Lindsay ever wrote. The old fire is still burning, but the lack of grosser fuel has given its flames tranquillity and radiance.

We have now reached the point in this study of Lindsay

where no surmises or conjectures need to be indulged, and
no arguments made, for the purpose of determining the
nature of the man and the composition of his genius. He
himself wrote a Prelude, or growth of the poet's mind,
and did it in the diaries or journals which he kept. These
become of first-rate importance with his years at Hiram
College. As with Wordsworth, so with Lindsay, the imagination was a mystical faculty, which saw into the heart of
things more clearly than the intellectual eye.

> "This spiritual love acts not nor can exist
> Without imagination, which in truth
> Is but another name for absolute power,
> And clearest insight, amplitude of mind,
> And reason in her most exalted mood."
> Prelude XIV, 188.

It is true that Lindsay did not have this insight to the
highest degree, for where it exists an intuition goes straight
to the core of an object or a person, and lays hold of the
essential. This is the case with Shakespeare, and with
Goethe. But what he did see was that the outer appearance
of things, the garb of nature, the language and the inarticu-
lateness of human beings, and the inexplicable shadows and
filaments which clothe the life of man, have something back
of them of which these are in a way the hieroglyphics, to use
a word that he often employed to shadow forth his speculations and his dreams. These he tried to penetrate; these he
sang; these he sought to fathom with unwearied patience.
What he knew perfectly well was that there is such a thing
as the mystic quest, and that he was predetermined by his
nature to follow it, as Merlin followed the gleam; and to
endure everything of poverty, pain, and misunderstanding
while doing so. He took the journey of the soul by the inner
ascent, to quote Dean Inge's words on Plotinus, the ascent
that leads to the presence of God, and to immediate union

with him. This desire and this faith cannot be touched, or controverted by skeptical logic. For what a man sees he sees; and what he desires with his whole heart to possess cannot be made untrue by satire or analysis. "Mysticism is an extension of the mind to God by means of the longing of love," wrote Inge, and the matter was never better defined. Nothing moreover more accurately describes the spirit of Lindsay. It will be found written all over his daily jottings, and in many of his poems, in all of them directly or indirectly. Whitman when calling his country to cultivate religion, morality, and beauty, when contending that the religious impulse was necessary to great literature, would have been satisfied with Lindsay as his son in respect to these things. For by religion Whitman did not mean a credal confession, or a church adoption, a baptism or an orthodoxy. He meant a moral conviction and passion by which man is linked to cosmic forces, to something beyond the daily life of materialistic effort, and by which life is dignified and uplifted.

When Lindsay's mind is carefully studied it will be seen that he paid no attention to the doctrine of rewards and punishments, and none to any heaven to be. He was among those who sought nothing beyond the stars "for a reason to perish and be sacrificed," but who sacrifice themselves, as he did, to earth in order "that earth may someday become superman." Thus saith Zarathustra, and thus said Lindsay in his own way, and as a matter of original thinking. Out of such spiritual passion is great literature made, which is the point that Whitman drove home. Lindsay had this passion, and never experienced any other. He had no period of Byronic pessimism. He was always the soul seeking beauty and God. Before he wrote a line of moment he had this innate urge, besides which talents, smartness, erudition, culture are nothing. However this flame which Whitman called religious can be the Shelley Prometheanism; it can be the eighty years' toil of Goethe, seeking to shed light for his fellows; it can be the communion of Wordsworth with nature, the courageous eye of Sophocles who wrote down the fate of man; it can be many men of the past, but it must be where great literature is. Without it there are generations of writers who shed reflected light, whose soil is thin, where the seed fails, crowds of rhetoricians, imitators, and hunters for fame, whose flower is brief.

We have seen that Lindsay cared nothing for mathematics and science. His mind was concerned with what he saw as a deeper reality. He knew that the eye sees only a fraction of the colors which stronger physical eyes can see. That being so what were those colors, and what was back of those seen and those unseen? Why take Lindsay to task on his mysticism when physicists assert that there are thousands of octaves besides the eleven which the physical ear can discern? These sounds that cannot be heard fascinated Lindsay's imagination, and concerned his mystical faith. We shall say something hereafter about his mental picture of the world, of his West, and whether he saw it truly or no. But now as we approach the prelude, the record of his mind's growth, it is important only to say that in this life Lindsay sat as one in an audience listening to music being played on a few keys of a piano, while he dreamed of what the whole score was, and how it would sound if the piano's keys could all be used.

In 1899 at Hiram College Lindsay started to keep six different notebooks. One was devoted to a study of the dictionary, to rhetoric, phrases, verses, and new words, "when nothing else." A second to culture; a third to homiletics; a fourth to style; a fifth to speaking; and the sixth to pictures. These books contain his most secret meditations, his most private reflections and prayers. But they are surrounded with no more sacredness than the revelations of Wordsworth's Prelude; and it is good for America to know how this young man of twenty was preparing himself for some work of worth in the world, though he then scarcely knew what it would be. It is valuable to know what thoughts he was thinking, what books he was reading to the ends of his aspirations; and how he was guarding the faith, and revering the memory of the illustrious heroes of the past, and giving praise to spirits and demi-gods, according to the injunction of Pythagoras. In each of these books he wrote the dedication, "This book belongs to Christ." Here now we may see what Lindsay was thinking in his heart of hearts in these schooldays at Hiram College. We begin with the one devoted to rhetoric and the like, "when nothing else." At this time he was reading Emerson and Lowell, and many other books. "Beware of adjectives and opaque words," is one of the first entries in this book. Ugly in the sense of hideous is a great word, he thought; and should be used oftener. Soon there is this reflection: "In the world there are two forces, nature which extends through every function of man, and love whereby man may be divine in power. Two beings, God and man. No commands of Christ are impossible. Follow every commandment vigorously. Get even with the devil. Comply with the conditions by which Christ keeps possession of men. . . . Do not despise letter writing. A circle of intellectual worthy correspondents is a splendid field for the development of a wide sympathy, a training in the suppression of the ego, and good practice in English. . . . I think that my first poetic impulse is for music; second a definite conception with the ring of the universe; third clearness of exposition. . . . I hold it an especial quality in a good poem, elasticity and suggestiveness whereby the reader may see his own emotions on a new framework. Thus there are a thousand Hamlets, though each one is Hamlet the Dane. People may never read alike at last. The privilege of private interpretation extends to non-Hebrew poetry. So when this man has not read this poem, as I felt it when I wrote it, but has yet retained the relation, a proportional value of each word, he has shown the possibilities of the poem rather than a lack of insight into the author's sympathy for the author's exact sentiment. . . . Angels and ministers of grace defend us from the snares of current literature. By all means let us read the dead masters."

"It would be a splendid thing to do for Poe, the great father of the American art of literature, what Carlyle did for Cromwell, that is to make his literary name great. It would take a lifetime of collecting critical evidence, and a summary of the literature of the world at the season the book appears. Now call it, What the Magician Has Done. Not by any means a panegyric, but a summary of Poe as the suggester of themes, as a strong literary influence, the raw material of imagination, from whom better workmen have been unable to withdraw. He did not start a literary fashion like any of his peers, to begin in some sort of iconoclasm or novel affectation, and wind up by a deluge of weak mannerism. He is a steady and growing influence, not the master of any school, but still the monitor of the art ideal; his treasures are in confusion like the lavished heaped up gold, etc., in the Assignation. The best of books might exhort young literary men to turn to Poe without any shame-facedness, or hesitation, but with discreetness and duly digested selection of suggestive inspiration. Exhort, beseech them to act upon the literary law, which Poe's work best illustrates. The chapters might be headed: 1. How he is a magician. Sketch of his actual work. 2. Our consequent modest claim and his real worth. That is the modest claim his partisans must make. Emphasize his main present claim, and his unexplored corners. 3. Literary fashions, literary monuments, how they rise and fall. There is neither rise nor fall in the power of the magician's wand. 4. In other languages a special case soon disposed of. Poe must reign mostly in his own tongue, for peculiar reasons. 5. How real his touch in influence is when it can be seen at all; how he calls forth all the originality to be possessed by the disciple affected, even when they swallow but a morsel of him. 6. The various literary spheres he has influenced, and how much."

Light is thrown on Lindsay's evolving mind and art by observing that nowhere did he give the same attention to Whitman as he here gave to Poe. Whitman was much closer to Lindsay spiritually than Poe was, in fact the two were very close of kin, and had many ideas of the art of poetry, its mission and spirit, which corresponded. Their insistence upon Americanism was a common note. On the other hand, the art of Poe was of little use to Lindsay, and furnished him with nothing, perhaps, except the repetend, and a skill in echolalia. The next entry may help to explain this inconsistency. "Under any of the inevitable world conditions men are never big enough for their duties. The world might be organized so that by bringing to bear the right personalities on the right situations Christ sociology might be put into a completely successful order; by the zealously preached or best enacted teaching and living Christ is the time set right. Here is the prodigious gap and the prodigious necessity for the spirit of truth, here indeed its only place to convict the world of sin, of righteousness and of judgment, in spite of frail human impossibility of being committed by the best and most spiritualized, strongest human agencies. Pray therefore for the completing power of the spirit of Truth in any message to be carried. . . ."

"A vocabulary experiment, or phrase experiment of profit would be to search the strange parts of the Scriptures, the obscurities of Job, and the ravings of the prophets, and find figures of speech and phrases. If good use can be made of them the skill will make them doubly my own as subtle allusions. Many of my concepts could be built of Testament phrases."

What became of this literary plan remains doubtful, considering that after all Lindsay did not saturate his poetry with Bible phrases and manner of speech, even to the extent that Swinburne did, who was one of Lindsay's early passions, and remained such all his life.

"When it comes to considering books that have most influenced the century I must not expect to read them all of necessity. But I must know of them each one, and be sure of the influence each one had. Then I will know enough. . . . The wisest way to write poetry, write it in prose first. Then choose a well finished metrical creation of Tennyson or some other as a basis, and imitate methods of rhythm and meter. I have a careless habit of following any length of line and any wild order of rhyme. Therefore this discipline is wisest. I begin on the Golden Rod Rhyme. . . . 'Giving form is eternal existence,' Blake said. And I know of no better way of epitomizing Browning's message. In Tennyson the sense of present, past and future, of tradition and ancient dignity, and coming glory are all his greatness. Browning's greatness is in the eternalness of the present crisis. . . . Now there is something of the essence of average human life in George Eliot; for when I read of Maggie Tulliver of thirteen, and then skipped to her romance of maturity, I felt as though I had forced prematurely love upon a girl of thirteen, violated the order of nature, been too impatient to wait four years to let the woman grow. It was an awful challenge to the conscience, or at least the scrupulosity. When I read up these skipped pages I felt as one making amends to an injured friend or neighbor."

"Shakespeare's plays are stories of families. The beginning of families, the ending of families, the destruction of families, the re-uniting of families. . . . It is no more wrong to impose a death on the race than to impose a marred life. Death is welcome to any manly man, but a marred life is something to fear. . . . Agnosticism is the meekness of those content with the unfolding of a real life."

Throughout this book, as in the others to follow, there are notes made of stories to be written, plots to be worked out, characters to be drawn. These are almost innumerable. At this point Lindsay set down the scheme of a story of David and Jonathan, whose love surpassed "the love of women, and whose self-sacrifice outdid very lovely women." Thus he would, by a series of such fictions exploiting manly love, explode the theories of the "dear old romance." To this point he here quoted the observation of Keats on the "generality of women" to "whom I had rather give a sugar plum than my time."

Lindsay indulged in many speculations upon the character and spirit of the Saxon stock. So in this notebook he recorded: "He whose dream of poetry is worthy of his Saxon kind is the one who seeks to chant a saga as fiery and bold as those of the gray-bearded in the hall Beowulf. There are bold hearts as many now sing to, who love best neither the words that are plain, nor the fancies that are fine, nor the voice that is articulate with well chosen speech. They love best the great chant that comes like the roll and the reel of ten thousand martial drums, speaking nothing to them but that they are men, and that the world is a wild flight of bold warriors, and that the joy of the battle coming is greater than any revel that has passed. Still for the sake of those who learn courage only through the chosen words of the battle cry, who cannot feel unless they first understand, for their sakes we must choose our words well, even in the heaviest frenzy, and maintain the conscience of art throughout the most primitive society. Thus we may make timid hearts bold, and quiet hearts bolder, and thus in the homes and schools and marts and forums of the twentieth century we will not forget that any of us, that the least of us are Saxons, born to dare, the race that shall dare forever. . . . The undying charm of classic fable has no charm for me. . . . Keats had flint and iron in him. . . . The genius of poetry must work out its own salvation in a man. It cannot be matured by law and precept, but by sensation and watch-

[66]

ful care—in itself. . . . Balzac's curiosity proceeds from curiosity. Thackeray's from sympathy. . . . Our fifteen- or twenty-year-old pear tree is a fine figure of speech."

"My first essay of ten or eleven shows I am for generalization rather than a power for doing it accurately. 2, A tendency to fly off at many tangents of thought that confuses the discussion, and makes paragraphs impossible. 3, A sense of climax, and a strong sense of dogmatic epigram (labor rules the world). 4, A sense that the world is a balanced bundle of laws. 5, A sense of the individuality, and strong personal oversight of the Creator. 6, A sense that the laws of the soul of man and the soul of God, and the laws of the roots of the trees are all in common. 7, A sense of the essential beauty of the world. 8, A sense of the principle of disappointment, decay as a part of the natural order, not to be feared, but to be understood. 9, A sense that all honest work ought to be respected. 10, A sense that the only social tie, and the only social motive between citizen and citizen is to be respected. God has provided others. But this is all I have recorded here. 11, Comparison of City and Country. A sense that man is fundamentally educated by the phenomena of nature, and that man is the divinely appointed ruler of nature throughout the universe. 12, A fundamental and disastrous irreverence for the paraphernalia of this world, the wrappings and mannerisms. 13, A reverence for wholesale ruggedness. 14, A mistaken tendency to see indifference in the souls of men, consequent upon their environment and deeds. Now all above I must never expect to understand and get away from. They are a part of me, the essential self. Any of these old opinions I may hope well to defend, and may never feel lost and doctrineless. I can defend them all with a whole heart, and a perfect faith, which will keep me strong."

"There are no masses, classes or asses among immortal souls."

"Good serious poems of the streets and alleys of Chicago, ash barrels, stray dogs, papers, old newspapers, old shoes. I say there is sentiment, real sentiment to be extracted from them. Muddy crossings. The great thing is to choose variety in your symbolizing and sweetness of your sympathy. Ash barrel—symbol of the burnt-out and worn-out art, and civilization personified by fashion, and social absolutism. To do this clearly and well with dignity and respect, and without sarcasm, but rather tenderness. The ash barrel is not only unavoidable, but necessary. Not all symbols see real beauty in the things themselves and leave them no further interpretation. . . . Twelve toasts, each one a sonnet, 1, To womankind. 2, To children. 3, To beauty beginning with the moon and ending with the voice of woman. 4, To America, phrases from the national songs uniquely played upon. 5, To the Saxon race. 6, To friendship in feasting. 7, To memories of rejoicing. 8, To old letters, hard to destroy. What shall I do with old letters? 9, To the greatest city of the world. 10, To the men of the world. 11, To the Mississippi. 12, To the mothers of America. . . . Write a series of odes, hymns, addresses, imaginary visions, etc., of a series of English poetic masters, imitating each master at his highest and most individual metrical triumph. The meter should be rigidly regulated."

"The great beauty of a dead master is that his work is all done, his life and many examples are all there to choose from, and no one phase of his development is too omnipresent to distract one. A great master treads devious paths before he finds himself at last; and his followers must stumble and be lost behind him. No living man in his lifetime should master me. If one dead master is outgrown one must turn to another. Ruskin must be learned as a whole, and one must read many lives of him before one reads many books of his. The great inspirations in him are the elements of his soul, always constant in their many contradictions of expression.

The thing to do is to find one stand he took, most central, most normal, and most strong and characteristic in his life, one gospel he preached, and one deed of success. From that one may look before and after. To find this viewpoint one must read several good biographies to eliminate the personal element of his historians. The truest follower of a great man is the posthumous disciple, or else the one who gets his greatest inspiration by happy chance at his master's best period, and is led astray neither before nor after. . . . No such man as Doctor Johnson could have been immortal in France. But in Saxondom a man has two immortalities, the lesser from his work, the greater from his personality, his ancestry, his habits, etc. We Saxons are eternally curious and affectionate as to personality, and achievement theory, but not as to art."

"It is of no use to tell what you know to be true to a man or a nation, unless, if it is information you tell them so that they soften their hearts and change their views. Truth tempered in the heated forge of argument does not soon cool to be used quickly, and those who burn their hands will refuse the sword."

We now extract from the notebook which he entitled Culture the main reflections bearing upon his growth as a poetical mind. "I love the human race until they begin to ask me questions. . . . It is not true that every nation must work out its own salvation. Is not the shiftlessness of France today the result of mixing the mind of Rome with the iron of Gallic barbarism? . . . How seldom you see a man in desperate earnest to be good. Humanity is not intended to be in desperate earnest all the time. Our earnest hours transcribe the limits of our liberty in our lighter hours. But there are as many desperate for goodness as for power, or riches or fame. All these constantly strenuous are rare. . . . The ideal Saxon is proud of his people, and simply loyal wherever he goes. He will learn new scenes, new people, but will go no further than to put the new on a par with the old, and find the most in common with either."

"Study now in looking at men to strip them of the clothing of thought and culture, and leave the temperament bare; it's nearly all of the man anyway. The greatest philosophers, deep within the most scientifically established system, are forced at the last to make a choice between two paths where it is merely a question of temperament. Carlyle would have snarled though an ignoramus; Max Müller would be an agnostic without studying every language under the sun and proving it. Byron would have been a beast without being a poet; and so the question is a foolish one, when we ask of the one great heart whence got this man letters? It was a great temperament after all and nothing more. . . . The ideal Saxon will see in the people from whence he came all the glorious functions they have carried out in the state and civilization, be it known or unknown. He will see in his best work what has been prophesied by their best self denial; he will see in every ambition their unselfish hope for him, he will see in life itself nothing but what they have seen in different terms and a different language before his day. . . . He can expect to be no better, and no wiser, and may well be thankful to attain their high standard and unselfishness."

"Perhaps all early love affairs should be strangled or drowned like so many black kittens."

Lindsay by this time was contemplating the art course in Chicago, which he afterwards pursued there. With this in mind he made this note. "It will be a great thing to study the race communities in Chicago. The best knowledge of the Saxons involves the knowledge of many other races for comparison. It is well to study the customs, the usages, weaknesses and strength of other races, their principles of organization, its relation to their temperaments and physiognomy. Study also the effect of the Saxon on the people.

Determine the core and heart of the Saxon, and find the simple secret that makes him what he is." We interrupt the diary here apropos of this last entry to say that Lindsay laid a larger foundation than he needed or ever used. Days and days of study and reading during all his apprenticeship bore on his work in only the most general way, and largely in a manner undiscoverable.

"Whatever is is right. Now this would not be a good doctrine in the East, in the presence of stagnation. But if you are on the skirmish lines of progress in the West, fighting your best, then whatever is is right. . . . Idle men have no right to this doctrine. It comes as a revelation, the last reward of the faithful, strenuous life. It is stealing the reward of labor too early to believe this before one has learned that it is duty to labor, for then it means that it is right not to labor."

"Do not grow so worldly minded that you can speak lightly of a past grief or joy or hope or enthusiasm. If you are so scornful of your dead self, your coming self will be equally scornful of you. . . . The law of the household gods—a book, a firebrand, a fierce attack on all nasty unhonorable things. Write in a new strong way how filial piety is vital in China, and love of woman, and every man's love for his castle are the central facts of all civilization. Fight for the home, and bitterly denounce everything opposing." One wonders if Lindsay was then familiar with the version of the commandment to filial duty which reads: "Honor thy father and thy mother that thy days may be multiplied in this country of Adam, that Jhôah thy Gods have given thee." Here it seems, however, was the genesis of his noble poem "Shantung, or the Empire of China Is Crumbling Down," written years after this time.

"The machine shop should be as much the fashion as the football field to keep our dainty darlings rugged and grimed. How can it be made an American fashion? Study it till you learn it and then cartoon. . . . Wrath of the people is the wrath of good. . . . By too close inspection of the confused cross-section aspects of the universe the pessimist, the atheist, the worldling all are made, and their souls at last destroyed. . . . Christianity has shown what is in men; nothing else has done it. So in the study of comparative race types, and race influences study their best Christian products, subtract all Saxon influences, and you have the man plus Christianity. Then look at the man. So mission stations of every sort are the best means of studying the various types of man. . . . The Saxon has a strong hold on the Sunday School Christ. He needs the secular Christ."

"Is it true that the days of courtesy are not the days of independence? Is man never to be still rugged, yet exquisitely gallant, still free, yet a gentleman? Does there need to be invented a new and beautiful American courtesy to save the manly American from being a puppy, a tuft hunter, an arrogant idiot? . . . The moral habits to which England owes the kind of greatness she has, the habits of philosophical investigation, of accurate thought, of domestic seclusion and independence, of stern self reliance, and science, upright searching into religious truth, were only traceable in the distinctive creation of the Gothic schools. . . . It takes a life work of a genius at agitation, Wilberforce, Garrison, Wyckliffe, to create a new public opinion. It takes a skilled master to rouse it even when present to keep it at white heat. But an ordinary man may discover an already present opinion, deep hidden and make it known in its mass to all its representatives, till all men shall realize how many others believe so, and united confident action be the result of such mutual discovery. This is the work of the cartoon."

Along the way later Lindsay's ambition to be a cartoonist will reveal itself from his activities and from the confessions made to his diaries. He wanted to be a sort of moral censor of the nation of men by highly conceived drawings, having no touch of satire, but rather stressing the beautiful and the good. No ambition was ever more hopelessly and groundlessly entertained. It was a part of his straying around when he was trying to find himself, and the problem of a livelihood more and more pressed upon his life.

He was not much in key with the literature of the hour. We find these words: "Howells is one of these kind pessimists who is plaintively optimistic for the sake of his sensitive audience. . . . The indecent is merely the misplaced rather than that which should never be. The disgusting is that which appears at radically the wrong time. What is loathsome is merely that which is out of its proper order."

"The latter end of my life from 45–60 will be the day of generalship, when I will be called to my missionary work as it were. But my beginning life must be spent in three countries, America, France and Japan. Now for five years I must master Chicago, as typical America, to the nth power, and make a name that will make my living. Then for three years France. Then for two years Japan. Then for ten years America. . . . Second love is best because it is a refutation of that first love fatalism to which so many surrender. It is well that they should take first love as a vision from heaven, but not as a decree of fate. It is a revelation not of one's destiny, but of one's self. The chivalric deification of love and constancy is overdone in this first love fatalism. It is perverted. First love survived makes us go at second love with our eyes open, with self-control, not being captured, but giving one's self. This first love fatalism has been the creed of so many maidens that when they surrendered it for second love they had no law or creed to go by, and felt themselves cheated horribly, unfaithful to themselves and the dead past, instead of thankful for the past, and equipped in faith in any present love, and present day. Only first love is blind; only second love is wise. . . . It is plain that

I must in Chicago learn the art of selection in all matters. Promiscuous absorption is fatal. . . . Within the next five years I must be the biggest man of my size in Chicago, by January 1, 1905."

"After my three years in France and my two years in Japan I will be about 31; January 1, 1911, will be my consecration day. It looks to me now that my equipment up to that point would involve the religious cartoons I have contemplated. But Japan for headquarters. Christ may let me be of such service to him, if I work hard up to that point. But I must concentrate and consecrate. . . . The crude instincts must be lived up to. They must be trained. He that is faithful in that which is least is faithful also in much. The crudest instinct makes us commonality artists, poets, actors, musicians in the rough, when the unlawful results cannot justify much impulse upward."

"I think that the poet should believe in art for its own sake, but the draughtsman inevitably moralizes. Artists always preach, if it is nothing more than their school of art. Art is pre-eminently didactic."

"The American imagination has had a majestic training in material things. And it has been strained indeed to stretch a web of glamour over the harshness of vast iron work, and crude brick work, masonry and the armored hosts of ugly Satan that people our streets in the person of ugly buildings."

"After marriage a man is in debt. He mortgages himself to his children, his after life is devoted in the main anxiety to the coming generation. Ambition is shattered forever. Wherefore a man is never larger than the day before he quits batching. Let that day be a far one for me. . . . The life of the individual is by then entirely finished and the man gives his energies to thankless children."

"Now at thirty years of age Christ began his service of suffering. Up to that time he followed out his own individu-

ality and his own environment for a complete knowledge and
mastery of himself. It is for me to do otherwise. Let it be
definitely understood that every inch of my will up to thirty-
one years goes to the evolution of myself, and the perfection
of the mental, physical, spiritual machine. Not till then
am I to choose any great scheme of suffering, and self-
spending. I have a world to save, and must prepare, prepare, prepare. Then it will be for me to save my world. I
will constantly expect at thirty years of age I shall choose
the chance of utter suffering, and the spending of self to
which I am best adapted."

"English government and American civilization will one
day rule the world. The English nation will spend herself
as Rome spent herself conquering the world, and teaching
it law and order. Then when the lesson is fully learned, and
America has meanwhile perfected democracy to a perfect
civilization England will lose her strength, and give liberty
to the nations of the earth. . . . At last I am attending my
choice of a college. It is organized within myself—the college of the love of the people. . . . Tolstoy after my 31st
year shall find me his literal follower. As he has consecrated
the novel, so may I consecrate art. And he is not Christ-like
enough. I cannot be utterly consecrated until I am utterly
trained—I would be a useless madman. But I have the
capacity for a deliberate monomania I know. . . . After
thirty every man I have taken hold upon to set afire for
Christ."

"It behooves the Saxon to change his idea of heaven.
Heaven is the New Earth it devolves upon the Saxon to
establish. That must be his religion, his ideal, his ultimate
heaven. The Saxon does not make love in songs and meta-
phors like the Song of Solomon, neither must his heaven be
expressed in oriental figures. He must translate them into
an Occidental heaven."

De Maupassant's literary rule derived from Flaubert is

copied into this book to this effect: "Whatever may be the thing one wishes to say there is only one phrase to express it, only one verb to animate it, and only one adjective to qualify it." He also wrote down what Lanier said of himself: "Let my name perish. The poetry is good poetry, and the music is good music, and beauty dieth not, and the heart that made it will find it." Lindsay denominated Lanier here, "the typical of the obscured Saxon singer." Of himself, he said, "I have just enough pedigree to keep me proud, but not so much as to choke or appall ambition."

"I would like to be a dragon with golden claws, and go out and fight the thunder and bite it as it rolls high in the air. I would like to climb to the top of the sky and fall down upon it and scatter it like dust, break it into infinite pieces. Perfect temperament, the perfect development of personality comes after the soul is broken and crushed by circumstances, and finally lit by coals from the holy altar, and offer of incense beaten small. That might be the title of a poem: Incense beaten small. . . . The grinding poverty of the Chinese nation has kept it virile. It has not the means of enervating luxurious living."

"The Japs have never had an open vision of the Great I Am. They need to be smitten into seriousness by a revelation of the one God who is alone in the world and the hell which is underneath civilization, and the Christ whose eyes are the fire."

So much for this notebook, and the growing mind of the poet as he revealed it here. We may say in conclusion of it that it contains fourteen pages of notes on Blake's poetry as assayed by Swinburne's book on Blake published in 1868; and voluminous notes from Gilchrist's life of Blake. We pass now to the notebook which Lindsay entitled Half Hour Memoranda of Culture, and which he dedicated to Christ.

"Seldom put down a poem," he wrote, "until it is clearly to be illustrated or cartooned; or better, put them all down with the action and appearance imagined. When you think a thought be sure that five of the master minds have thought it better before you."

"Reasons why I should be allowed the privilege of self education. 1, Every other sort has had a fairer chance. 2, I have never had a fair chance at myself. 3, I have initiated and fostered without help all my vast promising lines of development in large measure in proportion to the other possible lines. 4, The time to work on an idea is when it is burning in the brain and not when it is applied like a cold salve from without. 5, Ideas will not come on schedule time. Neither will thoughts. They come and go. They are like sunshine to be taken when they come. 6, There is a fixed law of routine within me, but one that does not correspond to anything without. It can be depended upon to keep constantly and earnestly at work on one of three things, drawing, writing and speaking. 7, I have. ambition that may be depended upon to be steady, fierce and relentless. 8, I have constant motives to ensure safe and proper direction. 9, I have ideals high enough to lead me on and keep me constantly unsatisfied with present progress. Wherefore it is safe, reasonable and logical from the broadest ideas of an education to allow me largely my own study, my own studio, and my own teachers. . . . If a man's body is the temple of God, are not his hours of inspiration the breathing presence of the Creator? . . . Plants develop when the sunshine strikes them. The only hours of real educational development in a man are when he is putting the shackles of his own making on ideas of his own."

"If I read twenty-eight days with a whole heart and with nothing else in my brain, then for three days take physical exercise entirely, I am ripe for four days of writing poetry or prose. This is a sure rule. I need to endeavor to be my most Hiram self in the world at large to the nth power. Let me endeavor to be master only in the things that made me know there a little for writing, but most for drawing. Let me illustrate a world animal as I illustrated the Hiram animals by a cartoon design illustration methods."

"I want to read all the great books and think over the great thoughts, and wrestle with them as Jacob wrestled with the angels. . . . Do not resolve to accomplish in character building more than the past has demonstrated you are able to do. Walk forward, but at a pace that will not kill your wind; but do not run into mental debt to yourself by resolving more than your normal will has met—do not overstrain the will. It is bankruptcy. Curb your imagination; simplify your aims."

"If one had to choose between Macaulay who never forgot anything, and Emerson who rarely remembered anything in an exact literal way, one would fasten on the man of insight, and let the man of memory go his way. The will of an artist is in his ability to forget the non-essential, and remember the essential. The characteristic of art is not memory, but insight."

"Our chief concern is to master this modern world, not the world of Cæsar or Columbus. . . . Let me withhold all energy from such enterprise as I have failed at in the past. As to the Y. M. C. A. Now this is a movement that should be expounded. It is becoming majestic in its extent. It is an army in need of a singer. For its uses I have an equipment of temperament, habit and method of thought. What Kipling has done for the Anglo-Saxon, that may be done for the people developed by this sort of work."

"It is a rare and royal spirit that will reconcile culture and manliness. Culture is like a bleating, bawling lamb, and mankind is a roaring lion, and they cannot divide the hours of the ordinary narrow human heart. Only strong Christian civilization, or a Christian heart can bring them into peace."

"What will be the day of judgment? It will be the day

when all our inward past shall be opened out to those that loved us to see every untrue inward act and thought and motive, everything false and selfish. Oh, woe and shame! Oh, those cursing, loving, reproving eyes! . . . There is the personal equation in everything, mysteriously involved in everything. Take suffering. To high souls it is a blessing, and a final expansion; to others it is a plain, straight down-right curse. And in like manner sensual or ordinary mental exhilarations may in separate individuals be blessings or curses. The principle holds widely and closely through the life of the soul, and in its religion. Mohammed was preferable to Henry VIII; one made the best of a poor religion, the other flunked at a good one. And Christianity has produced everything from Loyola to George Fox." . . . At this time Lindsay was reading Tennyson's "In Memoriam," and he here sets down many extracts from that poem.

"Doubt that comes rolling down after an unquestioning, hardened, weather-beaten faith, shatters it forever like a tree under the lightning. The same doubt in another soul may be a higher terrace from which to behold a grander universe. But believe me, my soul, when I say one may ascend terrace after terrace in this scale of illuminated doubt and the last shall be nothing but the dogmatic unquestioning faith we left so far below us in our childhood. Thus it is that tolerably right dogmatism is the best for the world, the preacher, preaching with a faith that comes with self control must preach to inspire a faith that is absolute, childlike, unquestioning and unspeculative. Too many men are going to hell to stop to let them possibly doubt it. We go from dogmatism at first to dogmatism at last. Let us preach of the heavenly city of faith we shall reach, not stopping to explain that we left it behind us, knowing we must reach it again to find our disciples there ahead of us, just because they believed and stayed behind us. Doubt may be illumination for the few; it is damnation for the many. The road from faith past doubt to faith again is too long for weak humanity to travel."

"The man of thirty should have run the gauntlet of possible human experience, normal and righteous; he should have embodied it in his masterpiece and with that purchased his fortune and his leisure. He should spend this fortune in further enriching and refreshing the sources of his masterpiece, so that new work shall be up to the standard set before, yet as fresh and great and unexpected. He should spend the first year of this leisure finding a wife, and the second, the most momentous of his life, in adapting his soul and his ways to this woman, and teaching her to adapt herself the best way to his work. That is a square trade. From his thirty-second year a man lives the past, he rises on old ambitions, he writes and draws and thinks old impressions, rearranging them. But he cannot see new things a new way if he would. So the ten years from twenty on must be a period of careful and slow building. From thirty on is the great leisure period of study and the comparison of one's experience with those of others, especially the immortals. If a man is a scholar at thirty it means he has lost ten years of his life hopelessly. Ten years of study would leave empty from forty to fifty, the days for scholarly work. From fifty to sixty God takes care of a man. At best, he has a chance to live over his youth with his physical and artistic progeny. At worst he builds a raft of the wreck of his life. From sixty to seventy if a man has lived perfectly and attained his youth again in its first full measure he may be a prophet, a sage, or a harper hoar, speaking with fire, and inspiring reverence. How wide must be the horizon, how multitudinous and alert and conscientious the array of experience from twenty to thirty to furnish a life."

"To feel at home even with a short poem one must expect to saturate with it. . . . It is well to study new words, but the great victory in English is to master simple every-day vocabulary, and drive it like a tribe of common slaves to build your pyramid. . . . Do not mortgage your future, not a day nor an hour with promises or resolutions. Look the present moment squarely in the face. . . . Shakespeare in *Romeo and Juliet* gives a lesser passion on the part of Romeo, transfused at its highest point into a greater one. . . . Oh, sing me the songs of Shakespeare—a poem to be written after all the songs are memorized. They are a splendid and unabused material from which one may use a lifetime for songs and rhymlets. . . . It is a very good thing to make note of possible situations, stories, and verses. What is recorded now may be used ten years from now, when one has run dry for a theme."

It may be said here that in these books Lindsay made memoranda for future poems, such as one on the drum, set down near this place to which we have come in the present diary. And frequently he noted plots for short stories, as for example he thought it would be worth while to write a story of a noble woman who became jealous of the abstractions of which her husband was enamoured. Most of these suggestions never matured into poems or stories. At this point of his life he had not yet found what his imagination could do, and what it was best fitted to do. As to stories he had no faculty for that sort of creation whatever. At this time he was thinking much of Shakespeare. One good poem on him should suffice for his own work. Sometimes he contemplated a poem of philosophical or analytical import, such as showing how accumulated bruises in the soul become intolerable, a truistic enough theme. Such bruises, however, are at first "laughed at, after being unnoticed, finally they are agony." Also he would like to write a panegyric on the heroism of women; he would like to study the science and art of allegory, and apply them to popular caricatures. To this end he would study Butler's "Analogy," Bacon's "Essays," Poe's "Raven," the "Fables" of Æsop,

the "Song of Solomon," and Bunyan's "Pilgrim's Progress."
He would welcome the poet who would mock and rail at the
skeptics, as Byron mocked and railed at the best. "One
should know one's kin, and get their secrets. If this is not
done it is useless to undertake anything larger by canvassing
the people of the world at large."

"I remember when I could not tell time, nor my right
hand from my left, and I had the same puzzled hopelessness
about them I have now about my French. . . . Not sur-
pressed, inhibited passion is the secret of a correct and
successful handling of any situation; but rather a calm
poised icy self-control that is the result of a conscientious
critical and artistic interest. In the arms of a frenzy you
have never succeeded in anything. You are mad when you
live out your heart. So dwell in the atmosphere of the judgment with its sweeter pleasures, its dignity, and its discipline. . . . To consistently hold with the past, or to consciously revise, this is my life. I find myself so far from
home sometimes when I might use maps of my own survey-
ing. . . . One cannot expect any recognition from the world
till it finally wakes up to a grateful realization of an enormous indebtedness. . . . How to be an Alexander Campbell,
and the result to expect. Those influenced most perma-
nently and importantly are the descendants of one's ad-
versaries who have forced through to exigencies of conflict
to take higher ground than they ever dreamed of. . . . Not
self-sustaining churches, but gospel-sustaining churches.
. . . Saints as spiritual sinners are often spirituelle. Yet
spirituality is often confounded with spirituality in art,
in artists, in music, in thought, in idealization. . . . The
power of democracy, the art of democracy, the construction of democracy. The skirmish line of civilization and the
skirmish line of art. The laws are the same. . . . When the
world needs truth the man will be found. . . . America is
the place where colleges are indigenous to the soil."

"Browning and Carlyle saw fit to surrender themselves to their mannerisms, having once formed them. Why should I not do so? It will take me ten years. I cannot acquire style by rules, though thereby I may discipline it somewhat. It is for me to study, copy or amend every legitimate trick of eloquence, and every way of emphasis and strong sort of mannerism. My mannerism is barren, lacking variety."

So now we proceed to the diary entitled Homiletics. He set down what he considered atheism. It was to view all things in disconnection, dull and spiritless. "No aspect of the universe, however awful and impersonal, may not have power at some season to guide and support the spirit of man. . . . A life that is reduced to the barest elements has yet a hold on the liberality of nature, and the affections of human hearts. . . . There is no harmony, no haunting melody ever heard by the spirit of man which he may not hear if he knows his books thoroughly. . . . Great art is never complete in itself; it is complete only in the imagination of the man who really felt it."

He was now reading Wordsworth's *Prelude*. Of him he noted, "there was no feeling in him which the world either repressed or twisted. . . . Superstition is an essential part of humanity. To try to separate it from Faith is to separate the soul from the body. A faith without the supernatural could gain no hold on the general mind. . . . It is a great thing to hold the hearts of all sweet, fickle, child-hearted people; child hearts are good for long. It is always by accepting the mystery that we make many mysteries plain. . . . Let us be radical then. I believe in prodigious general preparation. Be the man always you may be compelled to be sometime. . . . Platonic affection between sweethearts, and a pure faith between man and God are equally monstrous. . . . The rude songs of the Sunday school and the revival are savage; but they have the tang of sweetness. . . . In Revelation the saints do nothing but let their hearts pour out with gratitude and love. The most grateful of us would find an eternity of hosannahs a bore. Yet gratitude to Christ is the basis for our truest self abnegation. . . . The science of communion with God: Examples: Moses, Elijah, Isaiah, Christ. . . . Such Christianity as cannot be grasped in a childlike way by the child is not Christianity. Piety is a horrible word, occurring but once in the Scriptures. . . . Know that nothing is as logical after its own manner as passion. . . . A faulty poem may look like a scarred face. . . . Why be overwhelmed by the infinity telescopic above you? Why trouble about the fate of the worlds? It has no bearing on your revelation. Let us rest with untroubled heart between the sea above and the sea beneath."

"Environment of which heredity is one half is but one half man's destiny. The other half up to the death hour is planned to be filled with will. . . . If there is much to be said in praise of honest doubt, there is still more to be said in condemnation of the doubt that apes honest doubt because it is a fad. . . . I have long meditated, and will hereafter upon the Beatitudes as an economic code."

"Waiting: 1, The seriousness of life. 2, How to spend the time of waiting, watch and work. 3, The Christ-like spirit giving for humanity. This is a world of waiting. Working for souls is the only developer in the world."

"A free moral agent is the only agent worthy of God."

"My individual allegiance to Christ. He is my best friend, but I have grown up with him amid those who find him so, and I have never seen him taking possession of those who have known him not. . . . I have supreme faith in Christianity as a social force. . . . Laziness is cowardice. . . . To use only those things which have grown into my brain. . . . A perverted appetite remains as a desire after it has departed as a pleasure. . . There was a great deal

[84]

of Christianity in paganism, if one goes to the New Testament for his ideals, and there is accordingly a great deal of paganism coming out of Christianity."

"We shall never know what we lost by the absence of a Boswell from the Mermaid Tavern. . . . The truth of hand upon hand is not so real as the truth of mind upon mind. . . . It takes a great deal of life to make a little art. . . . Give to science everything but the garden of Eden. What this age needs is a personal devil. . . . Earth is the place of tombs; there are no graves in heaven, no tombs in hell. . . . Patent office models are all philosophical systems. . . . It is a dreadful thing to be religious and then be wrong about it."

At this point the diary entitled Disciples of Christ is germane to what we have just quoted. He refreshed his memory concerning the life of Alexander Campbell by referring to what Campbell did with reference to baptism. "He brought the baptism upon which all Christendom unites; the confession on which they all unite; the repentance on which they all unite."

Looking forward to a life in Chicago Lindsay resolved not to go to Sunday school but to use the time till church time in writing. "Evolution must make room for the power of Christianity. . . . Now let me burn out for God." He would draw a cartoon on the brotherhood of suffering, showing how only "union in Christ is common suffering for his name, the only orthodox Christians. . . . The denominations are not like Jonah—they will not offer themselves to be swallowed by the Disciples' whale. . . . Have faith always in God, and love Christ with fervor, but never forget to believe in the devil, the king who puts falsehood behind the face of beauty, and adorns with ugliness the truest hearts and duties of the world. . . . The one talent man was a striker. The parable was written for the one talent man. When he goes on a strike the cities go to pieces."

"An ideal student body: Every student an earnest disciple of Christ, a Y. M. C. A. man, a power in athletics, the earnest friend of every man in school, the Hiram spirit equivalent to a vital school allegiance to Christ. Results: Every graduate on fire for apostolic Christianity. . . . If Christ had been a statesman he would have been something of a Garfield, a Cromwell, or an Alfred or Cæsar. If he had been a theologian Campbell perhaps. There is only one law of life, that is consecration. Unconsecrated forces are lawless forces. Here is the mystery of evil. . . . Pessimism says, Quit, Let go. . . . We can do man's work without his spirit, not God's. . . . The highest art of all is the art of praying. . . . God help us all to be brave."

"January 1, 1911, is my consecration day. My father could set dates ten years ahead, and live up to them. Let me do the same. . . . Read history for perspective, read poetry for vision, read biography for courage, read criticism for precision. . . . Even God cannot conquer the free will of man, but a personality is a despot ruling the wills about him. Wherfore man with man is greater than God with man. . . . What this age needs is two personalities— the personal saving Christ, and the personal devil . . . this country will be roused as a whole against the liquor power only when it becomes insolent and overbearing beyond parallel. . . . There is only one art in the world—the art of loving."

In the diary on Speaking, also with the notation, this book belongs to Christ, there are not many observations to transcribe. Here Lindsay wrote, "I must come back to my old orations some day. The fire that went into them I will find there still, after a life experience to throw light upon them." Further on he committed himself to this resolution: "Be it hereby resolved that when it comes to a choice between a speech and a book or a picture, or a poem, from now to the end the speech must go." Also, "when I get to

Chicago I must not run away from any of the ideas and lines of thought and ambition already marked out in these notebooks. They are the flowering of all my past life. I must work out these ideas rather than add to them. My great danger will not be narrowness, but diffuseness. By a proper consultation of these, the works of the sage Confucius, I may keep myself to some uniformity of development."

CHAPTER V

THERE is one other diary started at Hiram on September 2, 1899, entitled Pictures; but as it blends coherently with the diaries which he began to keep when he entered the Art Institute of Chicago in the fall of 1900, it will be quoted in that connection. Enough has been taken from the other diaries to show the studious and thoughtful life which he led at college. He was bearing down very lightly all the while upon the purse of his father. In one notebook there is an entry which shows that he started the fall term of 1897 with $46.45, that his tuition was $16.00, his books $5.65, and board for three weeks $2.30, which seems well nigh incredible. He kept an itemized account of all his expenses even down to stamps and trifling indulgences in sweets. He was having meals plain enough, and not too abundant, we may well infer. His total expenses for his first year were $288.00; and for his second $348.00. It seems clear that with such economy so carefully practiced Doctor Lindsay could have sent him through Hiram. But he was not the only poet who turned from the regular courses to follow a reading path of his own, adapted to the self-development which he had conceived for himself. His marks at high school prove that he could have mastered the Hiram College studies, even to mathematics. What he was interested in, even though taught in the curriculum, he succeeded in. Thus we find that in three tests at Hiram on the evidences of Christianity he stood 90, 95, and 96, with a final test of 96; and that in Bible geography he stood 93. Lindsay's nature, his parental environment, his ancestry, the Bible influence which surrounded him determined him to choose the Hebrew culture rather than the Greek. He would have derived nothing from the study of that language and literature, since he cared nothing for classical mythology. And as for Latin, Virgil could not have been nearer to him than Homer; while Lucretius and Horace had no kinship with him whatever. By his own mental predilections, his tastes and his convictions he was preparing himself to be an American poet, of definite flavor, as much so as if he had had Whitman for a preceptor from the beginning.

Back in Springfield the poet's mother was frequently apprised of her son's activities at Hiram; and her letters show that she and Doctor Lindsay were more interested in their son's progress than parents frequently are. They were keenly solicitous for him to make wise choices in the exigencies that arose. Lindsay was sending home his orations and other productions; and in a letter dated in December, 1899, Mrs. Lindsay wrote concerning one of them, "it seems to me a very strong address. . . . There are decided marks of strength and originality as well as imagination in the address. These can be indefinitely developed, if you can keep your health. . . . There are some things that you must never forget in reading our letters or in writing to us. We are wrapped up in your welfare, and only want to do whatever will be in the end for the best in every way. While your father has always looked forward to having you help him for a time and then give you all he had in the way of a profession, friends and footing here, a great deal indeed that would be, and while he feels very much disappointed because you do not want to accept it, at the same time if you feel sure that you can, without any antecedents, acquire a better and more useful business by following some other line, then he is willing to do all he can to help you into it. His heart ache is because he fears you are throwing away a certainty of a very useful vocation for a very uncertain dream. If you are sure you have talent enough to make any one line of art a success, then shape your studies with reference to that. You seem to have in mind a large field that is certainly not occupied, that of Christian art, in the way of every day illustration. I do not know of any paper, except the *Ram's Horn* that does anything in that line. Our people are in the line of God's work for the 20th century. If they remain true to their calling, they will grow into vast multitudes. Our Cincinnati convention has attracted wide attention, and been favorably commented upon by leading journals everywhere. 'Our position' has been several times discussed in the *Digest*. The one characteristic of our people that impressed me most in our last convention is one that is never suggested by anything I see or feel in mingling with other religious people. It is the same characteristic that I find in your orations—undeveloped strength of youth, a beginning of growth; this is the strongest characteristic of our people, and it is not manifested in the Higher Critic, over-educated, wise, self-conscious class who think they are in the lead—folks just like them are in the lead in every other church, more or less—the real leaders of our people are such men as McGarney and Love, and McLean and Zollars: the simple Gospel, and the plea Back to Christ—the rallying cry for Christian Union, and the Good Confession are to take the Christian World. The field you think you have ability for is large and wholly unoccupied, so whatever you are capable of doing you would be sure of having a demand for, so soon as it was recognized. You speak of three lines of work, literature, speaking, and illustration. The two first are a great help to the last, but the last should be your final aim because there are thousands in the other two fields. In order to be a good illustrator and come into touch with the living masses of our people, you would be greatly profited by mingling with them just where you are. Nowhere could you have a better opportunity. If you can succeed at all in preaching occasionally, it would be a fine training for your ultimate purpose. As you say you need Latin and Anglo-Saxon, also French. You need also logic, and everything you can get in the way of literary training. You can certainly get enough in these lines in Hiram to take you to a diploma. It is not likely that you will ever try to graduate elsewhere. You ought to get an A.B., at least. Perhaps you can add enough later and elsewhere to get Hiram to confer an A.M. You ought to make fast friends of the most forceful young men in Hiram, for they'll stand by you like brothers in the future. If you're a Hiram graduate you'll have far more weight with them than if you never get through. You speak of having only two years of preparation. . . . Christ entered upon his ministry at thirty years. No man under the Jewish law was considered a full grown man until he was thirty years old. At that age priests entered their ministry. If your 'brain is like scrambled eggs' you are undertaking more than you can do well. When you came home last summer I felt alarmed about you. You were in a state of nervous exhaustion bordering on that dazed condition that ruined Arthur Wines and Geo. Brinkerhoff. You have inherited some excellent qualities from your father, and that tendency to nervous exhaustion from your mother. I am deeply grieved that I have given you such a burden, and yet that temperament seems to be inseparably united with the especial talent out of which you hope to make your future. You must, however, recognize the fact, you must at all times guard against that dazed condition. It troubles me often, but only when I am overdone. It bothered me much the year I was in Europe. Occasionally it was so bad that after a day of greatest interest I could with difficulty recall where I had been or what I had seen. . . . The study of Loisette has helped me a great deal. His system seems adapted to the weakness to which you are subject. Are there not some studies in the course for preachers that you could take with profit? Isaac Everett became a very excellent writer by procuring the best textbooks on grammar and rhetoric and studying them himself, practicing all the rules laid down until he made them a permanent part of his mental furniture. Surely anything in the way of rhetoric or teacher's grammar at Hiram would give you the line of work that you need. But if your brain is so dazed just now you need a complete rest and change. Don't study during the holidays. Don't undertake any more than you can master. You injure your habits of work and thought whenever you allow yourself to go to class with any lesson on a subject poorly prepared. Your whole make up in order to your substantial success in any profession or line of work needs constant and long discipline in thoroughness, exactness, promptness, regularity of habits. All these habits help to give one command of his powers. No general can succeed with a mutinous and half-organized army. Gustavus Adolphus is a character worth studying. His little army triumphed over much greater ones, just because of its strict discipline, alert action, and the perfection of control that the boy-king exercised. So you must get command of your forces. Take enough outdoor exercise, quiet sleep, complete recreation; not loafing, that is not the thing at all. Eat the right kind of food at the right time in the right quantity. Make all your habits subservient to your purpose. The Harmony of the Gospels you mention is a very useful study; in connection with it commit a little at a time to memory the choicest chapters of Christ's words, and Paul's. Better than any theories or opinions or theological studies is the Book itself with a good concordance. You ought to read the best of the Standard every week, and keep in touch with our brotherhood. . . . As to Chicago University next summer, we think you would lose much more than you would gain. You need the wildest, roughest life, the freest from study that can be gotten during vacation. You must have it if you ever acquire the constitution necessary for the life you plan for yourself. You have not the nerves to hold out. You must make a business of building them up. The kind of work you want to do is very exhausting to the nervous system. If you do not get a strong physical basis during the next few years you cannot succeed."

The letter then speaks of the possibility of the family going to Colorado for the summer. If so, "you can take elocution, a lesson each day, and read French for a short time in the morning, then spend the main part of the day in tramping. A collection of flowers and leaves carefully put together in a herbarium would furnish designs for later work. Nature is the very highest teacher of art. The artist who drew and painted the Rockies will be the great teacher of all artists to the end of time."

These admonitions and counsels from a devoted mother move one with their sincerity, at the same time that they go wide of what Lindsay needed at the time by way of advice in a great many respects, at least. She it was who filled him with the ambition to be an artist when he was a "curled darling," and now that he was feverishly bent on that vocation, and working himself into nervousness by studies to equip himself for it, he needed some one to tell him then and there what to do, and whether his ideas of Christian cartooning were utterly visionary, or were practicable and worth while. This good mother, having been education-bitten, tended to speak in mottoes, and to deal with the fate and future of her son by the handle of approved sayings, and church moralities. Her own study of painting and practice of the art in no wise helped her to see that her son was not especially gifted for drawing, or for any plastic art. Her infatuation with her church and her Christian enthusiasm sorely blinded her to the realities; and when for a moment even she thought of the *Ram's Horn* as a possible medium for Christian cartoons she was venturing the treasure of her son upon the frailest structure that one could imagine. The *Ram's Horn* was a publication of the time, of no circulation of moment, and of no literary importance whatever. It might be classed with **Brann's** *Iconoclast* or the *Appeal to Reason,* standing for Christianity and radical evangelism as those publications stood for freedom of thought and secular propaganda.

Lindsay's diaries and his letters to his mother showed that he was living too much within himself. He was having no intimate friends, boon companions, dear comrades; no convivial hours, no happy exchange of argument and opinion; no free faring, no happy abandon to the joy of life and of nature. He was all seriousness, all concentration upon the business of preparing for a great career, to commence like Christ around thirty years of age. And his mother, good and true woman that she was, educated and in many ways wise woman that she was, did not see her son's problems just aright. She is not the first mother of best intentions to fail. We are considering, however, Lindsay as a poet to be, and therefore it is pertinent to look into what he was receiving by way of direction, and what he should have had, the better judged of from this perspective. Nevertheless it seems clear enough that nothing would have made Lindsay an artist of any distinction; if anything would have done so, it must have come to him after he passed out of his own bewilderment, and away from the philosophies of his mother. He needed his imagination rendered more catholic, more plastic, more emancipated from the Campbellite theology. Lindsay had no dream of creating a Christian art out of the spirit which animated the Italian masters, but rather, even if he rose to something above Christian cartooning, to make the higher manifestation of his impulse a Ruskin-like contribution to the emancipation of a materialistic world, a business America. Even so, how were his hand and his eye to be trained for such expression? He needed much more than the average student an apprenticeship with an artist, in which to lay the foundation of craftsmanship. He needed to become proficient in the fundamentals of the actual work relating to painting and drawing. He needed all this much more than a congestion of mind with the philosophies and conclusions of Ruskin, with the history of art in Japan and China and other countries. He was predisposed enough to theory without feeding its faculties. He needed daily work with the pencil and the brush in order to body forth his ideas where they could be seen and appraised, and then kept or discarded. Instead he crammed his mind with much useless lumber; and in the end he saw that he was not an artist, but a poet. Perhaps a discerning mother might have perceived this in these Hiram days. There is consecration even when men are happy and giving themselves up to laughter and to humor; there is devotion in hours of gregarious association; but there is much in fellowship and in mingling with our kind. With Lindsay his personal contacts were too institutional; he saw his fellows too much all along as men to be saved, to be lifted. And this is only another way of saying that he had little feeling for people as people, but rather as objects to be fashioned, reformed, inspired with visions, and made creatures of the City of the Perfect, of a new America. So it is that he has no chants for people such as Whitman made memorable; and he is in no sense of the blood of Chaucer. To his last days in spite of a democratic manner, a gentle cordiality, a smiling friendliness, he was evidently attentive to the bishopric of his own personality and standing. Some of the masculine and vigorous affiliations of Robert Henri or John Sloan would have helped him. And it may be that he might have transformed or assimilated the counsel and educational influence of his mother so that he might have made as good use of them as Ruskin made of the Bible reading and other literary and moral discipline which he received from his mother. But at the last Lindsay's ideas yielded themselves more effectively to words than to paint, which is also to say that without ideas deftness of hand does not avail.

The letters of Mrs. Lindsay to her son while at Hiram throw much light upon his mind and its development; and one more may be drawn upon, written in the last year that he spent at that institution. By this time Doctor Lindsay had symptoms of breaking, of a change in the season of his life. Mrs. Lindsay spoke of this in somewhat ominous tones. The doctor, as it happened, lived eighteen years beyond the time of this letter. What she wrote of his health, however, sounds like a warning to the son to do his best while the father is in being to help him. By this time, January, 1900, Lindsay had decided upon a course at the Art Institute at Chicago, and evidently he was having catalogues sent his parents that they might be informed of the courses and the regulations and expenses. Mrs. Lindsay in this letter accordingly said, "Another pamphlet came today from Chicago. Your father will read it and then send it to you. We are not qualified to inspect art schools. We are not acquainted with one artist. The catalogues of art schools, I suppose, like all advertisements, may be half hoax, and should always be carefully inquired into before investing in them. This one sounds reasonable and practical. Possibly some very practical course of study by corespondence for a few months at home before you go away might save money and fit you to know what you need most in the way of technique when you go to school. It would be reasonable to suppose that the old schools in New York would be better in some ways, than Chicago, but they may be like the Eastern universities, slow mills that grind too fine for your purpose. Lose no opportunity of making inquiries. . . . We have sometimes wanted to know more about your studies and class standing. We do not know what you are studying now, nor under what teachers. We would be more interested in that than any other bit of information that you would be likely to think of. . . . As to your poem, I did spend quite a while trying to read it, but failed on a few of the leading words. You must remember that my time is more than closely occupied, I don't want to throw cold water on anything in which you are interested, but though your bits of verse sometimes contain strong expressions, and the practice is no doubt culture in composition, I do not see you in the future as a poet. Poets are certainly born, not made, and I do not think you have the flowing ease of language to give marked success in that line. I believe you can learn to write, however, and to speak, and ought to cultivate both lines—but—study ways of expressing the best you know of, the best in life to the masses of people. If you can learn to do it through illustration, it is a wonderful field. 'We as a people' have ideas that God is plainly going to give through some one or many to this nation and through it to the world during the next half century. I have no doubt of it. A man or woman carrying a great, God-given thought, though little more than ordinary in ability may be as *great a force as is the thought*. Then, too, the time must be ready for the thought—the simple story of the Gospel, the personal Christ, the Christ life, the necessity for the union of Christians—these are to be given to *a world that is ready*—by *a few educated people* who have not bowed down to *Culture and Criticism*. . . . Paul (educated) was a power that could project his mind into all classes. . . . I was at the Every Wednesday this morning by special invitation. The Rubáiyát was the subject. . . . I told your father that the observations and experiences this morning gave me great hope for your future, if you could see exactly the course to take. I go to the Every Wednesday about once a year. Some of the ladies are of the 'Culture Worshippers.' Very few have any understanding of life's purposes along the lines that I work with the Missionary Union, and the common people. I did so long to give them one little glimpse of it. They knew that I had reviewed the Rubáiyát at the 'Sunnyside,' so called on me, as soon as the paper was finished. I compared Omar Khayyam with the other tentmaker philosopher, Saul of Tarsus, and started a very exciting discussion in which I was twice roundly cheered. The women are (some of them) sincere, and if I ever have an opportunity, I will speak from their point of view, for the Christ-life. I sowed some seed this morning. 'You always fill me full of thoughts,' said Mrs. ——, after we were about to go home. Several others said similar things, and they were the strongest women of the club. I hope your study last year of Higher Criticism will be an antidote for all the 'wisdom' that I have studied in past years, for all the mist ideas that have come near leading me away several times. It's such a waste of time and strength. The wise thing is to study Christ, live Christ, teach Christ, in every way you can; but not as these schools; in the ordinary life, as a layman, it seems to me, I mean after the manner of a layman, not as a theologian; but you want to see that your life is shaped in a way that will secure self-support, money, that you may not only be independent, but have the means of helping others. There's plenty of Scripture for that. 'What Would Jesus Do?'—the book contains some vagaries, I think, as to business, not in the fundamental idea, but in the working out of the applications."

This letter evidently was not mailed the day it was written. It has a supplement dated Thursday in which Mrs. Lindsay returned to the subject of the "Rubáiyát." "I was awake in the night," she wrote, "and thought of several things: one was, in looking over Elihu Vedder's illustrations of the Rubáiyát yesterday some of them struck me as being very like your ideas and drawings. . . . I had in mind the possibility of a book illustrated, comparing the philosophy of the two tentmakers, Paul and Omar; or making Paul the answer to Omar. No other poem is likely ever to be written that will so touch every chord in the *human heart*, unenlightened by Christ, as Fitzgerald (for It's mostly his). No other treatise on immortality will ever equal Paul's. These two would make a wonderfully fine close-to book that I have had in mind for years, not expecting it to materialize, but as a dream of what might be made wonderfully attractive; a thought never given the world in a book, so far as I know: not a large book, but one copiously illustrated. When you come home I'll tell you. In the meantime study the Rubáiyát in connection with I Corinthians some Sunday afternoon, and look up the ideas of Christ along the same line. The *cultured* young men of this land, many of them, it is said, know the Rubáiyát by heart, and live by it, as their Bible. By the time you can come to the stage they will have felt the need of something better, at least the best of them."

In another letter she congratulated him on his poem "Dreaming," saying that it showed imagination, a vein of talent; but she was anxious to have him "adhere to your plan of educating yourself for your father's profession."

What the youth Lindsay was to do in business America passes understanding. This devoted mother wrote him long letters part of which were concerned with suggestions for pictures, and parts enjoining him to follow in his father's profession. He was dreamy and mystical enough without pondering the theological meanderings of a mystagogue like Paul, preaching "Christ crucified, unto the Jews a stumbling-block, and unto the Greeks foolishness." The Greeks long before had fathomed all such transcendentalism; and if Paul chose to "speak the wisdom of God in a mystery," "which none of the princes of the world knew: for had they known it they would not have crucified the Lord of glory," he might do so, as he did upon the Areopagus to his heart's content. All the while Lindsay was setting down his reflections in the notebooks dedicated to Christ, and strenuously trying in that way to clarify his mind.

Lindsay might admire Swinburne to the full, and commit, as he did, long passages from "Hertha," and the choruses from "Atalanta in Calydon." He might admire Keats as a spirit made of flint; but there was not a chance for him to get away from the Hebrew culture. It is remarkable that his Biblical studies did not affect his vocabulary more than they did; that his Biblical imagery came to him second hand, through the colorations of hymn writers, and the interpretations of Campbellite evangelism.

Leaving Hiram in 1900 an unfinished student, he was to spend the better part of a decade studying and teaching art. It was only by casting behind him the impossible, though he did not do this quickly enough; it was only by a courageous endeavor to get at reality, to learn what was true that he found himself. His full story may reveal what these art studies were to him in point of value, or whether they were worthless, as compared, at least, to a concentrated passion and practice of poetry.

CHAPTER VI

LINDSAY became twenty-one years of age on November 10, 1900. By this time Grandfather Frazee had died, after a long life of farming, preaching, and reforming the politics of his community. When the sound of so busy a man ceases, the silence is indeed impressive; and speculative spirits are inclined to ask what it was all about. Grandmother Frances Austen Frazee was living still in the old homestead near Orange, Indiana, and still affectionately interested in her grandson, whose orations, and art studies and verses, excited family wonder, but sometimes anxiety. Doctor Mohawk was no doubt greatly perplexed over so great a wonder bred in the quiet of his medical life, dedicated to Hippocrates. Grandmother Frazee having no responsibility in particular for the future of the youth, saw a few simple rules as adequate for his success. She wrote him a birthday letter, from which a few sentences will manifest her forward looking state of mind. This congratulation letter was belated eight days, for which she offered the apology of a better intention; then she said: "While 'tis true that according to our civil laws you are full grown, yet the Divine laws gives you nine years more to complete your Manhood. 'Tis the fewest that have had the opportunities of culture that you have had, a Father and Mother of the best of ability and principles and your own endowments of no Mean kind, the choicest of environments of all kinds. Now what next for your life's work? For all must work. Select your occupation never falter never get discouraged be firm and true to yourself true to your family true to your country and true to your God always relying on Divine assistance and you will be sure of success. According to my way of counting you have still nine years to become estab-

[101]

lished in your life's work whatever that may be but be established fully by that time and then never change and try some new thing."

The good lady's punctuation and lack of it, and her spelling have been observed as she committed them. The letter is only another piece of evidence to the point that Lindsay was surrounded by great affection, and to some extent was imbibing a harmless sort of vanity touching his central position in the interest of his relatives. This letter, however, put no idle dreams in his head about art. Likely she knew little enough about such things in that industrious life of a farmer's wife in middle Indiana.

Lindsay spent this summer of 1900 in study, as we gather from his diaries, one of which, commenced in September, 1899, was continued into this year. We find an entry to the effect that he saw Walker Whiteside play "Hamlet" in middle October, who demonstrated to him that "man is less of an animal than 'he' ever had thought." And so at this point we resume a study of the growth of the poet's mind, using first the diary entitled Pictures, with its notation, "This book belongs to Christ," which was projected along the months of this summer from the fall before.

"A novice in drawing," he observed, "should attempt 1 nothing ornate, 2 should strive for a simplicity, lightness, directness and force, everything should be sketched five ways. . . . A thousand years before Plato men saw the sun and loved Jehovah. . . . Unless you take precious good care you will fall under the domination of the check book, and that is worse than damnation. For work done without conviction, for power wasted on trivialities, for labor expended with levity for the deliberate purpose of winning an easy applause of a fashion-driven public there remains but one end—the oblivion that is preceded by toleration and cenotaphed with contempt. . . . Browning is southeast of Tennyson, as it were. Tennyson is an optimist and looks for the kingdom on earth. Browning is an optimist and looks for the kingdom in the individual. Tennyson cannot assume that God is without Time; Browning lacks the law of primogeniture, lacks that love of historical prospects and retrospects that come to the members of a proud old line. . . . The man of the world is the nearest to the Christ ideal of a man. Other worldliness is a damnable folly."

"What should a man be? A Christian love always. What should a picture be? The expression of the deep heart of man. Is there sunshine in a dandelion? Yes, and there is beauty and love and goodness in all art. He who would not paint a picture and be a dandelion (or a creative animal) must have his picture on fire. Lilies on the hill have been placed there by the artist, but he allows us to take them to the children of Easter to tell them of the resurrection. The grass of the field may be cast into the oven to warm the wanderer. Thus may man improve on art for art's sake."

"Never, never, never be a cynic, even a gentle one. Never help out a sneer, even at the devil."

"Christ the creator, the artist, the scientist, the poet, the philosopher, the statesman, most notably the poet in no mere rhetoric sense. . . . Teach the people the A B C of art if you want them to appreciate your pictures. . . . An artist is one who does fewer things than other men and does those things superbly, supremely well. . . . Be supremely reserved, be supremely sociable. . . . The corruption of the best is the worst. . . . I imitate men when they are strong and successful. If one will observe well a thousand successful men thus may a man live a thousand years of youth. . . . The greatest customs are those expounding the secular Christ. . . . The only thing that a man may do that is new is to write himself upon human hearts."

"There ought to be a poem, a poem that is grand and wonderful as the whole race, speaking of the myriads of the men in the stys as pigs, as Markham has spoken of the man with the hoe. The man with the hoe is a divinity in comparison with the White Man's Burden, the pig of India or Africa or China. Call up the ghost of Browning. What has he the apostle of individualism for these? What has Tennyson to say? Nothing but simple words and acts of brotherhood. When will the genius arise so strong that the strong shall fear him, so simple that the beast can understand him? Oh, the great poem has yet to be written. . . . The man who is too much in harmony with his time is a compromiser. . . . The fates deter us from the day when we repudiate a holy enthusiasm. . . . Mere noble emotion is not poetry . . . True criticism of art can never consist in mere application of rules. It can be just only when it is founded on quick sympathy with the changeful efforts of human nature."

"Angelico: spiritual beauty—highest—and Corregio, physical beauty. Dürer, Rubens, caring only for truth, third rank. Teniers, Salvator, Caravaggio of no rank, of a certain order in the abyss. . . . High art consists in neither altering nor improving nature, but in seeking throughout nature for the beautiful and bringing it by gentle emphasis. . . . We build all our satisfactions on things as they are not. This is a blunder. The imagination is to restore the past, or the unseen or the future."

"It is well to undertake to be a certain limited self, a consecrated personality, to be supremely strong, and direct and gigantic and virile in the territory already staked out. I am strong and large and extensive enough now in outline. Let the rest of my life be simply doing my simple best. I write pretty well. I must write better. I can't be a church pastor. Mustn't ever dream of it. I can dress better. I cannot be anything but a man of the people, and must learn this old tendency and strengthen it into an art. I must be much alone, and have a narrow routine of duties. I want to be perfectly conventional in all matters where I am not deliberately original, and would otherwise be ugly and careless. I must make haste to find the environment where I can stereo-type my conventionality into a perpetual type that I know will renew itself, and that will require thereafter no watching and no energy. But I must take root in a place in the socio-logical garden first. . . . Art as such has not possessed an efficient moral influence on mankind. . . . Now I read his-tory that I may be the better illustrator, and for this pur-pose alone did I do any of these things, study poetry, read novels, study designing, study paintings, study the mastery of men, study the art of mental, moral, temperamental and intellectual ascendency, study the careers of illustrators, study religion, speaking, culture, the Saxon races, the Dis-ciples, the American and French books. My one unwavering aim is that I shall illustrate. Let us never be mistaken."

"Where is my failure with my friends? I have acquired unconsciously the habit of Raillery. It must be totally sup-pressed. Where is my hold upon my friends? Let me con-sider and know. . . . Wherefore it is well for me to under-stand well what I am now, and to be zealous to achieve nothing else. . . . It is an honor always to go to the strong with your strength. It was an honor for Moses and Elias to come to strengthen Christ."

"First year Chicago. Second year New York. For five years no books, only the poets and Shakespeare, and the notebooks and an expense account. . . . Jeffersonian de-mocracy as an art is a thing to be desired. Let us by all means be artistic democrats."

"Behold, I shall be a Cæsar in the world of art, conquer-ing every sort, every language and people, and lead their kings captive before the men of Rome. (Wow!)"

Such is this diary recording the thoughts, plans, beliefs, and estimates of many things kept by Lindsay under the title *Pictures*, and which ended on the last day of September, 1900. The ambition to be an artist, with which his mother had filled him, was now to be pursued with feverish activity for some years to come, but as we have seen with especial reference to the work of illustrating, for which, as it turned out, and might then have been seen, he had the slightest talent in the world. What were to be the opportunities in the field of Christian cartooning can be discovered no better now than in those studious and misguided eight years in Chicago and New York. On January 2, 1901, he started forth on this long pilgrimage; and on arriving in Chicago rented with another student an apartment on South Paulina Street at $14 a month. The next day he registered at the Institute, partook of lemons and crackers for luncheon, and in the evening saw E. H. Sothern and Virginia Harned play *Hamlet*. We shall refer to the diary which he kept now to construct for the reader his manner of life.

He noted that he had luncheon for twenty cents, and saw the Field Museum, and read *Hamlet* at night. On the 11th he started to draw, but was nervous from lack of sleep, so turned to the reading of Ruskin, and general reading in the library of the Institute; then he heard a lecture on Japanese art. He was having creampuffs for breakfast, and reading Tissot's *Life of Christ*. His manner of diet is shown here to prove the economies he was practicing, and also that he was not eating food that ensured his health and strength. He attended a lecture on music at Fullerton Hall, became fidgety and walked to his home in Paulina street.

On the 16th he drew a foreshortened foot, and was told by one of the instructors to take advantage of the drawings of the masters. His food ranged in these days from chocolate cake to fig cake and bowls of milk. He read a book on the Holy Grail, and revised "The Battle of Love," one of his earliest poems; and he sent a poem to one of the Chicago papers. He attended church regularly, and was soon reading the poems of Blake. On the 28th he was too nervous to work at the Institute, and in the afternoon slept and read. That night he saw Bernhardt and Coquelin in "Cyrano de

Bergerac." He read Esther Wood's work on Rossetti and Ruskin; and once again revised "The Battle of Love." He was frequently having but bread and milk for breakfast.

On February 3d he taught a class in Sunday school, and joined a Chicago church. On the 4th he was ill, but studied Taine and sketched. A few days later he was correcting verse all day, including the "Dream of Lucifer," and became so absorbed that he forgot to eat supper, but later partook of two oranges purchased by his flatmate, whom he now owed $1.45. That evening he read *Romeo and Juliet.* His teacher at about this time told him that he was not drawing for mass and feeling; and on the 14th he wrote all day, and sent some poems to the Curtis Publishing Company; and also a poem entitled "Rose Rhymes of the Wayside" to the *Century Magazine.* Soon he was drawing the Medici, and daffodils, seeing Mistress Nell, and reading Scott, and *Hamlet* again; also Rossetti's verse. On the 21st he received rejection slips from the magazines to which he had sent the poems; but undiscouraged he started two poems with the subject "Pilate and Fine Linen." Again he corrected "The Dream of Lucifer," and turned to Lord Chesterfield's Letters "to catch his spirit." On the 24th he read Marlowe's *Faustus,* and drew glass bottles. He took "A Vanity" to the *Christian Century,* and read gynecology in early March; and now in this month he was drawing a picture of Dante and two views of Canova, as to which he commented, "I can't handle en masse, can't sketch or draw a flowing line." He was also now seeing such plays as "Monte Cristo," "The Gay Lord Quex," "Foxy Quiller," and "The Wizard of the Nile," and he toured through Chicago's Chinatown. He made a study of Doré's "Raven" and read the *Comedy of Errors.* Every Sunday he was teaching a Sunday school class.

In late March he was passed to the intermediate class, and was sending poems to the magazines, and reading

Lanier's *Science of English Verse*. At this time he had an attack of vertigo; but he did not relax his activities. He was now reading Omar Khayyam, drawing Lorenzo's profile and that of Brutus, and making a study of Vedder's drawings.

In April he transfered his residence to Kenwood Avenue and Fiftieth Street, on the south side of Chicago; and there started to read *Kim* and *Adam's Diary* by Mark Twain. He wrote a letter to W. D. Howells enclosing "The Battle of Love," which Howells returned with the comment that it was "frantic, frenetic and obscure." He started to write "The Ding Dong Doom Bells," which evidently evolved at last into "The Fireman's Ball," published in *The Congo and Other Poems* in 1914. He was reading the life of Poe now, also a life of Rubens, and Ruskin's *Præteria*, and Whistler's *The Art of Making Enemies*. He sent "The Dream of Lucifer" to Elbert Hubbard who rejected it.

On April 20 he confided to his diary that he was hungry, having spent but twenty cents for three meals. He was breakfasting on bananas and rolls. On the 27th he was too hungry to read, but managed to scrape together ten cents with which he got pork and beans; then he went to the public library where he read all day. The next Sunday he walked to church without breakfast, which he had later through the generosity of a friend. The next day he received twenty dollars from Doctor Mohawk, and bought needed shoes and paid his rent. His daily expense was now about fifty cents which he was trying to reduce. In May he was frequently going to the Institute without breakfast, and there drawing away at the head of Raphael, Apollo. He was walking interminably, reading Shakespeare, and Emerson on Shakespeare and Montaigne, and rewriting a poem called "Silence Borne from Afar," and for the first time composing a poem entitled "First Dream of Lucifer." In May he had no money for paper and in consequence could

not draw, and turned to reading Lanier's book on versifica-
tion. He began now to be troubled by insomnia. Somehow
he got paper and sketched some heads, because as he noted
"Full figures confuse me." A letter came to him from his
mother at this time. He made this entry respecting it. "A
letter from mama. Roasts poetry and theorizing. Says I
must decide on some definite line. I think I have." In a few
days after he was reading *Coriolanus* and Dooley, and writing his parents that on June 15 he would quit school and go
to work at something. In early June Mrs. Lindsay came to
Chicago and paid him a visit. He read parts of "Lucifer" to
her, with what effect we do not know. He recorded that she
made a speech at Central Church. He returned to Springfield with her, but in a day or two was back at the Institute,
having walked twelve blocks, a mile and a half, to his boarding house, where he was now able to pay his rent. It was
July now and for the first he was drawing from the nude,
and at night frequently attending the theatre. While comforting himself with Emerson he wrote to all the Chicago
newspapers asking for work to do, in which he was unsuc-
cessful. He drew the Elgin Marbles, and read Emerson and
Bacon, and had bad days with a burning stomach, the result
of too much soda water and chocolates. In early August his
teacher told him that his drawing was thin. He tried to get
work at an advertising agency, but was refused, and so
started to read a history of Greece. He was now sketching
perfunctorily, taking uneeda biscuits for food, walking and
reading in the public library, and sleeping when he could.
His diary confessed at this point that he was "on the bum."
Still he worked at revising the "First Dream of Lucifer,"
and read Byron and Shelley, and drew portraits, and saw
the plays. In the last of August he wrote "The Great Supper," something long pondered. He was now leading the
Endeavor Society and the prayer meeting, and attending
church and Sunday school as before. His work was again

criticized by his teacher, as all manner and no effect. A check came from Springfield on September 13, fifteen dollars it was, and he went home for a brief time. He returned to Chicago the latter part of September and got a job with Marshall Field and Company, in the toy department, where he wheeled and sorted boxes from 8:30 to 5:30 at twelve dollars a week. He was rising now at 6 and arriving at work at 8, and confessed to feeling good. On October 2 he made this entry: "I think tonight it would be quite possible to hold a place for 2 or 3 years at Field's by being extra useful this fall, and holding to that one place until I know enough about art at the Institute to get just as good an income as the big Chicago Art Reporter. There is nothing better than Field's except better wages with the pen, and that will not be so good for my health as swinging the hammer, nor so good for my art."

On December 5 we find this entry: "I guess the night work did it. On this date I quit Marshall Field's from sheer impatience. I may go home within a week if I can find an excursion. I have $15.90 in my pocket. . . . I have had a valuable commercial experience, am worth at least $6 a week to the men in the market place, and I can live on that. . . . I want to write this week 2 or 3 poems that have been haunting me, 'Mary of Bethany,' metrically an imitation of the 'Burden of Nineveh,' and the 'Pleasures of Babylon.' I desire to revise 'The Great Supper.' This has all been on my soul since before I entered Field's. I desire to break into the *Century*, if possible, make arrangements for some kind of a business start in January before I go home, advertising or some other thing. I should have done this before I quit Field's. I am not justified in my own eyes, though I have been prudent enough from the art standpoint. The night work at Field's spoiled all my chances at the Institute."

The distressing experience of Lindsay at this period of his life, and as recorded by himself, provokes a number of reflections. It is true that he was in his twenty-second year; but not less is it true that in point of practical mind he was still a boy; and he was most obviously one of those natures destined to a life of hard difficulty to earn a livelihood. He simply could not manage the economic part of life. Many men at his age cannot find their financial way, who for that matter become prosperous when they learn what they can best do and how to do it. But in his case it was more than doubly hard to do this. He was congenitally a mind full of vagaries, theories, dreams, and false conclusions, and reasonings based upon slight conception of the facts as a whole. His parents fully knew of these characteristics on his part. Mrs. Lindsay's letters admonish him to quit theorizing. It may be granted that Doctor Lindsay did all he could for his son. He tried to give him a medical education at Hiram, and the son would not accept it. He did send him some money to live upon while studying at the Art Institute; but not enough. And if he was unable to send more, especially while educating the daughters, then another course was open. He might have looked as carefully as possible into his son's artistic capacity and talent. If he then had decided that the talent was enough to justify him in great sacrifices to develop it, he should have gone the limit, even to the extent of trenching upon the educational opportunities of the daughters. On the other hand if he had discovered no spark of artistic promise in his son, he should have refused to spend a cent upon this art course at Chicago. By compromising between hoping that his generosity would come to something, and his disbelief in his son's artistic talent he involved him in this purgatory where he was struggling with art studies under economic conditions which kept him on the rack. One cannot see that Doctor Lindsay had any faith in his son's artistic talent; what one sees is a parental conscience which resolved the doubt in favor of the son for its own peace. Finally Lindsay would have been fortunate if he had worked under a foreman at Field's who, knowing of his interest in art, had relieved him of night work, so that his evenings could have been given to the Institute. Such luck befalls young men sometimes. That it is not a more frequent thing furnishes a commentary upon business, which Lindsay hated with all his heart, and with good reason. The night hours that Lindsay gave Field's and would have given them, meant only a few more miserable dollars to stockholders already gorged with profits; while if he had really been a man of genius as an artist the loss to the world by crushing it out by such slavery would have incalculably overbalanced any deprivation of extra dividends. Back of the officers of the corporation are the directors, and back of these stockholders, the widows and orphans who have invested their money! The corporation is par excellence the most dishonest device ever conceived for dodging moral responsibility and placing it always further back on some one else!

Lindsay could not be given shorter hours because of the officers; the officers could not give them because of the directors, and these could not give them on account of the trusting stockholders! All of these persons are thus hidden; and the man-machine goes on crushing out blood and flesh to make profits.

To read this record of Lindsay's life and studies, both at Hiram and at the Institute, is to think inevitably by way of contrast with Keats who went swiftly and directly to his appointed task of poetry, guided by Homer, Spenser, Shakespeare, Chaucer, Boccaccio, and Lemprière. In this year of 1901 Lindsay's reading was enormous, and the notes he made from the books he read of themselves involved immense industry. We may list those that he mentioned in his diaries: Many books on Sir Edward Burne Jones and Pre-Raphaelitism, on Ruskin, on Rossetti, on architecture. The works of F. W. H. Myers; Lives of Millais, and Watts; Taine's *The*

Philosophy of Art, the Ideal in Art; lives of William Bell Scott, J. M. W. Turner; books on contemporary English art, on Corot, Millet, Rousseau, and many other works. He read Vallance on the art, writings, and public life of William Morris. And let us see the thing which he got out of it, what at least he emphasized from reading it. It is this: "The world of advertising is a great place to test the art theories of Morris, for in it we live centuries in a year." Do we, and suppose we do? With all his hatred of business and its dominant materialism Lindsay when saying this was in a mood to fall from the pedestal of art, and become an advertising man. He might have done so then or later if he had had the slightest ability for such work.

Some way Lindsay was back at the Institute in September, 1902. On the fifteenth of this month he opened a book of daily report which he called "the book of common prayer of N. V. Lindsay," and as of old started to question, to probe, to examine and appraise himself. "In art at least," he wrote, "I am too subjective, whirled about by every wind of doctrine, not a fountain of inspiration within myself, steady and consistent." His doubt of other worldliness, heretofore expressed, took this turn for a kind of humanism: "In the philosophy of passion we must not leave the body for spiritual ecstasies, but remember that it is a scurvy thing to ever leave it behind. It should share the highest things of the spirit." Whitman might have said this, *mutatis mutandis.*

"Adopt the same attitude toward the technique of art that you do toward the rhyme and meter of poetry. Allow it to fall reflexly into line behind the conception as a whole. Concentrate on the main vision. . . . Always start art with a vision, a beautiful idealization of the thing you see, if it be only still-life pots. Let this vision be one-third art and two-thirds poetry, both as intense as possible. This is necessary when the theme is dryest, such as still life or scrawny models.

Cram them with epic feeling. . . . A thought that is nearer to letters than to art will carry me more promptly along, simply because my lettered imagination, my poetic imagination has probably reached its culmination, mediocre but mature. It is more sturdy for present use, at least, than my budding dreams of abstract color and ultimate form. . . . Could angels have done the work of Thomas Nast? He could had he tried. Roosevelt the dude entered politics, Campbell, the scholar, founded a sect among the farmers. Kingsley went into politics, Gladstone, Disraeli."

"But this rule must enter into the composition of all cartoons: they must be strikingly poetic, as well as terribly forceful, and unless the desire is to make them transcendentally beautiful, they will not be well drawn. . . . Truly if the Sistine Chapel expressed the church universal of the middle ages, one can by cartoons, by great, long powerful lines express one's love for the church universal today. . . . My art should contain beauty and love and goodness. . . . Who can hope to equal the art that has been? I can, and to excel it in this: to write it upon human hearts, to draw it upon human hearts. Let my art be perfectly polished like the blade of the Samurai, let it serve my captain, the secular Christ. . . . No sketches in the Art Institute catalogue are all posing, none of them are thought mediums. . . . In order to increase one's sense of beauty, one should not only find it rejoicing, but deeply dwell upon it and penetrate its farthest joy."

"What my routine now needs is more freedom of action, the resolve to do nothing unless one's best at any given creation; and the resolve not to waste a moment of time upon unessential things, especially within Institute walls. . . . Avoid analyses and learning, except it be in the immediate path of creation. . . . To study is to forget and lose; to create is to remember forever. . . . The Art Institute is a poor place to follow in technique, and such matters should be for the most part postponed for two years. . . . There is not enough of the dramatic, the romantic, the flashy and the stirring in the art world. We need the standpoint of Byron, Dumas, Scott, of Chicago rather than of New York, of Marco Polo and John Mandeville. There is not enough of Isaiah, Ezekiel, Job or the Song of Songs."

At this time Lindsay was reading Milton studiously; and he filled the diary here with many quotations and comments. Milton reminded him of the necessity of building "up a great vigorous, all powerful sense of beauty," as the main task of the artist. One night when committing confidences to his diary he felt that his main ideals "in drawing will be most readily achieved by the study of sculpture. . . . What is the attitude of a good Democrat and American toward the masters? Certainly widely differing from contemporary European schools, and their deduction from them. Our young Republic must inherit the masters, but scarcely their disciples. Let our deductions be always for the cause of establishing a simple American art. Instruct working along an unbroken line of tradition. Let him add to this a study of the notable American names, with a zeal to discover their distinct American quality, their special relation to the masters, ignoring as much as possible secondary European influences, but getting the biggest and most vital elements, the eternal stuff of art. . . . Find the absolutely native American painters, study, study, study them; and on this choose to live or die. One little thing done from the spirit of the soil is worth a thousand great things done abroad. . . . Through Whitman to Lincoln may be a path to artistic rest."

Here he incorporated in his diary voluminous notes made from the writings of Whitman, whom he was reading in this December of 1902.

"Everything worth winning in this world, art, religion, philosophy, even hearts, must be won many times, lost and

won again to be well won; or else there would be no growth.
. . . It is well to worship the pillar of cloud and fire, the
ever wandering, ever fleeing God, whom only the chosen
people shall follow and worship through the base wilderness. God is stronger than the solar system, weak as a dying
butterfly. . . . The Chicago fire should occur many times,
each successive time the buildings rising smaller, less expen-
sive, more economic, more beautiful. . . . America needs to
be gone all over again. We need new pioneers who will hew
down the stairways of horrible shame, and likewise the marble
halls of ugliness. . . . Chicago University needs an in-
formal, underground leader in matters of art, to whom all
will go who feel the desire for beauty rising up within them."

"My pictures heretofore have been idealizations, which is
reasonable, but they have been abstractions, which thing
must be restrained. Also my relations to the world and my
poetry are too abstract. Let me give up for the next six
months to a well selected and skillfully drawn and described
catalogue of the lesser world of beauty, as Whitman took
the greater world of Democracy. Let me search out the em-
phatic character of any distinctively beautiful thing; let me
draw it soul and body. Let me get a deeper and more realistic sense of character. Let me live a concrete life and write
concrete letters. . . . Try the rule to seldom undertake a
picture that can be finished in less than a week. . . . I need
to know a young architect with very pronounced views re-
garding American architecture, especially for the average
voter, and some young craftsman who has the stuff in him
of the same kind. . . . Some three months some time, if my
grandmother lives, I want her history from the beginning
as she can tell it, with the wisdom thrown in, especially the
atmosphere of the pioneer days and their ways and progress.
I want the origins of the Middle West civilization traced up
through my grandmother, and mother, for it is the Middle
West that has been making Chicago."

"Apostolic Christianity needs not so much to be changed in bone and sinew as to be clothed in a garment of humor and beauty. . . . Would that I could learn good intellectual manners. . . . This man Barrie puts my devout soul to shame. First, how by fasting and prayer to learn such infallible English. Let me be something of Barrie and Chesterfield in my attitude toward the men I shall know in the university. Let me learn to what sort of hearts has the wisdom of the age been entrusted, and what shall come of it. . . . Let us try sometime the philosophy that heaven is when we seek for God, and hell is when we find Him. . . . Let the poet, the artist, the devotee call himself a wooer for life, if he will be happy. Let Romeo remain forever on the balcony. . . . The thing that I might learn from Milton is the use of the inevitable word."

January, 1903, had arrived. and he noted, "Let me feel bitterly the need of a very Shakespearean technique and resource; let me not neglect to gather everything at the Institute. . . . I have faith in religion as an uplifting force; I have faith in the gradual improvement of human institutions. I have faith that every now and then a man occurs who is a glory to his race, and most every man has for a season a right to sunshine and air. I believe that art is worth while, that virtue is its own reward, and that the quest of beauty is worth a lifetime."

At this time he was reading Keats and Landor, and he observed, "Concerning impassioned prose at its best it is not a hybrid product, deformed child of degenerate poesy, but a great muse, sister to poetry, the muse made glorious forever by the Hebrew prophets, just coming into their power again. The next speaker of the age may well speak as Isaiah did. . . . Study the question of romantic idealistic vocabulary, full of rich dreams and traditional significance on an wholly American basis. Eliminate these kings, knights, princesses."

[117]

"American classic allusions: Liberty and Union, Log Cabins, Lincoln Rails, Honest Old Abe, the Little Giant, George Rogers Clark, Ladies of the South, Texas Rangers, Prairie Schooners, Indian named rivers. The forests and prairies our grandfathers found; wild flowers, grandma's old house. In general, the tradition of Lincoln in Springfield, of one's childhood in Fayetteville and Fairview, of one's childhood running around the yard in Springfield, one's dreams of Kentucky, and of Chicago as the child of this territory."

"Who has been the John Calvin of the beauty of God rather than the will? Hail to him when he comes. The church needs his theology. . . . A book of gathered information on art and sundry remarks concerning the God of Mystery and beauty, and the various means of worshipping him."

A new vision came to him in April, 1903, involving a reversal of his former ambition. "Once more let me note down something not to forget. It is tonight's theory of my work. It interests me tonight. Don't try to be an illustrator. Cast in your fortune with makers of single pieces of art, be they picture painters or sculptors or high class covers. But let your work be the first of its kind since Rossetti."

Somewhere in these days he was reading Pliny the younger, and probably Homer, since he noted: "Homer describes the garden of Alcinous with eternal summer." Altogether his industry at the Art Institute was prodigious. He made one whole notebook on English and American painters, which included some notes on Ruskin, and on Japanese Art. Another book was filled from his reading on architecture and gardens, English and Italian. Another book was devoted to English gardens, and to the architecture of Rome, Egypt, Greece, in which he copied drawings of capitals and acanthus and the like, and in which he set down the formula of a skyscraper. One whole book was made up of notes on sculpture.

This forms the mental history of four concentrated years in Chicago at the Art Institute, for the last year there was like the others. His Sundays were spent in church attendance, in teaching a Sunday-school class, in visiting the Field Museum, in reflection and reading. His weekdays were devoted to drawing, to hard study, to writing and polishing his verses. At the end of these four years he heard of Robert Henri, one of the teachers in the Chase school of art in New York. These to Lindsay were the oracles in art of the time; and so he set forth for New York still on the quest of finding himself, and preparing himself for the calling of reform in which he would establish a new era in literature and in art.

CHAPTER VII

IN early January of 1905, Lindsay, but newly arrived in New York City, had an interview with Robert Henri, in which he showed that genial and hearty and truly American artist some of his drawings. We will let Lindsay's entry in his diary tell the story of Henri's advice: "Told me of the undiscovered mystery of the figure and face. Told me my faces were too doll-like, my figures lacked action. I ought to get same mystery in my face I did in my designs. Then ought to study Beardsley faces and figures. I believe Henri has the simplest way out for me. Richardson recommended the Academy, Henri the human face. Richardson is right, but Henri is righter. I see that man Henri is the man I need. Richardson is right about the verses. I am bound I shall please them both."

The Richardson to whom he referred was at the time a magazine editor, to whom in the December just before he had submitted the following poems: "A Strike," "The Garden Toad," "The Moon Woman," "Bridal Veils," "Ghosts in Love," "Babylon," "Queen of Bubbles," and "The Tree of Laughing Bells." Richardson had advised Lindsay to write child's verses for adults, and to sharpen the significance of "The Tree of Laughing Bells," and, as a finality, to submit the poem to *The Delineator*. Lindsay was trying now to make his livelihood as well as to continue his art studies.

He went with his illustrations to *Harper's*, where the art editor assured him that such work was bound to win its way in time. That was well enough if Lindsay had not been compelled to eat somewhere and sleep somewhere while the success of the pictures was on its way to him. He thought he might find work with the American Colortype Company, so he went there and was cordially received, and even momentarily considered as an assistant in the art department. The chance, however, did not mature. On the same day he called upon R. W. Gilder at the *Century Magazine*, who was interested in Lindsay's drawings, which included three volumes devoted to Aladdin's Lamp, and two posters. He almost sold one of the posters, but didn't in fact sell one. Mr. Gilder kept the second and third volume of the drawings and some of the poems, and gave Lindsay encouraging praise, though he afterwards rejected the whole of the submission.

In March, Lindsay called upon Henri again, having an appointment with the artist for 1:30. Henri had not finished luncheon, but he wanted to hear "The Tree of Laughing Bells." Lindsay read it to him, and also to Mrs. Henri, whom her husband called into the room to hear it. Lindsay in his diary confessed that he went to Henri to get his assistance toward shifting from drawing to writing. Henri had given Lindsay the highest praise he had yet received on his drawing. If, however, and in spite of that, Henri should think Lindsay's writing better than his drawing, then that would be much toward a decision choosing that work. Henri in fact did think that Lindsay's writing was superior to his drawing, and gave the poet great encouragement. "He certainly gave me a big brotherly boost," Lindsay recorded in his diary, "and braced up my confidence a whole lot. . . . My confidence in 'The Tree of Laughing Bells' is by this time well established, owing to its having pleased such different temperaments as those of Henri and Richardson. If I can have a talk with Kenneth Hayes Miller, and Borglum on the same poem I feel I can make the art secondary at least for a time without doing violence to my nature."

During his first year at the Chase school Lindsay was

promoted to the life class, while the originality of his artistic conceptions excited admiration. He spent his hours out of school visiting exhibits of pictures, art galleries, and walking the rich corridors of the Metropolitan Museum. He explored the quaint and curious neighborhoods of the city, which had not yielded at that time to the innovation of the modern apartment building and the skyscraper. All the charm of old New York was still over such squares as Washington Square, Gramercy Park, Stuyvesant Square, and Greenwich Village. The great mansions on Fifth Avenue then flourished; and the red-brick houses with old-fashioned windows on the cross streets toward the Hudson River, and up and down the avenues on the West Side. We are given to understand that in this period of four years in New York Lindsay made many close friends; and it is true that he was always a man who evoked a certain affection, as well as admiration; but no one emerges conspicuously from the groups of intimates in New York, or elsewhere. No Alcott and no Thoreau ever came to him, as they did to Emerson, both to appreciate his visions, and to draw them forth into more concrete realization. He made his own fight, and won his own victories, largely because no one could share in the peculiar approaches which he made to life and thought.

In addition to his other preoccupations he was lecturing on art at the Y. M. C. A. The problem of making a living was on him, although he was receiving some help from Doctor Mohawk, but not enough to support him; and we infer that help was not any too graciously bestowed. Perhaps the father was thinking that the four years at the Art Institute were lengthening themselves into an indefinite period of education. After New York was it to be Paris? Lindsay was now twenty-five. The history of this Y. M. C. A. teaching is that Lindsay applied there to a secretary for some kind of employment, and being asked what he could do, replied that he could teach an art class. The secretary gave him leave to organize one, which Lindsay did. It became larger and more enthusiastic. After a few weeks Lindsay demanded compensation for this teaching and received thereafter $10 a week. The class was composed of policemen, street car conductors and the like, and as to race, of Italians, Greeks, and Jews. By this time Lindsay's parents had little sympathy with his literary and artistic ambitions, and he had resolved to accept help from home only when dire necessity drove him to do so. This is the report of an intimate upon his state of mind at this time; and entries in his diary corroborate this judgment. As Mrs. Lindsay had started her son on this hard path of the artistic career, and as she had studied art herself and must have known something of the struggles and defeats of beginners, even of geniuses, an adverse verdict on her attitude toward his work may be indulged. But it would be a hasty one, perhaps. Because Lindsay's drawings were not successful; and as to his poems, he was not exploring the content of existing philosophies, arts, and dreams. If he had been doing this, if he had been transmuting traditional themes in recognizable forms, his work could have been evalued. But he was on the eve of making new material, and of dreaming new dreams, and a new art, and with what should his work be compared to estimate its worth? Even now the meaning, weight and worth of what he wrote needs time to delineate its scope and its significance. For these reasons Mrs. Lindsay and Doctor Mohawk, too, are not to be summarily criticized. Mrs. Lindsay knew that many poets had written excellent poems by twenty-five years of age, Keats and Shelley and Byron, and Poe, and many others. There was a limit to the Springfield purse; and besides, other poets had struggled and endured privation; and if he were bound to be a poet, why should he not take the hardships that go usually with that calling? The result was that Lindsay did the best he could at this time on $10 a week, and got what he was forced to draw from Springfield. In the super-abundance of his spirits, and the fantastic wanderings of his imagination, which took little notice of the realities, he resorted now to a strange expedient, which was that of trying to sell poems from door to door in the streets of New York. Knight errantry has no chapter more extravagant than this preposterous attempt of Lindsay's to raise funds by a sale of the poem "The Cup of Paint," along the world-sharpened and business-bitten avenues of New York. We will let Lindsay's diary tell the story.

"I mailed 'The Cup of Paint' and 'We Who Are Playing' to about twenty-five of the leading actors and the leading preachers of New York. Each envelope contained the announcement that the pictures were sermons in the case of the preachers, and tragedies in the case of the actors. Also that 'my name counted for nothing,' but I wanted the work considered. About eleven o'clock in the evening in accordance with a plan matured for some weeks, stimulated by Riis' *Life of Roosevelt*, and also the example of Ancient Troubadours, I put twelve copies of the 'We Who Are Playing' in my overcoat pocket, and made a plunge for Tenth Avenue. I started at Tenth Avenue and 50th on the west side of the street. There were few places lighted up along the street, only the bakeries, the confectioners, the drug stores, the saloons and delicatessens. About one place in ten in my night's walk was lighted.

"Well, I tried a sleepy big shock-headed baker first. I tried to give the poem to him. He considered the thing for some time as I explained it, but finally handed it back saying he had no use for it. I thought there was a touch of class-pride and the resentment of my alms, and irritated independence in his manner. So the next place I said to the proprietor, 'I will sell you this for two cents.' At once I saw the thing take. My customer smiled, and said, 'newspapers cost only one cent, with lots more reading matter than this.' But he took two cents from his till all right. I said, 'you can see me the author, that is why I charge the other cent, and I made that myself.' He said, 'it looks like it,' and laughed, and we parted, I promising to come again sometime for another. Next man I tried was a black clown. He was frying fish in a little all-night lunchroom, a sea food place. I think there were three or four men sitting around. But I tackled the boss. He was a lean tired little man with sympathy in his face. He only looked at the thing. I stated my price, and he bought it quick as a wink. His manner plainly said, 'poor devil, you are trying to earn your living, and I wouldn't hold you back from it, knowing how it goes.' I charged him to give the verse to some other man or woman, if he did not care for it himself, because it was the best I could do, and I didn't want my work to count for nothing. Next place was a confectionery. Here was a pleasant looking young man, but stony-hearted in the matter of poetry. His manner plainly said, 'get out, beggar.' The whole town, the candy shops turned me down. They deal out sweets for the flesh, not the spirit. I must land a candy man yet.

"Two Chinese laundries had their doors locked, and the busy Chinamen only stared when I shook the latch. The last laundry door I passed was unlocked. I said, By Jove I will land one of these heathen. I will capture the yellow man by his heart strings. So I wandered to the desk. 'Good evening gentlemen,' but the five swishing flat irons swung like gliding pendulums. Not a Chink turned around. 'I have here a beautiful and unworthy little poem for your exalted and celestial eyes. But the heathen kept on ironing. 'Awake oh slumbering China, here is a message for you.' But it was no use. The only thing I said that got an answer was 'good night gentlemen.' And they all said good night in chorus, and with extravagant politeness. I must land a Chinaman yet. I will begin by saying good night next time, and spring the poem gradually. I walked down 10th to 42d. I met some prowling soaks on the cross streets, and most of the saloons on 9th and 10th ave had three men sober and one man drunk loafing in front of them. It was just cool enough to be pleasant for a soaked loafer. There were a few bad women standing at the foot of stairways, but not the obtrusive kind. Tenth ave was for the most part very still except for the intermissions that every city must have. 9th ave was still, except for the elevated. On this street I sold only to druggists. The confectioners and delicatessens refused. But with this difference. The confectioner is cold as ice cream in his refusal. But the delicatessen man is so genial you feel he has a kind breast anyhow. He is generally German. 'Every cent counts with us,' one said. But he laughed like a big brother, bless his heart. A customer in the same store stared straight in front of himself as I approached him. He outdid the Chinaman. He seemed to think I was one of God's American volunteers as a shoe string peddler. I tried wit, persuasion, everything I could, for two chilly minutes, but he wouldn't even say good evening when I left. The Chinaman, well he ought to attend a finishing school kept by Chinamen, and get a domestic finish put on himself. Even a Chinaman can say good night. For the rest of the evening of the hours, for the walk extended from 11:15 to 12:15 I decided to try drug stores.

"The first druggist refused me as though he was afraid I would whine and hang on his coat tails and weep into his hand, if he was not firm with me. But I bade him cheerfully good night, and he looked surprised. The druggist on the next block said he didn't see much art in that. Just then we were interrupted by a drunk. 'Beg pardon, gentlemen, but I am a poor bricklayer. I am not often in this condition. All I want is just five cents, five cents to get home on.' Did he want it? The druggist ordered him out. I sort of began to feel for my pennies when he was gone. This interruption past I presented my verse, and received my two cents, and wondered if I ought to help that poor devil on the car. Where was he? I didn't see him anywhere. The next druggist refused me, but an old doctor who was talking to him bought two of the verses for five cents, and told me to keep the change. This made five sales. Then I said, Now for Broadway. So over I went to Broadway. The first drug store there were men talking, in a loafing sort of way. When I laid my poem on the showcase before them two of them backed away in a very confused state. They were embarrassed by their over-hard heartedness. They didn't like the insinuation that there was any such thing as poetry in the world. Poor confused things! One of them backed against the wall, another turned his back and leaned his elbow on his hand on the showcase. The third looked straight at me, and made a great appearance of not listening. But as I pressed the matter and read the first verse he grew so confused that I pitied him and withdrew. Those three men did embarrass themselves dreadfully. They must have been plotting mischief. Maybe they had a notion that poetry is only found in books.

"Well, the next drug store, near Broadway and 53d there was a boy of about twenty, sole possessor. I said to him as I handed the picture to him, 'Did you ever do any drawing? Here is a little idea of mine. I am trying to earn my living. I sell these for two cents.' But he only gazed at the thing, silent as a Chinaman. At last he strolled behind the till and threw out two cents and said, 'This is a hell of a time of night to bring around those things.' I gratefully put my two cents in my pocket, and took the hint and went home to bed rejoicing."

"Now let there be here recorded my conclusions from one evening, one hour of peddling poetry, and that hour midnight. First, I am so rejoiced over it and so uplifted I am going to do it many times. Secondly, there is more poetry

in the distribution of verse than in the writing of it. It sets
the heart trembling with happiness. Thirdly, the people like
poetry as well as the scholars, or better. Those that bought
under all disguises could not conceal from me that they had
hearts full of dreams, and some of those that refused were
dreamers too shy to confess it to themselves. Fourth, I must
use more art and more persuasion upon these people. I did
not make any effort to stir their souls. I only let my work
speak for me. But I must get a fire in my breast that will
kindle them in spite of everything. Oh, they are my friends,
and I have loved all those that bought my work, and some
that did not. It is a perfectly natural relation to society,
as far as I am concerned. It is a situation in which I am
much more at ease than peddling manuscripts or drawings
from publisher to publisher. In this book I must record the
names of those hereafter who give me the warmest welcome."

The next night, March 25, 1905, Lindsay started forth
again to sell poems, of which he made this record in his
diary: "This evening at nine o'clock went to the man ——
who bought my first poem on the two cent plan. I gave him
a copy of 'The Cup of Paint,' saying as he woke up from
his daze on the table at the back of the store, 'There is another poem for you. I throw this in. I think I pulled your
leg on the last one.' 'All right,' said —— with sleepy cheer
in his voice, bless him. He understood."

"At the Klondyke fish market, a block south, there was no
sign of any sympathetic customer, as I looked through the
window. A stranger officiated at the frying pan. Some
evening I am going in and find that man who gave me two
cents so cheerfully. He had a large Adam's apple, a lean
neck, a little cadaverous face, sooty from burnt cookery,
and the eternal fumes of frying fat; but he gave me my two
mites and I must not be ungrateful. He was a sad sympathetic little man, bless him."

"Having thus borne in mind the warmest welcome of my last

[128]

trip, I started east for Third Avenue. About Fourth Avenue I decided to try the silent treatment. I walked into an Italian confectionery, —— I believe was the name. No customers present, all well. The folder found itself spread out before the eyes of the ugly stolid Italian girl at the cash desk. She looked up. I looked at her solemnly, turned slowly upon a dramatic heel, walked out with silent mysterious stranger stateliness. I'll bet that detained her a few parasangs. Next a prosperous grocery. The man at the back of the store, evidently the proprietor, didn't want that picture for two cents. Very busy, not interested. So to the stolid woman at the cash desk, with the red moon face, and the flour barrel shape, did I whisperingly present the picture for nothing at all, and walked out before she could give it back to me, or unbend the startle from her brows. When she shows it to the proprietor how pleased he will be!

"At last Third avenue and 57th. A bright street thronged with busy middle class shoppers in shawls, with arms full of bundles, children skipping rope, and having the time of their lives. A sort of continuous street picnic, and family reunion festival. Big bright stores in strong contrast to the shadowy side streets, and contrasting most dramatically with 10th Avenue at midnight two evenings ago. Here the places where there were no customers were as far between as the lighted stores on Tenth Ave. Another difference between 3d and 10th, 10th is very wide and cheerless, three times as wide as 3d, and tenth has low narrow sorrowful stores, and a more drunken and less prosperous Saturday night. And 10th Ave. the only happy people are the children. 3d Ave everyone is happy. 3d Ave is cosier too, for the elevated sort of roofs it over, and the trains go by with a rumbling and comfortable drum music.

"There is no use talking to people in a store where there is a customer. Time is money as long as customers are present. And besides the business atmosphere is not the poetic.

And it is impossible to talk poetry to one's best friends if there are more than two present, and one at a time is best of all. Poetry is distinctly a question of individuals, and a constituency is but an accumulation of individual isolated voters. There is no communal cult, at least I do not conceive it so. And when you meet a man alone it is no longer a question of business, and he is not able to entrench himself behind market place conventions, it is man for man, a duel of personalities. And there may be something in the fact that those who are susceptible to verse are likely to be those with limited business talent who are passed by by the Saturday throng."

"The first empty place looked prosperous enough, a Greek firm with two dreadful names, 924 3d ave, two or three blocks from 57, as I walked south. There was just a boy in the store. I wondered as I entered if the Greeks still loved poetry, and if that really was a Greek name over the door. There were beautiful things there, ferns, carnations, splendid roses. But the boy of twenty, of twenty-five was best of all. I have not yet learned to approach men with art, to radiate poetry from every pore. I am still a bashful suitor, and pleased with a gracious smile. And the fellow smiled with the sweetest good humor, he was really handsome, a brown boy, dark haired, with dirty thumbs from handling potted flowers. I said the picture was a gift for him. And he laughed with strong human good nature. It was plain he had a soft heart and a high spirit. I must call on him again. There was gentleness, and a wholesome willingness to take me at my word. I have come to this conclusion—to poorer people it is better to present the thing for a sale. That takes the air of patronage from the transaction. They take it for refined proud begging, which is a thing that they understand. It is a sort of carrier's greeting to them. To the rather prosperous middle class, however, it is better not to ask for money. They are not fearful of charity. They are more impressed by generosity, when it is proven absolutely genuine. Well, the flower man is my friend. Just for the sake of his hearty smile I will bring him another poem some day."

"At 880 3d Avenue at a delicatessen there was the proprietor and his wife, a middle aged tight faced, that is tight skinned shiny foreheaded red cheeked woman, not unpleasant in her manner, who greeted me with some curiosity as I briefly and awkwardly stated my business. She took the picture in her hand, plainly interested, and as I left the store I called from the door, 'I made the thing myself,' and with her curious, humorous and wholesome smile in my eyes I left her laughing. It puts laughter in the heart to see them take up with the thing so naturally, for all my awkwardness. . . . I flatter myself that the people who smile so kindly will not throw my picture away very soon."

Lindsay next tried a cigar store, finding a dragon man. "I made this picture for you," said Lindsay. The dragon retorted, "I didn't ask you to make it for me." "I want to give it to you," pleaded Lindsay. The dragon grunted, "I don't want it. Don't care for it at all." Lindsay in his diary proceeded to moralize for some pages on this man and his manner. It will be of no profit to copy it here; enough of such matter on other personages gives Lindsay's manner of thinking and reacting in these situations. That is the main thing here. Next he called in at a German pharmacy at Third Avenue and 53d Street. The proprietor was affable. Lindsay presented him with a copy of "The Cup of Paint," and went on. He had been scattering his poem and picture to passersby along the way up to this point. He had one poem left which he gave to a Swedish waitress in a restaurant, who seemed surprised that she was getting it for nothing. The experiences grew thinner as Lindsay walked on trying to sell or to give away his productions.

On April 8 he tried again to peddle poems, but obviously

[131]

it could come to nothing. A man of twenty-six years, soon to write great poems, was playing a strange rôle thus to spend time and energy on so profitless a venture. It is equally remarkable that he could moralize and theorize so interminably upon what he saw, or thought he saw. He was indeed full of the bookish theoric, and quite a fair mark for his mother's criticism that he was too much addicted to speculations. The conclusion is inescapable that Lindsay was feeding his vanity on these Quixotic jaunts at night about the streets of New York, and betraying something of an exhibitionism. He was showing no little bravado and gall for a man of sensitive temperament; and how he could go about on this visionary mission without being thought a little touched, and moreover giving that impression to people whom he approached, are things that one feels he could scarcely have failed to comprehend himself. The preaching, world-saving impulses were at the core of this peddling. The best that he got out of it was what he saw of the city, of human nature. He probably formed understandings these nights which guided his hand later in the writing of poems, even if he used nothing out of these experiences for direct and concrete subjects.

Soon after these nights it occurred to him that certain songs should be written in America in brass band style, harsh, popular, marching songs, of crashing iron, of men in a hurry, of roars in the street, of the rivers of money. Here is the genesis of his syncopated verse, his many scherzos. He now confided to his diary that it was better to dirty one's hands with coal or ashes than to do cheap and vulgar advertisements according to another man's cheap notions. "To conform to vulgar mannerisms, to please a vulgar popular taste, to play the fool for an indefinite period, till a cheap popularity is at last attained; to suit commercial engravers forever and forever, to cringe and to plead with publishers for permission to print drawings that they cannot understand—better than this is to heave coal. Better than this is to dig ditches."

These are sensible and brave words. Lindsay had come to them after having failed to be a Christian cartoonist, an advertising illustrator or writer, indeed, after having failed to be an artist at all despite the opportunities of the Chase school, and the association of Robert Henri. Many will wish that he had kept to his vision on the subject of not trying to please the mob. If he had done so he would not have taken to the lecture field, there to recite poems which audiences called for, not that they had any appreciation of poetry, but on account of having heard that certain of his poems were exciting. They, too, wanted to hear them, that was all. Lindsay, following the example of Herndon, might have bought himself a small hog farm near Springfield, and there in healthful work, in quiet and in independence, written the poems which grew up out of his vast experiences and studies. There he could have heard the "proud roar of machinery against the whispers of fairies," and sent "the souls of the buffaloes against Chicago."

By now Lindsay was beginning to dream of crucified angels, one of the features of "The Map of the Universe," later to be discussed. Was he not himself a crucified angel? No man, not Shelley himself, ever went forth into the world with purer and holier hopes and energies. Thus far he had done nothing; and he was beginning to see the rocky plateaus over which the vultures were wheeling. "Tell me the story of the crucified angels, and hold the jar to my lips, saying, Drink." "Let the angels be crucified upon a cross of iron. Let them be beaten with rods of iron. Let them preach against noise and money lust." All of this the man Jesus did, and the business interests of his day made way with him, as the bees kill the drone. It will always be so until the matter of bread and a roof are settled for all, for the weak as well as the strong, for the able as well as those who cannot take care of themselves, as Lindsay could not take care of himself in the hurry and roar of New York, where he peddled poems. Yet still he said, "God bless all beauty, and keep it pure, all love and keep it wise, all passion and keep it unselfish. We are in this world to redeem beauty from shame, love from stupidity, passion from selfishness." He would write a poem on Poe. "Morally he is to be damned, but he has an immortal part. Homer is high in heaven, do you think of him? Does your terrible pride burn you when you think of Milton, kneeling before the Mercy Seat?" No, but Poe was the magician.

This spring Lindsay saw Ibsen's *Doll's House*. He had read the play, falling asleep over it. But the dramatic presentation thrilled him. "The rebels for mine," was his comment. At 3 A.M. of May 16, 1905, he wrote as follows in his diary: "The time has come to centralize. I have tried everything and done nothing since January first. If I draw let it be from a point of view in regard to men—a point of view that will make Beardsleyism impossible. I will do nothing real till this Beardsley poison is out of me. I must let drawing alone until I am passionately possessed to describe something I have seen in the street, describe it in line. I have too many points of view, too many openings. Let me take one and stick to it. Hammer away till something happens. I am absolutely demoralized unless I can concentrate, and I can concentrate on but one thing at a time. Let me consider one good possibility, and hammer away till something happens. Newspaper work seems the thing tonight. Let me write for the newspapers, and do only such drawings in connection as absolutely compel themselves to be made. Let me construct the most artistic writing possible, be a specialist, if possible, on the street, and write away, say three articles a week. God help us all to be brave. Amen."

Lindsay at this time might have gone back to Springfield

and taken a place there on *The Register*, the Democratic paper of old-fashioned Jeffersonianism, which was always friendly to him. A column there conducted as William Marion Reedy ran *The Saint Louis Mirror* would soon have made itself known and felt throughout the land. The country then needed to see itself part of the time in the mirrors of a non-metropolitan environment, and to know that Fifth Avenue is not America all in all. Lindsay as a newspaper man in New York is unthinkable. He was unable to make himself into one, for which we may all be thankful.

The last entry for 1905 in this diary is dated May 31, 1905. It is worth quoting almost in full. "At half past one this morning my heart is hungering with desire to lay hold of, and live and die with the vision that possesses me. I see God in the greatness of his cold high beauty. I understand why the monks have counted their beads, why Michael Angelo carved the Night and the Morning, and painted the Sibyls. I have seen beauty that is cold as death, eternal as the voice of God, more to be desired than any earthly fire. There is peace in the shadow of these wings. Oh, my God let me attain to them for refreshment and strength again and again—give me this thing to hold to—let my Rock of Ages be granted to me if I can only have this vision for a moment every day I can do all things that I have been sent to do. The beauty that no man can name, deep as the ocean, high and cold as the stars. For a moment I felt my hands upon the fringes of the robe. I felt the eternal strength of the shadow of the Wings—yet I know it may never, never return to me. When I prayed my prayer in the jungles of heaven I learned how to repent, how to pray, how to kneel. Yet that vision has been gone for many a day. It may never return. Likewise this one may never return, these words will read cold and dead to me. But the coldest part of Keats, of which Arnold speaks, the principle of

'Eternal Beauty in all things,' the part in Keats that stands higher than the bloom and the ripeness to serve this thing day and night, to feel the secret understanding with the spirit that will enable me to go for strength, and cool many foolish passions, this is my prayer. I have seen my God face to face —how can I blaspheme Him ever? Why am I made to forget what to love, to lose, the dream I worship, to be stupid, to be shameful, to be hot with fool fire, to be paralyzed by the struggle for life, to be daunted by the stupidity of men? God make me to look you always in the face, and see your stern eyes on my soul. Then if I am weak I can wait for strength, then if I am wounded I can be healed, then if I am still selfish I can at least be worth something to men, serving my God, I can serve them."

When Lindsay kept saying that he must concentrate one wonders why he did not do so, that is if it was in him at all to act, to work, why did he not draw some of the scenes and faces which he saw on those walks while peddling poems? Why not a picture of the Negro frying fish, or of the two men plotting mischief as he supposed in the cigar store, or of the crowds in Third Avenue, the children playing, the shoppers with their arms full of bundles, of the types he saw in the Y. M. C. A.? It is easy to ask these questions; it is just as easy to answer them. Lindsay's mind was not fixed upon the human face, nor upon people as figures in the human drama of the city. He saw them as souls to be saved in a world made beautiful. And in truth even now he was more intent upon fairies and butterflies than on people, in whatever aspect they might be presented. Thus his life in New York went on with lecturing at the Y. M. C. A. and with dreaming and theorizing. He hoped, he studied, he prayed, he wrote, he dreamed. He had no faculty for the practical things. And he had not yet clarified his mind on the thing that he should do, whether to paint or to write, for which reason he could not concentrate, as he termed it. He was soon now to take a long walk, and find in the outdoor life and the events of the road a solvent for his congested mind, a binder together of his incoherent mental wanderings.

It was a way to fly from the pragmatical spirit which he had inherited from Grandfather Frazee, from the perturbed imagination with which his mother had endowed him, from the iron city which had not accepted him. It was an incomparable recourse by which to assert a growing rebellion against business America, the machinery of city life, from too many books, from too much introspection, from the atmosphere of academicians and culture, and luxury in which he did not share, nor for that matter want to share; from everything grown intolerable with which he had coped in vain in the effort to be an artist, and to maintain himself. He had done many things, teaching, lecturing, conducting students through the Museum. He might have made a living at some manual labor as John Masefield did when he worked in a saloon. One wonders why he did not do some sort of labor, for which there was chance in abundance in New York. It would have been good for his physical being, as much so perhaps as walking. But the soul of Saint Francis was reincarnated in him; and Johnny Appleseed was his archetype. He therefore now took to beggary and the open road. Nothing more contributed to the growth of the poet's mind than the walking tour from the South north in 1908 and the one West in 1912. Many of his best poems came out of these vagrant expeditions, and they seem to have clarified his imagination and concentrated his visions for much of the most distinctive poetry that he ever wrote.

CHAPTER VIII

LINDSAY abhorred the tyranny of convention, and loved the freedom of the untrammeled life as much as Whitman, almost as much as Johnny Appleseed; for he never quite took to the wilderness as the latter did, and he returned to Springfield eventually, "the city of my discontent." But a central fact in understanding him is that he was a profound Jeffersonian Democrat, a non-conformist in the practice and art of poetry and pictures; and in spite of his Campbellite rearing the matter of religion did not escape his original analyses. He mixed with Jesus of Nazareth a lasting reverence for Prince Siddartha and for Confucius; and his mysticism led him to Swedenborg and kept him there as long as he lived. As to the practical life he had a wary eye against being caught in the trap of routine labor of every sort. He was willing to starve, but not to be shackled to business, to the system which standardizes the lives of the young, and uses them as it does any other raw material. These resolutions were aided by the fact that there was scarcely anything of a practical nature that he could do. For the rest he could not teach as Longfellow did, nor edit a newspaper and translate Homer as Bryant did; nor could he follow the simple life of homekeeping as Whittier did. He was not precocious as Poe was, and won no prizes, and sold no stories, and developed no prestige for himself by which he could start magazines, or review books. In the spring of 1906 as he was approaching his twenty-seventh year with no profession, and no means of gaining a livelihood, his economic outlook was as dark as possible; and Doctor Mohawk and his mother must have been greatly concerned for him, if they had not by that time erased anxiety from their minds with the determination that he must get along the best way he could. If he was to have his own way, there was no other position for his parents to take. Lindsay himself, as far as one can gather from the autobiographical notes which he was daily making, seems to have decided that, somehow, some way he would live, and the future would have to take care of itself. This state of mind had by the trial and error of these previous years evolved definitely as a central point of his thinking; and in this mood on March 3, 1906, he sailed with a New York friend, Edward Broderick, for Jacksonville, Florida, intending to walk back north from that place. In a *Handy Guide for Beggars*, published in 1916, Lindsay made a report in part of this tramp, and of a subsequent one taken later through New Jersey and Pennsylvania; but Lindsay's prose chronicles always lacked continuity, and that order and clearness which make an intelligible story, and fully present travels and experiences. A very much fuller idea of what he did and saw and felt can be had from his diaries in which he set down in the freshness of the moment what he was living, and in the words that came to him at the time. These diaries therefore furnish the chance of seeing how poems came to him and just when, how his mind was forming itself, what he liked and disliked, and just how he was faring toward the man and the poet he became.

In three days after sailing on the boat *Iroquois* Lindsay with his friend was in Charleston, warm, gray, and beautiful. He went to the old slave market; he walked through the slave stalls, and felt as if he were being stifled among bloody tiger lilies; and there he reflected upon the luxury that this market once bought and sold, and of the beauty and happiness and dreams that were bartered there. In imagination he could hear the clanking of chains and the rattle of skeletons. But when he left the stalls and stepped to the sunny street of this old American city, with its ancient charm unspoiled, all the houses turned to gold. Yet despite all this the city was to him a tomb overgrown with magnolia and haunted by crickets and mocking-birds. He did not see the old estates on the Ashley river; and he made no mention of the beautiful churches there on Meeting Street, one of which was designed by Sir Christopher Wrenn, and in whose yards such celebrities as Calhoun, Timrod, Hayne, and others found burial. Perhaps he did not know that Timrod wrote "The Cotton Boll," a poem as distinctive as Leopardi's "La Ginestra."

The next day the *Iroquois* was in Saint John's River, which seemed a hundred miles wide. A fog hung low over everything, and banks, source, and outlet were obscured. Lindsay called it the "white river of souls," and felt that the boat was bold to go forward. On the 8th Lindsay and his friend disembarked at Sanford, a town forty miles south of Jacksonville; and in the afternoon they started to walk to Winter Park, fifteen miles west. They passed through the jungle of Florida, as the day ended in a golden sunset, and a full moon. The college bells were ringing as they entered the village at seven o'clock. They had traversed a country of primeval palm swamps and turpentine camps, and of cleared spaces where casava and watermelons were being raised. The houses stood in the midst of orange groves; and as the moon shone the sandy tracts turned white under the moon, whose light sifted through avenues of old trees, looking like gray smoke. They were too late for dinner at the boarding-house, with the result that they repaired to a grocery store where they fed on canned beans, sardines, Uneeda biscuits, lemonade, and root beer, with a total expense of thirty cents for both.

The next day Lindsay obtained the consent of the president of the college to give a lecture to the students in Knowles Hall. In the afternoon he went up and down Main

Street inviting students to the lecture at 6:30, while his friend was at the office of the local newspaper where he was offered the editorship. Nineteen students appeared at the lecture, and Lindsay called it a glorious experience. He was ecstatic over the clear-eyed boys, the young gods, and the girls with kindly hearts and the sort of rapturous youth that departs when college days are ended. These travellers found lodging that night at one of the cottages, and the next day set forth for Orlando, four miles distant.

Here Lindsay obtained the consent of the secretary of the Y. M. C. A. to let him have the use of the hall for a lecture that night at eight. Three old men came to hear the poet, one of whom looked like Spurgeon. They were Confederate veterans who quoted Poe, but declared that Burns was a greater poet. The manner of these old men made Lindsay conclude that there might be "forty thousand in Israel who have not bowed to Mammon, though they may not come to my lectures." After the lecture Broderick passed the hat. The veteran who looked like Spurgeon put twenty-five cents in it, the one who looked like Carlyle put in nothing, the one who resembled Haroun Al Raschid contributed ten cents. After the lecture a drummer approached Lindsay and began to talk about his business. This drummer confessed that he wasn't much for poetry, but that he liked to help a man who seemed to want to go to the bottom of the subject; and as he had given a quarter the night before to a sleight-of-hand performer, he could give something to poetry too.

The next day, March 11, Lindsay started to walk to Tampa, forty miles southwest from Orlando. For some reason Broderick decided to go thither by train, leaving Lindsay to the tramp alone. This day he walked twenty-nine miles in nine hours. His observations of natural life and of flowers along the way are unusually acute; but his feeling for nature never inspired poems dealing directly with her in the Wordsworthian or Shelleyian sense. He noted, however, on this walk the thistle-king, the profusion of violets and pearl flowers, as well as numerous turtles, snakes, and flocks of cranes. The swamp by moonlight thrilled him.

His mind was working under the stimulus of the open air and the walk. He noted that a poem should be written on the subject of the path beside the railroad; and the following subjects for poems suggested themselves. They are set down here to show how he never used all the material with which he stored his mind, and how much of such material in the process of his evolution was discarded and forgotten. Here is the list of subjects for "little stories": The arrow shot into the heart of the sun; What the red-clay lady said; What the white-sand lady said; What the turpentine-tree lady said; What the fire lady said; What the orange-and -tangerine-and-grape lady said; Cardinal birds and mocking birds; Buzzards; The palmetto lady; The pecan point for the arrow; The palmetto lady and the crane. He observed that the men around were whistling "The Mocking Bird." "Without the shedding of blood there is no muse," he recorded. "There could be no mocking birds without buzzards. Let buzzards devour our bodies. What do we care?" That night Lindsay slept in a lumber camp, and had lodging and breakfast for fifty cents. The proprietor of the camp told him that he could make ten dollars if he would stay and give a lecture; but Lindsay was intent upon making one hundred miles as a record, and so departed. That night he had arrived at Lakeland, thirty miles from Laughlin, where he had lodging and breakfast for one dollar.

The next day, the 13th, he walked eight miles out of his way, and upon retracing made forty miles during the day, from eight in the morning to ten at night. During the three days he had covered 100 miles, arriving at Tampa at the hour mentioned, where he went to a hotel, had a bath, and slept "like a stove."

The next day he received a letter from Broderick, who was taken ill at Lakewood, and had decided to stay there a week. Lindsay, therefore, put in the time trying to find work in Tampa. He had taken with him on this tramp some copies of a pamphlet-printing of "The Tree of Laughing Bells," bound in a red cover, with a design of bells around the title printed in an open space from which radiated innumerable cones and spikelets like the petals of a sunflower. The date, 1905, appeared below his name as the author. The poem is as symbolical and less intelligible than "Childe Roland to the Dark Tower Came." It is as incoherent as Poe's early work.

Lindsay exchanged three copies of "The Tree of Laughing Bells" for a breakfast, bought by a travelling man from Mobile, who first read the poem and then decided to be generous, not only with breakfast, but with luncheon, too. That morning Lindsay looked for work, and toward noon found it in a paint shop. There was a strike on, and the proprietor needed a sign painter. He was not wanted to begin the job till the next day; so he spent the afternoon looking for odd work. By this time Lindsay was hungry again. He met a produce man who took him across the street and fed him. Finding that Lindsay's feet were blistered from walking he assigned him to a cot behind his office for the afternoon, and that night gave him supper consisting of two raw onions, bread without butter, bacon, and bad coffee. Still Lindsay characterized him as standing second "on the roll of the merciful today." Moreover, he bought a bed for Lindsay that night; and the next morning gave him twenty-five cents for breakfast.

If Lindsay had had the skill of James Whitcomb Riley at sign painting he might have been in good fortune now. He reported for work at the paint shop, and made some pen-and-ink signs, which were not satisfactory to his employer, and he was dismissed. That afternoon a letter came from Broderick, and Lindsay decided to wait for him to come on. He spent the afternoon gossiping with a hotel porter. Then the produce man came to the rescue again, and gave him another night's lodging. The next morning he sold a copy of "The Tree of Laughing Bells" to a lawyer for five cents, with which he bought rolls for breakfast. He then bullied the hotel clerk out of a cent and despatched a postal card to Broderick, asking him to come on. He wrote a poem now entitled "The Blood of the Mocking Bird." Broderick arrived finally, having walked from Lakewood, and the two went to Sanford by rail, and from there to Jacksonville by boat, on which they had excellent meals, and saw many alligators in the river on the journey.

It was Sunday, March 18, in Jacksonville. Broderick had had enough and took the boat back to New York. Lindsay went to church, and then started north, walking the ties of the Atlantic Coast Line, feeling that he was "taking a plunge." He made ten miles, where he abode with a man named Edwards, the third on the roll of the merciful. Edwards had been in want himself and could appreciate the like fate of a fellow man. Lindsay was given supper, which consisted of biscuits with dough hearts, a greasy dish of pork and greens, with a terrible flavor. There were only chairs enough for the children, the father and the guest; the wife stood up. After supper they repaired to the fireplace, where pine knots were burning. Here Lindsay found what he called a tender and appreciative audience as he recited poems on crickets, fairies, and "The Tree of Laughing Bells." His host asked him to write a poem on a ten-ox-team, which Lindsay promised to do. After this evening Lindsay slept before the fireplace on the floor, one comfort under him and one over him, and a pillow which dated from the time of the Flood. Breakfast the next morning consisted of boiled cabbage, biscuit, and salt pork; and Lindsay resumed his journey, walking four miles to Cranford, where he arranged a lecture in the schoolhouse, and got lodging from one of the local ministers, who was also a section boss, and patriarch.

That night Lindsay lectured and gave a poor show, he thought. The little boys squirmed in their seats, and the collection was but eighty cents. He then repaired to the fireside of the preacher, finding that the household was "fanatically and realistically Christian. There was no doubt of the presence of the Spirit." The minister sang gospel hymns in a strong voice to the weak accompaniment of the wife and children. The singing was followed by prayers, in which the themes dwelt upon were honesty, godliness, temperance, faith, and love.

Breakfast the next morning included corned beef, biscuit, sweet potatoes, and hominy. It was now March 21, and Lindsay chose Macon, Georgia, as his objective point.

He went to the station and bought a ticket to a small village a few miles beyond, hoping that the conductor would let him sleep past it. But the conductor was too alert for such an omission. He woke Lindsay, who got off, and walked sixteen miles to Fargo, Georgia. It was 200 miles to Macon, and he was having a taste of the "long, long road," which became the refrain of a poem on Andrew Jackson many years later, one of the most beautiful of his poems. On the way to Fargo he enjoyed the hosts of bluebirds that filled that country and the "lustrous brass bespangled ooze of the swamps." Arriving at Fargo in the afternoon he would have telegraphed to Doctor Mohawk in Springfield for fare money to Macon; but there was no money order office in the village. He was completing arrangements for a lecture in Fargo when the landlord of the Lumberman's Inn suggested that Lindsay ask the freight conductor for a ride to Macon. Lindsay repaired to the conductor and showed his Y. M. C. A. letter of recommendation, which was referred to an inspector in the caboose of the train. The result was that Lindsay got to ride from Fargo to Valdasta. In the caboose a stove was roaring with pine knots, and a Negro Adonis was polishing the lanterns. Lindsay was happy now and greatly enjoying this lark. He was saying "By Jove" ever now and then by way of exploding his abundant spirits. The conductor finally warned him against the expletive, saying that the inspector was religious and did not tolerate profanity. The inspector was a dried-up old man, whose shirt collar was chewed from many washings. He talked much, ranging in topics from total abstinence to educational reform. He thought there was going to be a great war sometime with the whites ranged against the people of color all over the world.

On reaching Valdasta Lindsay waited for the general superintendent, and when he appeared, he showed that official the Y. M. C. A. letter, but without effect. The superintendent said that he had no authority to let Lindsay ride. Lindsay turned away and began to talk to a drunken farmer from Texas, who was broke and had given his ring to the telegraph operator for the cost of a telegram sent home for money to travel on. The money had not come. He still had twenty cents, and proposed that each of them take ten cents and buy tickets to the nearest station. Instead Lindsay boarded the next freight train, and arrived in Macon, March 21, at two in the afternoon.

In Macon, Lindsay made his headquarters in the office of a lawyer; and soon became acquainted with one of the intimate friends of the late Sidney Lanier, who showed Lindsay many musical scores written by Lanier for camp orchestras. This friend hesitated about the merit of Lanier's poetry; he was sure that he was a wonderful performer on the flute. In Macon, Lindsay received more copies of "The Tree of Laughing Bells," sent on from New York, the printing cost whereof cannot be explicated. Grandmother Frazee may have paid the printing bill, as she sometimes did for poems or leaflets. Lindsay was in Macon ten days, and there won the friendship of a woman by reading to her a letter from his sister, at the time the wife of a missionary physician in China, the lady in question being the president of the local missionary society. She gave him a supper of corn cakes, waffles, rice hominy and gravy, and steak, for which he read her "The Tree of Laughing Bells." Another lady furnished him with luncheon when he left Macon for Forsyth, where he presented a letter of introduction to a Forsyth citizen given him by a Macon acquaintance.

From Forsyth he walked to Barnesville, sixteen miles, and spent the afternoon in the postoffice. Later he begged accommodations of a family there, and was taken to the hotel where he was furnished lodging and breakfast at their expense. He went on, finding peach cider at a Georgia village, for which he beat down the storekeeper to four cents for a glass of it. He was glad to leave walking for a ride on a load of wood with two "crackers"; and on the way saw a chain-gang and a gray-headed Negro, a trusty, who was their guard. By the way, at times, he rested to make notes in his diary. At this point we find the entry that he would write an article on wandering as a fine art, on the same principles of going against chaos as he had already depicted in the cover designs, using their principles of pride, whim, change, surprise, and colorful pageant, whatever this can mean. He left Barnesville with five cents' worth of stick candy, some graham wafers, and a five-cent can of devilled tongue.

Along the way he heard talk of the new régime and the old régime in the South. Hoke Smith was then a regnant influence there, and he was anti-corporation and anti-Negro. Lindsay heard much of the battles of the Civil War from people he met now, just as he heard about them in Illinois when he was six years old. The diary now contains these entries: "The search for beauty is still the only thing in which I have real faith; but the reality of friendship promises change in art and life. Of course, the preacher can forcibly remind us that he said so by authority of his Master long ago. It is easy to be unctious and orthodox. Almost every day I find myself in a glow of wonder over the tenderness of the Southern hospitality. I do not stay in any one place long enough for people to lose the glamour of romance. They are actors in intense little dramas from the hour I knock to the moment I go."

At Sunnyside, sixty miles from Macon and forty from Atlanta, he found hospitality with the widow of a captain in the Civil War, in a house of departed glory. "I have had supper, bed and breakfast in the most spiritually beautiful house I ever entered," is his notation in the diary. The lady was herself a poet and a friend of Mrs. Lanier, widow of the poet. The captain mentioned had taken part in the naval expeditions of the Mexican War, which were directly concerned with conquering California. He had been on the staff of Perry's Japan expedition; and the house was full of Japanese and Chinese objects of art. The walls were hung with prints of Perry's ships, and of the cruisers *Sumter* and *Alabama*, on which the captain had been an executive officer. Nearby was a little house where the Laniers once lived, north of which was a cornfield which had inspired Lanier to write his poem on the Corn. Lindsay's hostess emphasized the religious side of Lanier's poetry. Also at hand was a patriarchal house which had dwindled to the size of the Frazee homestead in Rush County, Indiana; and Lindsay was reminded of the "sharp tears of the Confederate defeat. Into these walls have been poured all that I am able to realize of the South, strength, dignity, and sharp sorrow."

April 7 Lindsay arrived in Atlanta. The diary now contains these words: "I believe I have arrived at a principle. A man can live on one meal a day, if he is sure of that meal, and does not wreck his nervous system worrying about it, and pays 50 cents for the meal, and eats it at night. As a corollary I suggest he need not pay for sleeping quarters. He can sleep out of doors. Tonight is my choice to sleep under the stars."

The next day was Sunday. Lindsay wrote letters the night before till one in the morning, and the lights in the hotel office were turned down. Then he went to the railroad station, but was put out of there by a lounger. He sallied forth and walked a mile on the east side of a street trying to sell "The Tree of Laughing Bells," in drug stores and candy shops, receiving uncivil treatment everywhere. It started to rain, and he hastened to the postoffice, where he wrote letters till four in the morning. He then slept on the steps of the postoffice till five, after which he went to mass, where he "had some comfort out of it, though I sometimes dozed on my knees. The priest was a failure. I could not hear his voice."

Nearby was the largest Christian Church in Atlanta. At eight the janitor came, and opened it. Lindsay asked him for the address of the pastor, and getting it, went to see him, arriving before breakfast. He told the pastor, however, that he had had breakfast, thus uttering "the first lie of the day." Nevertheless, the pastor's wife dragged Lindsay to the table. She was glad to see him, as well were the children; but the pastor was preoccupied with his sermon. After breakfast there was a chapter from Daniel, and prayers. This pastor knew Lindsay's missionary brother-in-law, and so Lindsay became identified. Sunday school followed and was a treat to the poet, for there he met some New York acquaintances. In church he slept peacefully through the service. The pastor's wife invited Lindsay to dinner, but he refused. There must have been something lacking here, perhaps on the part of the pastor, in a recognition of the fact that strangers are sent by Zeus and deserve hospitality, according to Homer. Lindsay, however, left his bundle at the pastor's house, and went to the hotel to write letters.

After this he repaired to the headquarters of the Salvation Army, and saw on the wall the sign, "Why do you sware? Would you like to be swareing when Jesus comes?" Here Lindsay, for fifteen cents, slept till the next morning at six-thirty, and with "a grateful heart." He reflected now that if he could secure as much as fifteen cents a day he could have a bed in New York, and his "future would be made, providing I combined it with other things as wise. If I had a free desk or studio corner in the Association Building somewhere, and a five-dollar lectureship, I could pull through."

After paying a tribute to the Carnegie libraries along the way, as an influence in favor of the higher standard of public buildings, he resolved that this journey should be a real pilgrimage till he reached Washington. "That is a city I must study in a practical fashion. Between here and there let me search for the rare spirits, sell the book and write the letters."

A man named Jones now came upon the scene, a lover of Browning, but unlearned in art "like most of the poets." He let Lindsay have fifty cents. He recognized at this point that "my words are all in a lump when it comes to feeling out a character," and he longed for the vocabulary of Edith Wharton. He never more justly judged himself. People never meant very much to him; and just as he couldn't draw the human face, so he could not describe men and women. When he poetized heroes like Jackson he was indulging in lyricism which is not portraiture of necessity. In Atlanta he might have engaged to be on *The Constitution;* but they heard that he was soon going to Europe. He tried to interest that journal in a correspondence plan, then in a poet's corner; but they were cold to both suggestions. One of the editors loaned him $2.50. He attended a lecture by a local academician on Browning versus Tennyson. In a private colloquy Lindsay discussed the problem of good and evil with a professor there, and he noted in his diary the definitions of pantheism and dualism and optimism. "If God is omnipresent," he observed, "He is able to crush out evil if He will. So it is no more absurd for the Christian Scientist to call evil perpetual, yet in a minority." He respected one more religion after talking to this Christian Scientist.

Here in Atlanta, Lindsay gave a talk of an hour and a half on Pre-Raphaelite poetry, gathering in an honorarium of $10, $5 down. His lecture at Winter Park had netted him but $2.85. A woman came forward at the lecture, the most brilliant of Atlanta, we are told, who suggested to Lindsay that he study sociology. The lady had taken a number of courses at the University of Chicago. On April 15 he left Atlanta on a street car going north, with Asheville as his destination. "Let it be recorded that the vividest impression of landscape comes the first half mile after a week in town. This time it was noon before the ecstasy left me, and the light of common day came again. I must certainly turn some of this winter's experiences into verse, and put the wandering poems in the first half of the book, and give them some such title as 'The Songs of a Tramp.' The first pages should contain my greetings to the various types of hosts and hostesses I have met. The next should contain verses setting forth the principles of life as I have had them forced upon me, the few undoubted things, such as when you work with a man, you love him. Next greet the various types of creators and creative minds, the scholars, the poets, the editors. Finally should come a judicious arrangement of little verses, covering the widest territory I have covered, the mountains of Colorado, Halstead Street, Chicago, Tampa, New York. There should be more souvenirs of these places, four lines or so, epigrammatic records, mile-posts of travel. This should be sent to all the people. Arrange to use all the verses in the book that I have written, by having the middle section 'A Tramp in Fairyland,' and the third 'A

Tramp in Soul Land'. . . . There have been many pilgrims: Christian in 'Pilgrim's Progress' wandered one way; Lucifer wandered the other; Dante had occasion to remember in what ill bread he fares who clambers up and down another's stairs. Whitman has gone afoot in America; the angels have gone on their pilgrimages to the stars. There have been wanderers with and without determination. Tennyson followed a moving light, the Gleam. I have searched for the hidden treasure of Aladdin's lamp." Ah, yes, Lindsay would have had a magic lamp of some sort with which to be delivered from the prison cave of his own ineffectualness, by which he might have built himself a castle of dreams and indolence, maintained by wealth for himself and some Badroulboudour. The vow of poverty can so easily yield to splendor, itself being a sort of splendor of denial.

Nothing yet so far as we have gone with him has revealed a heart interest. In a man so vital and imaginative such celibacy seems remarkable. But he had his moral scruples, as we shall see later. There are further plans for his book of the wanderlust. "It should contain my sermons on the new Christ, and all other things I would wish to say as a priest of art, and cannot say by word of mouth. That is my only chance to evangelize peacefully. . . . My book should contain the form of my gospel for each type of man I am to meet, a little sermon for each man, scholar, poet, editor, teacher. *A Pilgrim's Message* would be a possible title, or *I Prophecy the New Earth,* or *The Songs of a Dreaming Tramp,* or *The Passer-by,* or *The Dreams of a Rhyming Tramp,* or *A Beggar from Fairyland.* . . . I will do without everything for the sake of being my own master. . . . I had better be a beggar than a trader tied to the machinery of his task. In this world he finds no pity. But the beggar's world is full of brotherly kindness."

We may go on a little further with this projected book, one of the many visions which Lindsay had without materialization, when it did not come to a poem at last like "The Litany of the Heroes," in which pages of ruminations were reduced finally to a few stanzas. Lindsay was really afflicted with a species of megalomania, as Whitman was for that matter; but where Whitman sought to make a nation of comrades and to spread the dear love of comrades over America, Lindsay was concerned with moralizations of a lower order, so that his descent from an artist to an anti-prohibition lecturer was neither so violent nor so incongruous as one might think at first. "My book," he went on, "should contain the biographies themselves that men have given me by the fireside. Why should one be eager to live first-hand with so many biographies waiting to be digested? Let there be a section of the book called fireside confessions, or what they are willing to tell a stranger. Or begin with a verse to the effect that people will tell a stranger what they will not tell a friend, because he passes on and is not there to witness the inconsistency, the every-dayness of tomorrow. The stranger has the same glamour for them they have for the stranger. The gleam is on his face, for them as it is on their face for him. And with so many of my friends seeking out errors for the sake of its jewels or its ashes, let me keep together the jewels of their confessions rather than hunt jewels of my own. Let me say to my soul, 'Hold, my friends are sinning enough to learn wisdom, let me sin no more than I must, let me remain cold that I may record their wisdom.' "

On April 22, Easter Sunday, Lindsay left Atlanta for Highlands, North Carolina. He had several days of tramping over cotton plantations, and through peach orchards, stopping at houses where he got his noonday meals for nothing, but paying forty to seventy-five cents for supper, bed, and breakfast. By the middle of the week he reached Gainesville, sixty miles from Atlanta, and lodged that night at White Sulphur, a little beyond. He was near the Tallulah Falls now, and the Blue Ridge Mountains were in view.

Four days later he took a bath in a millpond under a railroad trestle, and waded all afternoon in a water slide, such as is described in *Lorna Doone*. An old man with a mule came along and gave him a ride into Tallulah, where he repaired to the postoffice and received a letter from Atlanta, the remaining $5 due him for his lecture on poetry there. He then bought a pair of plough-shoes for $1.50, spent $1 for souvenir postal cards for "the folks," and then put up at an atrocious boarding-house. The next day he devoted to Tallulah Falls. He went to a store and bought cheese and crackers, which he munched as he walked down the canyon. He sat on a rock in the sun and watched the falls, luxuriating in the solitude. Then he went in bathing. "I suppose it was the sweetest drunkenness of my life. I never laughed so much alone. The water with its roar, and the sunshine and the splashing, and the smooth rocks to stretch on, and the solitude were a cup running over. I threw logs across from notched rock to notched rock in the rapids, and laid down in the current that swept me against the logs. Swimming is a dull sport, but wrestling with an ice-cold fall is great." He got under the falls and took a shower. "And the music in my ears was the one line over and over: 'Sweet, sweet O Pan, piercing sweet by the river.' I was in and out of the falls till the sunshine completely left the valley. . . . I never came so near to the glory of living, and I am sure there is a nymph in that water, whiter than a cloud or a lily, whiter than snow or a feather—my queen woman is there—she has changed from raven-black tresses to eternal white beauty tresses." That night he changed his boarding place in the village, but got a bed infested with bugs, and at breakfast confronted a snappy revenue officer.

On Saturday the 28th he walked all day crossing many trestles. Finally he left the railroad track and crossed the Tennessee Valley encircled with mountains. His feet were now sore from the long tramp, and a stage came by, which

he mounted for a fare of twenty-five cents for a ride of
three miles. On the way to Highlands now he reached a log-
house late in the day at Mud Creek Flats, where he found a
genial man with a fifteen-year-old daughter, planting sweet
potatoes. Inside the cabin was an ugly, tired, sick, faithful
wife who was cooking supper in a Dutch oven. There was
a big fireplace, too, with a back log. Here Lindsay obtained
hospitality, and made a full meal on biscuit and corn bread,
after which he read "The Tree of Laughing Bells" to the
family. The host enjoyed the poem, and became confidential.
He had been in prison for moonshining. Nearby sat his
"beautiful, Saxon, flaxen-haired, smart" children, and the
ugly wife, who in the firelight became transfigured as she
kissed her baby. She looked then like "The Forest Bush
mother and child," Lindsay recorded.

The next morning Lindsay resumed his journey, and
crossed into North Carolina. It was Sunday and he met a
boy going to Baptist Sunday school. The teachers there
were a man and his wife, who took Lindsay home with them
to dinner. At Sunday school there was a promising student,
who had a minute knowledge of Christ and the alabaster
box woman. His face "and little body were those of a
cherub." Lindsay gave him "The Tree of Laughing Bells."
He arrived in Highlands in the evening of this day and went
to the house of some people to whom he had been directed
by a friend. The woman of the house cooked him an excellent omelet, gave him brown bread and sweet milk, and a
couch for the night. The host was a Pennsylvania Dutchman, "earnest, scholarly, and a botanist, superintendent of
the nursery at Highlands." He had tramped all over
America, and was full of Spencer and Huxley, an anti-
socialist willing to die fighting socialism. He seemed to Lindsay like "a doctor out of one of Ibsen's plays." Lindsay
could get up no lecture in Highlands, the place being a
wealthy summer resort. After a good supper with the nur-

seryman, Lindsay started toward Cashier's Valley, but turned to the right once too often and had to retrace to the Cashier's Pike. After passing through groves of enormous cedars and by many waterfalls he came at 8 P.M. to a log-house which "had the best blood I have seen in mountaineers." The family was completely civilized, wrote Lindsay. He was placed in the loft to sleep, covered with homespun blankets. The house had a loom and a spinning-wheel, which the hostess worked. The family said little, Lindsay observed, but "were full of force and beauty." He resolved to dedicate his next book to these people of the Blue Ridge.

He departed and climbed Mount Toxaway. He noted now in his diary, "If I cannot beat the system I can die protesting. I can give things away and keep ragged. Count that day wasted in which you are not giving away the work of your hands." The sincerity of these utterances cannot be questioned.

At Asheville, 200 miles from Atlanta, he saw the Vanderbilt gardens and was entertained hospitably enough in a house there. He thought now "it will not do to make a profession of depending on hospitality. What is generously given should not be perpetually received." His studies in architecture and gardening helped him here to appreciate the landscape display of Biltmore. It looked to him like the Dutch Gardens, like Lord Bacon's garden, like the Italian terraces. From here he tramped toward Cumberland Gap, 100 miles away, in Southwestern Virginia.

The first day out of Asheville he made twenty miles. He was now penniless. A man was willing to give him lodging for the night for thirty cents. Lindsay substituted his shirt and collar for the money, much to the host's disgust, who was a silent man ruling a grim household. He was partially deaf and could not read. Lindsay was bedded with a crippled child. That evening Lindsay read "The Tree of Laughing Bells," being compelled to trumpet into the ear of this dour North Carolinian. The diary now reads, "Hospitality now wanes, and I am far from home. I do not seem to have any fight in me today. Five dollars in my pocket would give me all the nerve in the world." Where was the soul of Johnny Appleseed at this hour? Were there not the stars to sleep under in this May of North Carolina? The diary now shows how far he was from the full philosophy of the road: "My book must have a few dreadfully cynical poems about money, dedicated to the merchants of the world. I must say, Brothers, though I have rebelled, I must acknowledge sometimes that there are few things more honest than a trade. The soul is so seldom its high self in extremity that it cannot emanate enough spiritual glory to give a fair exchange, even for a night's lodging, and we must get back to a money basis. . . . Once I set foot in Kentucky I will cry 'enough,' the trip is done, unless a merry heart comes from somewhere. I have books but hardly care to sell them. It is at least 150 miles to the Gap. I face a week of pennilessness that seems to me almost dishonorable. Spirit! Spirit! Courage! These are the things I need. Why the soul should be gone from me I do not know. As long as a man's heart glows he can face anything. I am in perfect health, and the sun is warm, and I have 20 books. Let me then go forward."

He now encountered a Negro preacher with whom he walked for many miles. Coming to Little Creek, Madison County, North Carolina, he was a quarter of a mile from the ridge of Ball Mountain. Here he received hospitality from a generous woman who gave him corn bread, beans, and buttermilk. She looked like the cartoon of a peasant in *Simplicissimus*, and played the banjo famously; while a sister named Diana danced in plough-shoes and red stockings, with her waist half open at the throat, around which was tied a blue handkerchief. This hostess was managing the little farm alone, her husband being in prison for moonshining. She was glad to have "The Tree of Laughing Bells." Look how quickly the temperamental spirits of Lindsay were raised! "As far as the raw material of womanhood is concerned I could love her forever," was his tribute to Diana. "The hills have done wonders for me." And he set forth again with "visions of brown-eyed womanhood to make me forget the perils of the way. Farewell to the fairest of all North Carolina. Biltmore and all its glories is not arrayed like the tigress who toils with the hoe because her husband is in state's prison"; misdefended, the tigress had confided to the poet, by a lawyer named Lindsay.

By May 12 Lindsay was in Unico County, Tennessee, and was being entertained where there was a fine fire and an attentive audience for "The Tree of Laughing Bells." The mother and her three children looked like Yao San; and on the wall were some photographs of Japanese. An old grandfather with a head of hair half gray and half red listened to Lindsay read with great interest. Lindsay was now in the land of the Southern Republican—no Democrats between Flaghand and Cumberland Gap. In the hills he attended a Hardshell Baptist church, and stayed with some pious, rough people. He started to read "The Tree of Laughing Bells" to them. In the midst of the performance the young woman and the old woman left the room unceremoniously. They returned and Lindsay, not sufficiently persuaded that they did not want to hear the poem, but that they should be converted willy-nilly to beauty, prevailed upon them to listen again. The old lady grew angry now, and told Lindsay that she had no use for such lies. She wanted something with the gospel of Jesus Christ in it, the Old Book was enough for her. The result was that she would not accept the poem as pay for his entertainment, and Lindsay was compelled to leave owing for it. He went on, and met a woman missionary from Jacksonville, Illinois, who was also tramping. Lindsay offered the poem to her, and she refused it.

At Greenville, Green County, Tennessee, he was received into and slept in a store in the midst of wheat fields. He discovered that the Negro minister had taken him greatly out of his way. But there were compensations. Across the way from the store was a camp of gypsies, "Who live better and cleaner than any people since Asheville." The gypsies asked Lindsay many questions and told him that he was entering the land of hospitality. Along the way now through the valleys were numerous snakes; but there were many rose bushes in luxuriant bloom in the pretty yards of the farmers. On May 14 he reached Greenville, and stood under the shadow of the monument to Andrew Jackson with its epitaph, "His faith in the people never failed." "It is an atrocity," observed Lindsay of the monument. "A poem should be inscribed to the grave of the statesman who failed." Lindsay had been educated on the calumnious histories written to degrade and erase from favorable memory all the men who had striven against the capitalism which the Civil War and its justifications created.

At times Lindsay moderated his opposition to business and commercial America, and was inclined to think of art as a salt and a spice, and as an occasional pleasant surprise. It was so now as the diary makes evident. "The busy American cannot reorganize his whole life for the artist." And now at Bull Gap, Tennessee, he stayed at the house of a thrifty German, whose farm "reeked with energy and promise." He loved this man in five minutes, is the confession. "It seems to me I understand the great American people for the first time in my life. I swear that the small college is a mighty force when it puts the salt of ambition into such a small household." This is a reference to his host here, who had attended a small Baptist college.

Tramping further on he was given a cup of water where "two beautiful girls were harbored. Their grace and youth were metropolitan." Seeing many roses on the way led him

[159]

to this enthusiasm. "The rose is so encrusted with tradition that it is a marvel she is not a mummy. Yet she has a face flushed with foolish adorers and languors still. I have searched for the immortal everlasting woman, and today I find not her but her flesh reflected in these petals. And here are yellow roses burnished in the sunshine into little suns. But the true soul of the rose is red. What church can be without you? What priest or what soldier can scorn?" Here follows a long rhapsody on the rose, with many historical references. "O, rose of Tennessee," is the conclusion.

At a picturesque spot he was ferried across Crockett's Ferry, giving the ferryman "The Tree of Laughing Bells" as the fee. He was not ten miles from Cumberland Gap, after a week of walking, having made 200 miles. He was now looking forward to Springfield, where he would cram for the trip to Europe. Finally he passed Cumberland Gap, and saw the stone which marked the conjunction of Virginia, Tennessee, and Kentucky. He was now ninety miles from Richmond, Kentucky. At Middleboro, Kentucky, he was provided with a pair of shoes and three envelopes by the Y. M. C. A. secretary, in the "usual frosty style." At Ferndale, Kentucky, he found an excellent hostess, but the railroads had spoiled hospitality to tramps. He now had a dream. It was "of a land where rhyme was coin of the realm, and the richest in rhyme was feasted most of all. I have feasted on corn bread and milk—a feast to him who will have it so—who has walked twenty miles. Hospitality is as sacred an obligation to the guest as to the host. My heart is full of happiness. It must be the sun that has come right after a rain, or maybe because I have quit waiting under a cliff for a freight train."

At Artemus, Knox County, Kentucky, he was entertained by a storekeeper, and recited for the loafers in the store. He told fairy stories to the children. "The Tree of Laughing Bells" proved a good medium of exchange here. At Coaksburg a teamster gave Lindsay entertainment. Richmond, Kentucky, was still thirty miles north. He walked on, but got a ride of thirteen miles, and arrived on a Tuesday night at Richmond. It was the latter part of May. By advice of Aunt Eudora Lindsay he applied to the Campbellite minister for lodging, and received it. Here the diary ends, and one infers the tramp ended. Richmond is about 80 miles from Louisville, and the latter about 120 miles to Orange, Indiana. Here still lived Grandmother Frazee; and on June 4, 1906, Lindsay arrived there. On the 23d he sailed on the steamship *Merian* from New York with his father and mother bound for Europe. Perhaps Doctor Mohawk thought that he would make another trial toward establishing his son in some kind of settled life by giving him a vision of foreign lands. However that may be, the growth of the poet's mind was still progressing.

CHAPTER IX

LINDSAY arrived in Liverpool July 5, and directly visited Lincoln, Ely, and Cambridge. Sailing from Harwich he went to The Hague, and from there to Amsterdam, thence to Hanover, Dresden, Nuremberg, Würzburg, Frankfort-on-the-Main, Mayence, and Cologne. He went to Brussels, to Antwerp, and spent one week in Paris. Going back to England he devoted several days to London and its neighborhood, and two days paying a visit to Oxford, Warwick, and Kenilworth. According to his habit he was keeping a notebook or diary, and from it one may see what was passing through his mind in these days of opportunity. Doctor Mohawk may have tightened his purse strings at times; yet not many fathers of means as limited as his would have taken a son of twenty-seven years on a trip of this extent, especially when that son had not given any sign yet that he would find himself, or in any way make his way in the world. Furthermore, if study and travel make a poet, Lindsay's equipment as one was already equal to those of many great names, always making allowances for his spiritual ecology, which somehow sensibly emasculated him. His religion softened an intellectual fibre none too hardy at best; it made him myopic to reality, and timorous about facing the malice of life and the evil of a dualism of which he was so clearly convinced. His Christianity was too much of the atonement variety implicated with the efficacy of blood and the mystical power of baptism and the Holy Spirit, and too little of the philosophized sternness of Milton. Briefly and to use a behavioristic term, he was conditioned as a Campbellite, petted as a curled darling and a prodigy, which, added to a disposition never to mature to the toga of virility, gave him problems enough. He was hence destined to fall into soft attitudes of morality and adorations and penitences which were too sweet, and to embrace principles which took his vitality in body and in mind. It will not be difficult later when the subject is reached to trace these cultural factors and their feelings into his poems. We shall see him wrestling with himself now as in this entry; "The next time I should write verses, even if they are not polished. They should be as raw material to be polished at leisure. I fear me I will not be able to turn the last note-books into verse—the moods are gone. . . . In the great synagogue of Amsterdam I felt tempted, I was even eager to bow to and kiss the law after the Jewish manner, and to do it honor, as the host in a Catholic church."

The following comment on Rembrandt is interesting: "Rembrandt has painted the burghers with their flags and their flagons, the solid Dutch burghers, and put mystery upon mystery around them. Here is a master a shoulder higher than other masters, and a magician without blemish or littleness. They have compared him with Shakespeare, yet there is no man in literature with whom to compare him. He has re-established the word 'magician,' an honorable title, a worthy title, a glorious crown. Consider the Presentation in the Temple. There is more mystery in that little frame than in all of *Macbeth* or *The Tempest*. There is gentleness, and nothing sinister, neither gorgon nor hydra, such as Poe would have used, for he could make no mystery without terror."

"It would be a pleasant variation from the first trip I took through the country to make a picture drawing expedition. . . . To draw the farmer's children and his dog; to put my experience as directly into pictures as the time before in words, and to give the farmers all the pictures but my best." Truly why did he not do this from Tampa to Richmond, since he was trying to be a cartoonist, and a creator of the human face and figure?

"Let us seek rather to live the fullest, most self-expressive life possible, to unravel the secret of the imagination, or the hand that still dwells hidden, to bring these before my average fellow man on the road, and to trust him. . . . There is an extreme in realism in the carved Christ and the two thieves in the Nuremberg exhibit before me. With the exception of the dying faces, and the rather dramatic and decorative hair, the corpses might have been taken from a morgue. The Nuremberg wood-carvers know how to make the Angels fly. They are real angels, a sort of bird, non-human, of the naturalness of heaven, having no aspiration or thought there, but identified with the clouds, as the birds are with the leaves of the trees."

"The first danger of the new art is chaos from struggling too hard for freedom . . . the second danger is weariness from too much surprise. . . . I ought to be a higher class lecturer this year than last, probably should dress for the part. . . . Some day I must be able to know Ruskin thoroughly. . . . Let me consult Professor —— on getting myself in training for a permanent professorship, or in some way connected with the Columbia Art Department. . . . This U. S. needs to be taught Beauty, and from no small rostrum. I have something for the men of learning, for the men holding fellowships. . . . Let us be prophets of Beauty, in this our Nation, half begun, and still to grow. We see by comparison with Europe that nothing yet is fixed in America, all, all is yet possible for our land. Let us take heart with great courage."

"I have known one woman who set me one day to seeing visions of beauty higher than Nirvana, and gold and glorious as Minerva. And the next, and ever after she was only a ragged panther. . . . Some day I should write a preface to my series of poems, after they are written, stating the history of the visions, and giving in outline the whole statement of them."

"If I had been born among Mohammedans who are unscientific, I would have believed myself called to shed blood for my visions and to have died fighting . . . if born among German philosophers, and endowed with power of thought rather than vision, I might have made a scholar's religion like Comte or Nietzsche. But I scarcely think one thought a year, and visions come in cataracts. . . . With these visions burning heart and conscience away, I might in some ignorant stratum of society have built a better city than Salt Lake City or Zion City. But I am fortunately free . . . having no genius of leadership."

"The flower of the Holy Spirit is the most wonderful and dangerous flower in the whole Universe. I have for good or ill eaten of it. And I have the desire as all those who eat. I would compass heaven and earth to make one proselyte."

"I would go through smoke and flame to prove these very visions come to me. The martyr's crown would be sweeter than honey to me. Therefore let my friends thank me that I do not disturb their little world. And let me give thanks to all of them who have given their hearts to beauty. All hail to the artists to whom every day is a revelation to be recorded, to be written or painted, and to whom the face of nature is a perpetual and ever-changing vision in the ever-changing light of the eternal sun. They, too, like us have visions in the night more glorious than Mohammed, but they are not troubled with the religious fire, that ate his blood and mine. It is by mingling with the artists and striving to be altogether an artist that I am able to refrain from street preaching the things in this book. I have said in my heart, 'Let me be a good magician rather than a false prophet!' "

He resolutely set his will to this rôle, and for this reason he was sensitive when any one divined the preacher, the evangelist, behind the mask of the poet. Such criticism always stung him.

"In taking my trip South I lived up to portions of Aladdin's lamp. I should live up to all of it before I write at all. I should know Mormons and Zionites, and Mohammedans and Buddhists. I should know missionaries in every land. I should try for myself every holy worship, even as in the Amsterdam synagogue."

"But whether I had been born in Islam or China, I would have made some new religion. It is inevitable with me. By knowing artists I have learned how the making of a religion or of a picture have much in common, though they are not the same." So Whitman said in "Democratic Vistas": "In short, as though it may not be realized, it is strictly true, that a few first-class poets, philosophs, and authors have substantially settled and given status to the entire religion, education, law, sociology of the hitherto civilized world. . . . Democracy can never prove itself beyond cavil until it founds and luxuriantly grows its own form of art, poems, schools, theology, etc." Lindsay was now preaching these same doctrines, whether under Whitman's influence or not; but more evidently largely out of his own peculiar genius.

"This morning in this town of Frankfort-on-the-Main I wake with the resolve to see the world, and put it on record from my standpoint. Five years from this date I shall be upon my way. From now till then I should be gathering information on the right points of view, and doing all the preliminary study. . . . My tours in the spring and summer should be gathering the right standpoints for foreign observations, and maturing my eye as a traveler. I should be able to carry on all the functions of life and travel at the same time. I should be able to write verses, draw, and record progress. With my decorative poems I should be able to make pictures of architecture. But whatever the next five years makes me that I should be able to go all around the world. And I should choose such a trip that I should be able to be fully myself, every inch of it. . . ."

"I must learn to develop such standpoints as have been given me to see all the mysteries that can be seen in broad daylight, to make my heart pure and contrite that in the exultation of the Puritan I see far and fairly. It is the constitution of men like Bryan to travel better if they are base. It is like the blood that strengthens the lion. But it is our fibre to be more exalted in power as we become morally sweet, and I will willingly be a Pharisee if it enables me to see better the shadows of Rembrandt, or the gentleness on the faces of men. Spiritual pride is a sin, it is the sin of our experience. Men must sin to see. . . . What is the matter with a long walk or two, one from Texas to Alaska, the other from New York to San Francisco?"

"The improvement in my style is considerable since I took my walk South. One more three months of that sort would give me a working grip on prose. Brevity and sharp edges and power of insight are still beyond. But they are nearer than real powers of thought. Real power to think will be the longest coming."

"I can never draw well, but some of my walking tours should be devoted to drawing that I may have full command of my resources in 1919, if I desire to do so more than the souls of butterflies, if I desire to deal in the face and form and ways of my fellow man. It seems that architecture, being a decoration, should in the end be easy for me to draw. . . . Must I always understand the work of my fellow man better than I understand him as his soul? Hardship gave me the gift of understanding for a moment in the South; but soon the vision grew dim. It is only in floods of gratitude, or the sudden lights of strange scenes that the face of man grows deep to me."

"No man has written America's art constitution, as Emerson wrote the American scholar. The New Englanders knew nothing of art. It was an evil period all over the art world, and what they knew was wrong."

"Once in a hundred years my heart is swept by the spirit. Let us not be ashamed to kneel in that hour, as I am not ashamed to jest when jesting time comes, or quarrel when quarreling time comes, or dream when dreaming time comes. So let me pray when my knees are tempted to bend, and my head to bow. Let us not be stiff-necked, let us not harden our hearts after the manner of Pharaoh."

On August 1 there is this entry: "This is my first night of Paris. Tomorrow the Louvre but tonight and this afternoon my heart is searching the Taj Mahal, and the temple of Nokko. Have I not seen Cologne cathedral, the greatest blossom of the church? The Catholic church is as holy as Cologne cathedral can be to its devoted worshippers. . . . What blossom shall arise from Oriental Christianity? When the Catholic and Protestant have wasted China and had their religious wars, till all that land in lip service owns either Peter or Paul—then a new Chinese Protestantism should arise. By this force or some other new fires will burn in the East, from which shall burst flames of Art. In a thousand years immemorial China transfigured, Russia ripened, America will show a wonderful new art History. . . . I must go to Jerusalem, Constantinople, Saint Petersburg, Mecca, Kamakura, Calcutta, Benares, Llhasa. . . . Every artist sees pictures in the air. The only differences are mine seem to be on religion, a ritualistic, a prophetic import, and the sense of their religious life is as clear as the sense of their pictorial life."

"Let us worship world wide the divine spirit in man, and record and prophesy concerning its blossom. As for conflict in our poems let it be the line drawn everywhere between new beauty and old stupidity, and old beauty, and irreverence. A series of essays or verses from remote stations of the conflict would be well. Let us in a sense visit the star frontiers, and view each crucifixion there."

"Now there are other magicians beside Rembrandt. In Correggio's Marriage of Saint Catherine in the Louvre, the shadow that hovers between her and the infant Christ is a shadow from the Greek Elysium. And in the faces of Leonardo's Saint Anne holding the Virgin upon her lap, and other of his there is psychological magic, the wisdom that has made the serpent the type of wisdom more subtle than any beast of the field. Yet it is the wisdom, not the wickedness of the serpent; the smiles are according to the Scriptures, wise as serpents, harmless as doves."

"In the presence of the Venus of Milo I have gleaned eternal beauty, the highest sort, much beyond what we usually feel even with our favorite poem or picture. And I have felt this eternal beauty in the pathway of bronzes alternating with golden sarcophagi, marble, yellow with time; I have felt it in this avenue that leads up stairs to the Winged Victory; and I have felt it from Titan's Entombment in the great Rubens' room. This has been the highest point of Europe to me, and the room of the Italian Primitives has had a deal to do with the result."

"I have been taken back and forth in the world, yet feel as though I always stayed at home till I started South. That was living for the first time. It seems the beginning of wisdom to me, the first time I have really revered and followed the divine. . . . It is worth while to be alone. It is worth while to mix with one's fellows. It is worth while to be one's self on the road, and to study to be that. In a little chapel in the Louvre this morning these things come to me: One cannot be completely one's self unless alone. There are a thousand gracious nerve filaments that only expand themselves and unroll in solitude; in the garden of the soul there are whole anemones of sensitive plants that contact with another personality, however delicate, will cause to fade out. The life that is lived in this solitude, this beautiful life is reached in our best pictures and verses, and this in the end shared with others who take the book and the picture to their solitude, and live it over again. No matter how we strive, no matter how we struggle, we cannot be sweet spirited, nor mightily minded, nor high dreaming among our kind, as alone. Only orators, or actors, or great singers have this privilege. It's not given to the artists and the poets. . . . On the other hand there is a great seasoning of the soul that comes by mixing with men; and these things solitude and society are contrasted abruptly and splendidly in travel, in meditating along the lonely road, or from the mountain top, and in mingling with the family by the hearth at the close of the day."

"The moods of poetry are for the most part the moods of solitude. Let us not rebel because we cannot carry them into every day, we cannot afford to be mooning, brooding creatures in the presence of our fellow men. I cannot resist thinking how inevitably different this European trip would have been had I gone it alone, on funds of my own sweating, or alone at any rate. How many more of the ghosts of history would have risen, how many past nations would have stirred in their graves. As it is when I reflect hereafter in solitude upon these scenes it may be the ghosts will come then. And I almost saw one at the tomb of Napoleon, though my father was there, and an impatient commandant ordering us out, and a restless group of sightseers. But to have done it right I should have come to Europe alone; I should have spent all day in solitude before I entered, and there should have been no one else there. And the rest of the day I should have been alone, only remembering. Why, I gathered more dreams and visions from the log cabin of Andrew Johnson, tailor at Greenville, Tennessee, than from this thundering conqueror. But I feel sure that some day alone with the tomb of Grant or Lincoln, as in the East, the grave of some Tamerlane, this tomb of the emperor will come to me with grace and power. In some quiet corner of a Colorado desert, as a procession of the world passes before me in the air of the desert shall I not then think the keystone thought of my youth, and write the ripe soul word that shall be sown for the second harvest of my middle age? . . . The world I know will not be the real world but from the dust of all the pathways I have trod shall be shaped beside me a basket of clay, and from that clay I shall make a little earth, my earth, as I have seen it; and then it shall be my Eve, for she shall bear my great thoughts, my Cain and Abel. . . . Real poetry is not based on the verse one has read, but on the men and women one has met, and what one has seen them do. . . . In the end a man can expect to understand no land but his own. But having met its many phases he can meditate when he is far from it. . . . It is not a virtue to do without money, but it is commendable to carry through one's plans, though penniless. Lack of funds should not stop me a day."

"Concerning death sometimes we desire it: from desperation, exasperation, or from world weariness, from mere numbness of soul. Then on the other hand we fear it, lest it should check us before our work is accomplished. Your true philosopher stands between desire and fear, if he has already done enough work to subside into a philosopher. He should be prepared to meet it any time upon the road. He should have nothing to lose, he should have his face serene for disaster."

"It is a great thing to mix action with our work, if the action is normal. That sense of being written at the time and on the spot is a great help to Childe Harold's Waterloo description. This is the strength of occasional poems, when they are truly occasional. Poems that bear the reminiscence of great action, The Recessional, The Charge of the Light Brigade, have a value all their own. Poems written at great places in memory of other great places—this is worth while."

"What do you poor little people mean when you say, 'Go

[171]

get experience'? I tell you I was Solomon, the son of David, king in Jerusalem; and the Queen of Sheba came walking to me upon the crystal floor. What do you lovers mean by saying, 'Go gather kisses'? I have written the Song of Songs, read it and be instructed children. What do you traders mean when you say, 'Learn to buy and sell, and get gain'? I tell you it was I who burned the bonds of Charles V. What do you mean when you say, 'Put on your goodly apparel'? I tell you I was Sir Launcelot, and wore the stateliest plumes of all; I tell you I was Louis XIV, and I was the king of France, and the tailor was my prime minister. Do you say, 'Go forth and do battle'—I tell you I was Tamerlane, I have been Attila. If you say make a religion, preach the dreams and visions, I say I was Mahomet, and other dreams and visions beset me, and I drew the sword, and what did it profit? A little civilization, a little architecture; but the Sahara is still the Sahara. Do you say, 'Foolish boy, live while your blood is young, get children, and let them do you honor'; I say I was Confucius, and set in order the precepts of Obedience, and the thousandth generation of my sons burn incense at my tomb, and what doth it profit? Also I knew the bitterness of ungrateful children, and their gratitude or their ingratitude have become shadows of the past. Nay, nay, the dust of the road shall make clay on my sweating face, and the eternal road shall lead me on, till I have traveled every foot of my ancient dwelling places, and gathered such wisdom as is there distilled from a thousand memories. Let me gather the last beauty and the highest this whole earth can give. I have the blood of youth, but I shall spend it in accordance with my heart, which beat with temperate age when Homer sang in our village the song of Troy. And I wandered with him. And I met Dante in his wanderings, and young Milton came to me; and I was the aged Galileo, and we spoke of the stars together. Many times I have journeyed—this last journey I make in search of

Aladdin's lamp, which is to say Supreme Beauty, and Suprem Wisdom, and the essence of all magic."

"Let me gird myself for my roadside priesthood, the teacher of the mysteries of beauty in the church of Beauty. He who in his heart of hearts reveres his functions as a teacher needs little other life. Let him attain to cleanness of mind and patience, and let him live the dignity of his mind, and there will be no dignity lacking. The life of a teacher need never turn humilities into humiliations—all things necessary to his office are of inherent dignity. I have lived so many lives let me spend all this body on this one, and dissipate my energy on nothing that is meaningless, and whether I eat or refrain from eating, let it be in the glory of the God of Beauty. As to the history of art I am determined to know so much that what I know now is a child's knowledge."

> "What is my price for good old dreams?
> What is your price for rest and bread?
> Any dreams are free if you welcome me,
> We are friends if we break bread."

"I must wear my dress suit this winter in making speeches. I must make the sort of speech a man makes when he is really interested in municipal art. If I made one good sermon a week on the holiness of beauty, or two or three in the winter, let them be big speeches. If I exhibit I should have some pen and ink on the principle of the soul of the butterfly, only four times as fine, as big."

"In studying the Metropolitan this winter I should seek to get under the surface of pictures of undoubted standing, and sculptures also. I should spend the entire evening on two or three, no more; yet should not make them wearisome. Then a month on Greece, passing from sculpture back to architecture, and comparing both with Egypt and Cyprus. Then drawing the line between the Greek and Roman pieces, an evening with Naples bronzes, and the Parthenon model. Then the medieval remains, the chests of Germany up stairs and down, and the Gothic casts. Then an evening with Notre Dame. Then an evening with the early Italian casts up to Angelo. An evening with Angelo involving a careful analysis of him. An evening with the drawings of the old masters. An evening with Hals and Rembrandt. An evening with Rubens and Van Dyck. With these men much history can be linked. An evening with the early Englishmen. An evening with the Barbizon school. An evening with the Chinese ceramics, the Japanese swords and armour, the medieval armour. That might be studied along with Notre Dame or the early German Gothic. The room of musical instruments of all nations might be made the matter of an address on music as one of the arts, but no archeology, please. I must make my classes great events. I wonder if I could make the Metropolitan addresses real, popular events, which can mean something in the history of New York? I can at least hold out until I am sat upon."

"Looking upon the Egyptian remains it comes to me with the force of an avalanche that Egypt every hour of her life was one vast ritual. Was not her priesthood dominant for thousands of years, were they not magicians ruling mystery? What must have been every day and every hour in this land, when every appointment of a life was ordered and formulated with the things that make mystery, from the giant pylons at the temple gates to the pyramids, from the pyramids to worship of the gods of every day? The perpendiculars and horizontals of mystery are with them all, the flat gold surfaces, the solemn head-dresses. And consider what the processions must have been, the ceremonies every hour of the day, the teaching of the ritual after death was so enthralling! What must have been the experience of life? If the soul had to struggle so far amid terrors to meet Osiris, how must it have yearned pale with bitter ecstasy, or been mesmerized with fear before the impenetrable mysteries of the priestly establishment. When the priest walked abroad, how much more he must have carried of terror and power than that Belgian priest I saw pass in Antwerp with all the people kneeling because he bore the Host to the dying. What intricate reactions must have been between god and god, fear and fear, shame and shame, grandeur and grandeur in a civilization all magnificent superstition! What little room for the things of Greece and Rome."

It was superstition as a plaything, a spectacle that always engrossed Lindsay's imagination. It was a show, a circus. His Christ was out of Santa Claus, his paradise out of the baubles of Christmas. He made nothing of Egypt and its dreams of the divinities of fertility and death, which compass the wonder and the life of all things. Osiris of the mysteries never became anything more in his writing hands than Santa Claus; and the comment we would make after the pains taken to incorporate such meditations from his diary is that such profound material as the Egyptian culture dwindled in his hands to popcorn, tinsel, fairies, circuses, and spangles. This is another way of saying that these hieratics did not belong to him. He played with the hieroglyphics much as one might do with a crossword puzzle, seeking to find some symbolical representation of America; and if he had done so it would have been fantastic, but not important.

"And another thought that has been struggling at the back of my head, a question of ratio: The Catholic system has a few candlesticks, a cathedral, a half dozen priests, and we have high mass. The trappings are simple compared to the vast array of trappings Egypt has left, the vast range of the material of superstition. How overpowering then must have been the thing based upon these sphynxes, these mummied cattle, these canopic jars, these multitudes of impassive, mummified kings."

"I must make speeches if I am in the Y. M. C. A. Chalk talks in that room just off the lobby. Once a week is all I can possibly do well, prepare for along with the Museum. For this I can ask three dollars and a half a night. I might ask for a little dribble of money from home, say two dollars a week. Then with six dollars from the Y. M. C. A. I could make out. Or with seven dollars from the Y. M. C. A. I need no home money. . . . America must be magnificent, she has no other chance. She will be magnificent, as a merely ostentatious gaudy failure, according to the sort of interest her people take in the matter. She cannot remain indifferent. She must choose between gold and gilt. . . . When shall the American eagle scream, on the Fourth, on the day after election, on the triumph of an honest man? But when a great art man does a great work does she scream? She hesitates, she fears she will scream in the wrong place. The people do not care, and the critics are not heard. . . . If we cannot be sages let us at least be scholars. I think there is a deal in the Chinese reverence for more thorough acquisition."

"We do the same things from New York to San Francisco, and wait to do them all at once. A man that does not move us all moves no one. It is the result of the mechanical unity of the nation: the railroad, telegraph, newspaper, public school, and political uniformity. The same set of magazines on every Carnegie library table. Hearst papers, from San Francisco to Boston. The same six best selling books read by the gum chewing typewriter girls from the Philippines to the offices of Philadelphia. The two or three political parties writing platforms which shall induce the follower to vote the straight ticket, and make the mugwump impossible. Every advertiser in the land plays upon this principle that the American people do not move unless they move all at once. And indeed by a thousand interwoven and all embracing systems is the American citizen being involved. But what are the chances for the still small voice of art, among the megaphones and the automobiles? Here is a chance to plead for the voice of the minority, for the voice of the masters. . . . There is much to be enjoyed in Greek sculpture, set by Immanuel Apollo with hair and harp strings of gold which outshone the pale Galilean in comeliness; and when we shall see him there is no beauty that we should desire. Yet the new Immanuel shall not be outshone by him. Immanuel shall inherit that glory and transcend it. I shall carve me an idol called Immanuel, of ivory and gold, and it shall be as much an idol as the face of eternity; yet it shall outshine any idol yet made, a graven image of my holiest dream. Yet it is a simple idea, and will not take many words to infuse it into the whole book. And it is such a grand, constant, over-sweeping idea, that it will keep mv soul burning like an eternal lamp."

"Into the Egyptian drawings one can put all the plea for magic and the soul of Poe. Into the Greek and Roman the whole spirit of Keats and Swinburne. Into the medieval there is to be gathered in the Paulist Father Church. Into the Renaissance the souls of angels—into the East the soul of Buddha—into the Saracenic the sharp sword of Mahomet, then of Omar. And into modern art I must choose one man and paint the whole period his color, that these things may be massed. And in the chapter on the art of the future the soul of Immanuel."

Truly it was necessary for him to choose one man, rather one great object of devotion around which he could accrete his various passions and idolatries. He was never really to do this. The result was that his seed was scattered, from which trees of a size sprang here and there, but no over-topping boughs into which all his strength was sent. Thus Lindsay was a product of that multiverse American life which no less standardizes itself as to non-essentials and fails of a genuine culture. He was not in truth wholly satisfied with his Campbellite faith; if he had been his imagination would not have roamed to Catholicism and to Buddha. He found no place to rest his heart politically, because there was no such place to find. Painting and drawing eluded his ambition; he had no æsthetic creed, save such as he drew from the prophetical agitations of the Jews; and when after going about galleries and reading books he chose Hebraism instead of Hellenism he finished the course of his meandering, and obeyed his nature and his parental influence. There will be a few more diaries to deal with in giving the history of his growth as a poetical mind. When all of them have been covered, and they end with his tramp West in 1912, it will be clear that he had no visions and formed no ideas after these days; and that all his poems to the end of his career oriented themselves out of these years and their books, pictures, and tramps. He did not grow after about forty years of age, even if it may be said that he grew after he was about thirty. He never became philosophical, he never found the hieroglyphic that he searched for. He ended his career as a poet with moon poems, and poems on fairies, and other juvenilia, after a plentiful harvest of great poems.

On this trip back from Europe as the boat neared America, Lindsay had a vision which became the subject of a poem later of haunting quality, of memorable music. This experience reminds one of the story which the venerable Bede told of Caedmon, the cowherd in the monastery of Whitby, where at night the inmates of the monastery used to entertain themselves by singing to the harp, while Caedmon retired for meditation, because he could not sing. This is the language of Bede: "This he had done at a certain time, and leaving the house where the feast was in progress, had gone out to the stable where the care of the cattle had been assigned to him for that night. There when it was time to go to sleep, he had lain down for that purpose. But while he slept some one stood by him in a dream, greeted him, called

[178]

him by name, and said, 'Caedmon, sing me something.' To this he replied, 'I know not how to sing, and that is the very reason why I left a feast and came here, because I could not sing.' But the one who was talking with him answered, 'No matter, you are to sing for me.' 'Well, then,' said he, 'what is it that I must sing?' 'Sing,' said the other, 'the beginning of things.' At this reply he immediately began to sing verses in praise of God the Creator, verses that he had never heard." So it was that Caedmon, according to this tradition, composed verses which have been rendered into English and are of this tenor:

> "Now must we hymn the Master of Heaven,
> The might of the Maker, the deeds of the Father,
> The thought of His heart."

So on the night of September 4, 1905, Lindsay in his stateroom on the *Hamerford* saw a vision; and this is the record of it in this diary: "Last night I saw Immanuel singing in the New Heaven, with the church, his bride beside him, and his friends gathered round in a bright grassy place. And now I remember that at first Immanuel was singing almost alone, and the bride was a later half waking thought. The real dream was Immanuel singing wonderfully, as became a son of David. He was almost as simple a shepherd as David, and his robe was Angelico red. But it was the strain of his song that was happiness—how can I write the gray memory of that song? His lips scarcely sang at all, it was his harp that sang. And some one listening behind me said, 'It is Immanuel.' That was the word that came with the dream. As to the half waking thought that came after I said, 'This must happen from within the deathless walls of the New Heaven, in a place so far within the bright walls. Let me write the song of Immanuel, his happiness when all things have passed away, and all things are become new, and he can breathe with a child's heart the new native songs of heaven, not the grand new song, but the tender memory of the glad new song. For in the singing he was thinking over all things that had come to pass. His head was bowed over his harp, with thoughts as he sang, and a part of the thought was song.' "

Lindsay had been looking at sacred pictures, and thinking of Poe and from him in the wandering ways of dreams it was natural to arrive at Israfel, and his harp with the unusual strings, and then to Immanuel, the Christ, who was bowed over his harp—but in thought as Lindsay wished he himself could be. Let this be the explanation of this theophanic vision rather than ascribing it to some form of ophthalmic migraine.

Out of this vision and, in December of 1907, Lindsay wrote the poem "I Heard Immanuel Singing," with its gospel melancholy, such as one finds in old hymns like "I Will Arise and Go to Jesus." But also it has sunlit spots, though rather of that light which shines upon Beulah Land, and upon the "beautiful shores" of a sepulchral eternity. Written in iambic trimeters, it ripples along with easy music as it celebrates the Rose of Sharon, the Holy City, and the green hills which Immanuel has made into thrones, emphasized by the Poe repetend. One could scarcely write such a poem and disassociate the figure of Immanuel from the Oriental imagery of the Hebrew prophets, and the writer of Revelation. For this reason and because of the character of Jesus, which the character of Christ has not left behind in the mythopœic process of its creation, no poem has been written on this subject as purely beautiful as Shelley's "Hymn to Apollo," or to Pan, not to mention the Homeric hymns.

CHAPTER X

THUS in September of 1906 Lindsay was back in New York City, leading the life of an art student again, though in no Bohemian fashion. When he went out with other students to the cafés he took sarsaparilla instead of beer, and he was set down as a poor mixer, though a genial spirit. He was aloof and puritanical. His hard and fast orthodox convictions, his intense originality kept him out of intimate comradeships. His abstentions were not dramatized but wholly natural. He did not like beer, he did not like tobacco, he abhorred lapses of the flesh; though, according to the testimony of fellow students, he was tolerant of the sins of others. He impressed every one as a man with force of character, of definite individuality. He was soon known as a mind fascinated with snails and butterflies, fairies and the moon, and the silver glitter of Christmas decoration, and those other trivia of childhood which he never ceased to celebrate to fifty-two years of age. He was distinguished for his familiarity with Milton, Poe, and Swinburne, and one wonders what he thought of Swinburne's poem "Before a Crucifix." His improvidence was one of his conspicuous traits. Once when his worn shoes let the snow of the walks upon his feet he put the money he happened to have for a new pair in the charity box of a Catholic church; and later, in Chicago, when he had begun to derive some money from the sale of his poems, he gave to the editor of a small magazine there the very considerable prize money which he had recently received. It happened that this editor was of no consequence and the magazine undeserving of existence; but these considerations had nothing to do with the fact that Lindsay was carrying out his Christian benevolences.

Lindsay was to continue his residence in New York until 1909. He did not become an artist, nor a Christian cartoonist, nor a newspaper writer, nor the editor of a poet's corner. He failed to find himself as an illustrator. He spent the years between 1906 and 1909 in teaching and lecturing, in calling upon editors and trying to interest them in the verses which he was writing; and he was producing to some extent. In January of 1907 he organized a class for a literary study of the writers of the New Testament, and at the church of Saint Luke and Saint Paul, he led this class. The fee was one dollar per person for the course of ten evenings. His mother's career and interests had marked his life so deeply that he could not escape following in her steps. His dreams were full of plans to reform and regenerate America, to save it from commercialism, and to invest it with the soul of beauty. The diaries have already given us much of this program of a new day, of Utopias, and an æsthetic localism. All these days the Metropolitan Museum was Lindsay's constant inspiration. He studied the pictures there over and over again, and almost endlessly. There was not much of interest in Lindsay's external life. When the story is told of his drawing snails upon windowpanes, or making a lunch of one orange and nothing else, or munching at a stick of peppermint candy, the record of his bodily life is complete, save to make mention of his walks about town, his recitations from Swinburne and Milton, and his church devotions. He had no heart interests, and no Shelleyan elopements, and no police attention for spouting, such as Shelley encountered in Ireland. He led the village life in New York, though he was acquiring the city wisdom while remaining a villager. He was a good Campbellite, a Johnny Appleseed spirit in the very heart of megalopolitan sensualism and luxury. He did not acquire the Eastern accent, he did not look for an heiress through whom to solve his financial problems, he did not try

to become respectable or cultured, nor did he aspire to rich
men's tables, nor to the friendship of powerful persons or
magnates; nor did he attempt to shape his poetical utterance
to the epicene fashions that prevailed at the time in the
magazines, thereby to sell them poems. If he built a literary
foundation too broad for his use, if he did not make use of
all of his gathered material that he planned to make, yet
what he read and studied and thought, which was dictated
by his originality of mind, grounded him so firmly in himself that the passing scene and all of Vanity Fair left him
utterly untouched. He went his own peculiar way with a
happy self-confidence that placed him with those original
minds who remain themselves, even if they fail of their
dreams. For these reasons he was an admirable young man,
and may well touch hands with Milton, whom he constantly
meditated. One can sum the whole matter by saying that the
money infection which attacks so many aspiring natures,
and makes imposters and mummers of good minds, never
entered him; and on this score we may be thankful that he
could do so little in the way of a practical self-support. If
he had become a Christian cartoonist, for example, his ruin
would have been sure. The growth of the poet's mind is not
yet complete, so we again turn to the diaries.

In January of 1907 Lindsay opened a notebook "based on
the first serious effort to find out what is true, what is right,
and how to move the innermost souls of men in matters of
the whole life, rather than art alone." Didactic poetry may
be an inferior sort; but what great poetry is not backed by
a great morality? The laughter and satire of Rabelais are
inspired by an ethical passion, an æsthetic vision as intense
as Milton's. They only took, as it happened, according to
his genius, the direction of monstrous buffoonery of an absurd world. Even Byron understood this truth of great
poetical art when commenting upon the genius of Pope;
and Shelley knew that Æschylus shaped his vision of the

mystery of life out of a titanic dedication to the hope of uplifting the human race. Let us turn to Lindsay's first entry in this notebook.

"Now I can worship Immanuel till I discover the truth. The poem of Immanuel finished this December, and my soul growing because of teaching my art class, and the few visible results upon the work of a few students. I feel a certain exchange between them and me in the matter of art in the Development, and in the Fire-side talks. I can speak confidently on beauty, I know what is beautiful; but I cannot speak confidently on truth."

Having written "I Heard Immanuel Singing," in December of 1906, one wonders why he did not publish it in his first volume, *General William Booth Enters Heaven and Other Poems,* which he brought out in 1913; but he did not give it forth until 1914, when he issued *The Congo and Other Poems.* He was accustomed to revise and rewrite his poems, and it may be that he did not get this one in the form he desired it until 1914.

"Lyman Abbott is not very satisfactory on the conversion of Paul. No matter how genuine to Paul we have no notion of the absolute truth or falsehood of it. I would prefer to have it accepted as an hallucination, and so described. How can a great truth be based on an impossible experience? I would prefer that Paul's conversion be the result of thinking, observation, natural experience, and struggle, such as we all must have who take life seriously." These remarks furnish some comment on Lindsay's dream of Immanuel.

"I have sufficiently adequate experience of God in my own life to make a beginning, not as a theological formula, but as a force, a creative paradoxical quantity, a force very close to identity with protoplasm and the sap of nature, and the presence of the sun, yet a personality, a whimsical personality, mostly pagan, yet forgetting his vast inconsistencies and accidents and blind blood storms in the veins of nature and animals, forgetting there to be a still small voice to men who aspire, a Gleam to men who dream; a religious presence to the Hebrew, a mystery presence of infinite wickedness and darkness and power to the Egyptian and the Hindu, a vast sky and an army of devils to the Chinaman, and to the Greek beauty; and to me in my own soul the desire to create, the reverence for the Creator, the companionship with those who are artists, and at last the hunger to stir men so that their lives may be set in sure paths and ordered and built in beauty."

"The next step is to discover the real state of mind of the historical Christ toward his Father. The historical Christ means little to me, it is the Immanuel of the millennium that means more. Nevertheless he is a makeshift of the soul, and the relation of the historical Christ to this curious God I know must in some manner be made out immediately. The Immanuel Christ of the millennium was a thoroughly convincing deity according to the old art life that accepted everything truly beautiful, and in beauty moods he reigns. But in the search for truth I am alone with this curious nature-God-experience of mine. Was Christ's experience based on real facing of the facts of his life, the God he actually knew, or the God he dreamed he knew? Was it a spiritual short-circuit in the head, the flash of a fuse, like Paul's vision; or was it a true hand to hand contact? Was it a series of abstract statements, or the passion of fanaticism? How shall one know he has a piece of the truth? He cannot go after all beyond his own experience, he can never apprehend what he has not known, he can merely rearrange the material. The best he can do is to put himself in the path of experience, what appears to be the truth, as rigidly as he may. It is a question of keeping the mind physically clean, of accepting that as true which appears so at one's calmest, most physically healthful moment."

"I feel like getting on my knees and adoring forever

something I can adore forever, that has no waning light, that perpetually shines, if it be the sun or the moon to kneel, feeling my soul go up eternally without pause in a perpetual cold ever smouldering incense to a deity that can never change. How the dreams go! How the world of the spirit shifts and changes, and how change wearies! I would like to kneel till my hair is gray."

"Oh, to have fire, fire, perpetually in my heart that I may give it freely to all who come. If Christ was a great structural character consistently built up from temptation to Gethsemane, always consistent with his teachings in every act of his life, which I doubt, Gethsemane was the last act in the great character building, the final stone. But if it was merely the seer's agony of loneliness, the gathering of resolution to make good at the trial, the faith that a man must die to make good his doctrines and hold out the little inconsistencies of his life, and make it consistent in a large way, it is much more believable, like the consistency of Socrates."

"There was a certain roadside socialism about Christ that made him akin to the artists indirectly. And there was music in his words. And he was a carpenter, which is a craftsman. No religion is a success unless it is fanatical, a social success, I mean. Only the surrendering religions propagate. The question of surrender is now that of complete, and passionate surrender to the demands of one's fellow men—a new type of social Moody, who shall call on us to give all our strength to what our fellows ask of us."

"Now, though I be unworthy, it is an eager desire of mine to so learn the age of Pericles, the age of Augustus, the Renaissance, as art producers, that I may be able to establish some fixed national doctrine of art, an art ambition for the nation that shall have perpetually as much as she has a Constitution."

"To avoid all the errors of past republics, and to inherit

their virtues has our Constitution been constructed, and though an imperfect instrument, promises to outlast and excel all that have gone before; though it contains germs of its inevitable decay, and like the Roman system of law will break down at last."

"Let us seize these three ideals: Beauty, Freedom, Holiness; let us stamp them upon the innermost spirit of the land; let us write them into such perpetual phrases that further generations shall find new life in them. We must have them all."

"This also is true, that all these men who learn from me live over certain portions of my past life that I would otherwise have almost lost. One of them has acquired my last year's enthusiasms for Swinburne, another acquires an enthusiasm for Tennyson that I myself had long outworn; another acquires a zeal for Henley that was mine beforetime; and now forgotten. Thus these men listening to my interpretations of these past enthusiasms bring them back to me in a sense, I remember in their company a past I lose altogether when alone. I am in a hall of mirrors, yet each one so colored and curved that though I am reflected, yet with sudden and interesting additions."

"Christ anticipates all his critics in most everything, yet he is inexplicable. The substance of Christian Science might account for his healing, and be the law of resurrection. But the substance of Catholicism is suggested by his assertion of authority, and his transference of authority to the apostles. The substance of Greek fatalism, fatalism anyhow, by his persistent prophecy of his crucifixion, of the persecution of the apostles, of the fall of Jerusalem. The substance of pantheism is suggested by his desert prayers, his attitude toward the fig tree, his nature parables, his roadside Bohemianism, his epicureanism by his interest in publicans and sinners, a gluttonous man and a wine bibber; his asceticism by his single life and pure teaching. His socialism by his

Sermon on the Mount, his tolerance by his joke about the tribute money."

"It requires much history to make one stroke of art."

"Is the real Christ the one who is in the imagination of Christendom, or He that lies concealed, entombed in the bosom of the human race, because of their weakness? . . . I must know the Thebes of Rameses as though I lived there, and the Athens of Pericles as though I lived under his helmet and was buried with him; and the Rome of Augustus as though I had cut the sarcophagus of his time."

Lindsay never learned any of these things; and as it turned out he had no use for learning them, as his genius took its final and definite form.

Further on he observed that religion was like sex, since argument against it only deepened its strength. He thought this happened by opposing Christian Science. And now at this time some woman came distantly into his life. The diary contains a poem in which he wrote that if she were a "pebble I could crush and drink you; If you were a fire I would burn like dead leaves; If we were two lion cubs I would devour you." But "Our life and desire would destroy one another." Who this woman was remains a mystery. She passed out leaving not a wrack behind. His prose comment was: "This poem written day before yesterday while I was writing other notes in this book gives me much to reflect upon the two sides of man, the three sides: the beast, the father, the worshipper. Let me rein the beast, let us prepare to be the worthy father. Let us worship."

"One thing I have been seeking is a Christ I can fervently and unfalteringly worship, and it is hard to find. The historical Christ is a doubtful figure, the Christ that actually was has to be reconstructed and destroyed piecemeal; he is in the end a battered historical relic, and we must submit to what scholarship has to say concerning him, and our own reason and speculation and honest study of comparative religion leaves him an insufficient deity. 'What hast thou done that all the world is blood?' "

"But now that I have friends with whom I interchange my life there is a Christ that is not a figment of my fancy, nor a poetic phrase, nor an illusion of mine. It is the Christ that is in them. Now a real worship can be given to this Christ. At least for today I can build a chapel in my heart to the Christ that is in other men. In dreaming of a religious revival that will stir all hearts deeply, yet stir up no dogmatism, it is possible I have found it here. It is the religion of humanity, and varies with humanity. It can be as great as the human race, at least in the West. I must give myself up entirely to my fellow men, to the society and machinery of society about me, the multitudinous chances to teach and work for a long time; and then when my selfish self takes time to rest and dream again the disciple of contact will show in the fibre of the writing."

And so he had arrived at Rousseau without reading him. In April of 1907 he was making speeches once a week in the West Side Neighborhood House, at the College Settlement, the Jacob Riis Settlement, the Christadora Home, and the Union Settlement. His audiences consisted of policemen, jewelers, pearl button burners, politicians, and union labor men. He was talking to them of Praxiteles, Leonardo, Raphael, Rembrandt, Van Dyck; and, with poetry for a subject, of Tennyson and Kipling. At the Christadora House he addressed Jews for the most part from nineteen to twenty-two years of age, on their favorite topic of art. He opened at the Jacob Riis House with a talk on Kipling to about twenty people. At the College Settlement he had as many as fifty in his audience at times, whose ages ran from fifteen to twenty-five. He told them of Botticelli, Raphael, Murillo, Corot, Burne-Jones, and of the Greek temples. Despite these activities his life was soon to run thin in New York, beyond the sustaining limit. Evidently he did not realize this, especially just at this time; but it turned out to be so.

On May 17, 1908, he started on a walking trip from New York through New Jersey and Pennsylvania. At Newark he slept in the Salvation Army quarters, and was compelled to wear vile pajamas while his clothing was being fumigated. He stopped at Lafayette College at Easton, Pennsylvania; and stayed with a coal miner at Shickshinny. He tramped in the rain, to his great discomfort; and kept a western course along the Susquehanna River, and stole rides upon box-cars, and drove with drummers, and was refused a bed in the hay, but was given one on a lounge by a relenting farmer. This diary contains various prayers, and the beginnings of verses to Christ, and one fully written out, entitled "We Who Know We Have Sinned." Finally, on June 8, he entered his "Conclusions." They were in these words: "As long as I continue to do my best to write I am producing my reasonable share of this world's goods, I should give every one as free access to my work as possible. In return I can ask of society bread, shelter and clothes. I should take pains to ask of those who can part with them easily. Be it here highly resolved that I am my own master henceforth. If my father refuses to be reasonable I will not come back, I will not write henceforth or forevermore."

Yet at this moment he was drifting back to Springfield, and didn't know it. He was soon now to enter a realm where the fiery imagination of youth and the mounting energies of great vitality would beat themselves against a civilization of small merchants, and the parasitism of lawyers, and the hypocrisy of politicians and courts and legislatures, and the imitative aristocracy of country clubs, and the counsels of banks affecting their metropolitan dependency in the money affairs of the town. Sinclair Lewis, perhaps in chief, has made clear why youth revolted against the American village at this time and before, and since. Lindsay himself revolted against it bitterly; and when he wrote of censers swinging over Springfield, he had in the back of his mind the feeling that the town in spots needed fumigators as well. It was no easy matter to return to Springfield, one may be sure. He was not to come back as an artist, as one who after these years in New York was returning with distinction. After nearly a decade of absence devoted to art studies in the intellectual capital of America he would return with no ambition achieved, with nothing but some verses, and the material for many verses, of which few could know at this time, and concerning which fewer would care in this "city of my discontent." Thanks to poetry and the passion for wandering, he was not to be overcome by boredom, nor to be wasted by the suffocations of Philistine environment. He would not be seized upon by dissipations, such as destroy so many American youths in these places where they cannot express themselves or find themselves, or become honorable workers at something. In New York as the result of his ardent nature, his high ideals, he had got into no fads of life, no strange cults, no empty radicalisms, no social extravagances. He went there a Jeffersonian; he left there a more thorough Jeffersonian. Robert Henri, at the very first, liked his verses better than his drawings; and after these years of study he had no skill at composition, no eye for realistic effects, nor indeed for verisimilitude, no deftness as a draughtsman, no æsthetic beyond delicacy of line, and for scrolls, for a sort of Spencerian penmanship applied to the depiction of flowers, crickets, bees, censers, and the like. And as he returned to Springfield so he remained to the end of his days in respect to drawing. As to poems he worked at himself, as Shelley did, till his being took fire and burned away the absurdities that encumber all but his best poems. For neither the plastic arts nor poetry thrive in a mind which sees everything from a strange angle, whose deductions are upon the basis of unrelated premises, whose categories are mixed and illogical. Art and poetry must have logic. Lack of logic was the vice which defeated his art ambitions, and weakened his verse. It was when the sincerity of his feeling, his passion, burned all non-essentials away, and left nothing but the pure jewel of his imagination as the residue, even though amid the ashes, that he succeeded with verse.

The cast of Lindsay's mind as here summed is clearly shown by the ample selections which have been made from his diaries. His manner of thinking and imagining have thus been explicitly revealed; and by considering them we are better prepared to study his poetry at a later part of this book. That he would not ask his father for help again, that the world owed him food and lodging for poems, or because he was writing poems may have some comment. When he tramped the country trading rhymes for bread, he found the rich, the exploiters hidden away, after having built churches which had no bread, and established libraries of indices of expurgations, or selections made with reference to the existing standards of finance, patriotism, morality, and other things. All such powerful persons were absent from the roadside; they were in the fastnesses of the hills, and by the sea, walled away from intrusion. There was left to Lindsay, therefore, the Y. M. C. A. and the Salvation Army quarters, and these financed, for that matter, according to a definite standard of charity. For the rest there was no one but the log cabin by the road, or the frame house near the meadows; and upon these the burden had to fall of feeding the poet for verses, or for verses to be written. At last the woman putting out the washing, the coal miner at Shickshinny, the old woman to whom the Bible was enough, the woman running the plough while her husband was finishing his term in prison—these were the human beings upon whom fell the responsibility of giving Lindsay bread and a bed. These were the "they," the society who should not let him starve; for in every case of need the burden falls not upon a group, a body politic, a "they," but upon some individual who chances to be near when the man in need passes. If a poet cannot sell his verse in the literary markets, if he cannot paint pictures and sell them, if he cannot earn a livelihood in some occupation or kind of work, if he must tramp, these are the "they" upon whom his support falls. It cannot be called a sane and workable solution of a poet's livelihood; it is at best a makeshift, such as it turned out to be with Lindsay. For at last he found a way to live, even if it was by lecturing, which he had often written in his diaries he would never do.

But as he reached the threshold of his activity in life it seems clear enough that he had not achieved that clarity of mood, that stablization of his mind out of which instruction to his fellows could flow. He had not found peace in his Campbellite faith, and the wisdom of the East, and the influence of Swedenborg had not reduced his spirit to tranquillity. He was full of fears, and even of doubts, against which his flaming hope dashed itself with evident impotence. Somehow he lacked the happiness that a certain sort of pantheism brings to some souls; somehow nature did not mean enough to him, and the figure of Immanuel meant queer and startling things. In his reading of Emerson he did not take to heart, even if he came across those words in the Address to Divinity Students, in which Emerson counselled his hearers to live after the infinite Law that was in them, and to keep company with the infinite Beauty which heaven and earth reflected to them in all lovely forms. He was subordinating himself and praying for greater success in subordinating himself to Christ's nature, and making an idol of some composite Immanuel—which after all did not satisfy his longings. He was still left in vacillation, in fear, and in distress of soul. "Once leave your own knowledge of God, your own sentiment, and take secondary knowledge, as Saint

Paul's, or George Fox's, or Swedenborg's, and you get wide from God with every year this secondary form lasts."

Emerson might have put in the name of Jesus, too, as he does by implication elsewhere in this address. Stated less theologically, Lindsay needed to stand on his own feet, and to face life with a courage as original as he faced the art of poetry.

It was therefore an inevitable consequence that his message to his fellows for a time now related to the trivial question of prohibition.

CHAPTER XI

WITH Lindsay the Lehr-jahre and the Wander-jahre were always combined, and not ever in succession. He was a traveller and adventurer about America seeking the soul of the U. S. A. He did not tramp about so much for self-improvement, as in youthful wonder. He was expressing flight and escape, sometimes from fatigue, sometimes from intolerable dissatisfaction with New York or Springfield. His distribution of poems was in lieu of sowing apple orchards, and was perhaps in imitation of Johnny Appleseed. He was always either consciously, or half unconsciously, carrying out some dramatic impersonation of this sort. But not as Plato did he ever meet a Dio or a Dionysus at the court of Syracuse. Plato hunted for the philosophic king, for the city of the Perfect, as Lindsay sought for materials for magical Springfield; but when we come to *The Golden Book of Springfield* we shall see that his mind was unable to find in the American scene the stones and the mortar for his new city. They were not in existence to be found; but his mind was not of a philosophical cast, and when he came at forty years of age to build his republic, his city, he would have been as well off for that work as if he had never read anything or dreamed anything beyond the fairy stories of the Grimm brothers.

The words of Diotima in *The Banquet* well describe Lindsay: "Those whose bodies alone are pregnant with this principle of immortality are attracted by women, seeking through the production of children what they imagine to be happiness and immortality and an enduring remembrance; but they whose souls are far more pregnant than their bodies conceive and produce that which is more suit-

able to the soul." It was Lindsay's soul which long before
this period of life had become pregnant, and he was sworn
to the Uranian Love. "Those who are inspired by this divinity seek the affections of those who are endowed by nature
with greater excellence both of body and mind." What
would have advanced Lindsay at this time would have been
a lover, that is some man or woman who could have drawn
him out and along the way, and by the exercise of affectionate intuition shown him how much there was and how
much there was not to his visions, the vision of Immanuel
included, and perhaps especially so; and how much there
was to formal church going, to Sunday school, and to those
other interests which had been made engrams in his nature
by maternal influence.

There are these words in *The Banquet* which well describe Lindsay: "What is suitable to the soul? Intelligence
and every other power and excellence of the mind; of which
all poets, and all other artists who are creative and inven-
tive, are the authors. The greatest and most admirable wisdom is that which regulates the government of families and
states, and which is called moderation and justice. Who-
soever, therefore, from his youth feels his soul pregnant
with the conception of these excellencies is divine; and when
due time arrives, desires to bring forth; and wandering
about he seeks the beautiful in which he may propagate
what he has conceived; for there is no generation in that
which is deformed; he embraces those bodies which are beautiful rather than those which are deformed in obedience to
the principle which is within him, which is ever seeking to
perpetuate itself. And if he meets in conjunction with loveliness of form, a beautiful, generous, and gentle soul, he
embraces both at once, and immediately undertakes to educate this object of his love, and is inspired with an over-
flowing persuasion to declare what virtue is, and what he
ought to be who would attain its possession, and what are

the duties which it exacts. For by the intercourse with, and as it were, the very touch of that which is beautiful, he brings forth and produces what he had formerly conceived; and nourishes and educates that which is thus produced together with the object of his love, whose image whether absent or present is never divided in his mind."

Where in Jesus will such profound and subtle words be found, such intimate instruction and guidance in the matters of the loftiest and finest import of the soul's welfare, and by consequence having to do with the progress, the freedom, and the beauty of the state? All of the precious wisdom of Plato, of the Greeks, indeed, has been obscured from all but the few by the grosser moralizing of Jesus, which has made for harsh regimentations, for tyrannies, for unhappiness of the mind, that real un-Epicureanism. And if Lindsay had never found a purer art through Plato than that which he achieved through Jesus, because incapable of such high development, he might have freed his spirit from many anxious obscurities of soul by looking with direct eyes upon the beauty of Hellas.

So it was that Lindsay needed a lover, an Aspasia of a sort, or a Harmodius through whom he might have been educated and drawn forth to slay the tyrannies that circumscribed his growth, and even his secretest reflections. No amateur poetess would have sufficed, no "ragged panther" would have done aught for him except to have harmed him. Even Doctor Mohawk, his father, made into a confiding friend, and assimilated at his best, and for what he was best to be used might have been of great benefit to Lindsay now. But whether Doctor Mohawk would have done this or not, he needed some one to save him from the descent which he made now from art studies to campaigning about the country for prohibitionists, those off-shoots of all introversions and evil denials. It was a falsification of the facts, a half look at the facts that made the campaign against the saloon the success it was. Arguments were brought against it which in the vehemence of fanatical debate could not be immediately answered always; for memory sometimes fails when voices grow too loud. And thus a sane dealing with the question required that the distinction should be kept in mind between the good saloon, which was to be kept, and the bad saloon which could be put down by proper administrative policy. That was the course which a wise and just state should have followed. Any other was the same as abolishing all religion because of the Holy Rollers, the Footwashers, Mohammedans with polygamy, or what not.

This is enough to be said about Lindsay's anti-saloon talks about Springfield and into counties which adjoined Sangamon. His notebooks show what he made, what his expenses were, by whom he was entertained, and other things. He was making his living at this time in this sort of work. One feels that he was somewhat ashamed of it at the time, and that later he tried to minimize its character. He was wont to reply when charged with this kind of zealotry that he had once worked in Marshall Field's store, wheeling boxes, and that he had bound sheaves in the wheat fields of Kansas. The extent of the work in Field's store has already been reported; we shall see about the wheat fields a little later. The fact remains that he never stuck to any gainful employment for the length of time which he devoted to the cause of ridding Illinois of the saloon in the name of Sir Galahad, and Jesus. But so far as Lindsay's growth is concerned, the history of his mind, there are much more important matters to consider. As hard as the New York life may have been, it was a kind of flying high above the inescapable curiosities, and face-to-face criticisms of Springfield. And like an aviator dumped from the sky into a field of bulls, Lindsay found himself back in Springfield, compelled to make his way the best he could, and to lead the life of the mind in as much peace as he could command.

There had been rebellion in Illinois on the part of the young long before Lindsay's day. When I was a youth there all of us who did not get jobs in the abstract office there to record real estate transfers, who did not become the manufacturers of cigars, or begin as clerks in the stores with the hope of one day owning the store, or take with alacrity to the practice of medicine or law, or raise chickens, or vegetables, or in short do something else which made us permanent denizens of our villages, were in rebellion. The church choked us to death, the constant ringing of prayer-meeting bells filled us first with melancholy, then with resentment; the moral intermeddlers which broke up every dance and frowned upon every amateur dramatic venture set our nerves to bristling with pugnacity. We had nothing but each other, and we were few; and except for the sustaining voices of Whitman and Emerson we should have sunk to the dregs, worn out with the struggle against the prohibitionists and the Sunday school workers. A few of us survived and fought our way out. I am giving reminiscent pictures of my own town, where one aspiring girl wrote every week for one of the town's papers a column called "Culture's Garland," where another taught school and used her money to travel and read, and where another as a city editor castigated the forces of tyranny every week, making himself bitter and doing no harm to those obtuse and stubborn souls. It is true that Springfield in 1909 was not so deep sunk in Zionism and gloom as this; but probably it was redeemed from them largely in those particulars in which Lindsay could not share. He hated athletics, and the kind of people who constituted the country clubs. Playing golf and then after the game resorting heartily to highballs and food did not appeal to him. With politicians he would have been at sea, and he despised them. None of the diversions which made New Salem a joyous village though of less than a hundred people interested Lindsay at all. He was not a hunter. If he had been he might have spent happy days around the bottoms of the Sangamon River in the duck season, or over the meadows and fields of autumn when the quail are calling. Not thirty miles away lived John Armstrong, a famous fiddler and hunter, and man of hospitality, with whom Lindsay, one feels, would have found infinite delight and surcease from what offended him in Springfield. He never played with John Armstrong. His associates were his former school-teacher, a group of Single Taxers, and the pastor of the Campbellite Church. It was his right to choose his own friends and to go his own way. At the same time it was the right of the Springfield people not to admire his way of life; and it is easy to see why they did not do so.

Any budding poet or novelist, whatever his behavior, and whoever his associates, would have doubtless incurred suspicion and even unfriendliness, however democratic and human some of his companions may have been. For those who are thinking and writing crave solitude and dread contacts that rub off their glossiness of individuality; and these ways are unsocial and may easily be interpreted as exclusive and patrician. Again the question was asked, Who is this man who has been studying art in New York and now is back here telling us how to live and what to do? Is he not the son of Mrs. Lindsay, the church and missionary worker, and lecturer on art? Is not his father Doctor Lindsay who drives by with his old horse and buffalo robe, and in all these more than forty years has not changed, or followed the lead of progress? Besides, Lindsay had a manner which sometimes amused and sometimes infuriated those who met him. He stood with his head thrown back, his eyes half squinting in elephantine fashion, the better to scrutinize whoever was addressing him; he was a little pontifical. And after he became famous his dignity was that of a bishop, except with very close friends, and except as it was moderated by a hearty laugh, which after all was sometimes too loud to be all heartiness. All the while he was a cordial heart, and a man of real simplicity and urbanity. His mannerisms were handles which unfriendly people could seize with which to belabor him. Very soon now his propaganda, his talk of socialism, his drawings of censers swinging over Springfield, his animadversions on Christianity as practised, his pleas for the city beautiful, his piety, his solitary appearances as he emerged from his home and wandered about town, became the subjects of criticism and ridicule. He told me one time that he was practically booted out of Springfield at last. When the story of this interregnum of his life is told, no one can be in wonder that he met that fate, all things considered.

On July 19, 1909, Lindsay, at Springfield, issued what he called *War Bulletin Number 1*. It consisted of four pages, nine by twelve inches, printed at one of the local union shops. No inference could be drawn from this publication except that he was making war. At the head of the first column was the title "Why a War Bulletin?" He proceeded to answer the question in this fashion: "I have spent a great part of my few years fighting a soul battle for absolute liberty, for freedom from obligation, ease of conscience, independence, from commercialism. I think I am farther from slavery than most men. But I have not complete freedom of speech. In my daily round of work I find myself taking counsel to please the stupid, the bigoted, the conservative, the impatient, the cheap. A good part of the time I can please these people, having a great deal in common with all of them—but— The things that go into the *War Bulletin* please me only. To the Devil with you, average reader. To Gehenna with your stupidity, your bigotry, your conservatism, your cheapness, and your impatience. In each new *Bulletin* the war shall go farther and farther. War! War! War!" This was hardly the spirit with which

[201]

to tempt nickels from Springfield pockets for the support of poetry; it was not the James Whitcomb Riley way, which made the Indianian the most beloved man of his city.

Then followed a story written by Lindsay, called the "Golden-Faced People," being an account of the Chinese conquest of America. Only nine years had elapsed since William McKinley conquered the Filipinos in order to put down Islamism, and fill the islands with Methodist spires and hymns. It can scarcely be conceived that Springfield wanted heathenism to overrun Christian America. But not taking the matter seriously they thought that Lindsay was cracked. This was the content of the first *Bulletin*.

The next one by announcement in this was to contain "an attack on Conventional Christianity as it is practised in the remote and nefarious village of Morristown, New Jersey, the wealthiest little burg in the United States. The paper will contain many a lesson for those who make sudden and ill-considered attempts to be good."

War Bulletin Number Two was issued on August 4, 1909, in the same format and size as the first one. "Why I Fight" headed the first column. The explanation which followed was comprised in a quotation from Sartor Resartus. "What art thou afraid of?" asked Carlyle; and he proceeded to eliminate death as a thing to fear, and ostracism, and all that the Devil could do against him. So Lindsay had plucked up his courage, always in need of being plucked up with words, "let us be brave," or the example of others; and having become heroic he had written the leader to the first *Bulletin*. The promised attack on conventional religion now appeared. It was the story of Lindsay's reception at a Mission where he had been compelled to wear vile pajamas while his clothing was being fumigated. "If you have any friends in Morristown please forward them this *Bulletin*" were the words appended to the article. He announced that the next number of the *Bulletin* would be in the form of a seventy-page book containing his verses, and entitled the *Tramp's Excuse*, which "I will give with both hands to any one who will confess that he reads poetry, who will try to read it through twice, who will write me a brief letter when he is done." However, the next number of the *Bulletin* was not of this character. Instead it was the same feuilleton, and dated August 30, 1909. In this he set forth "The Creed of a Beggar," in which he announced that he believed in God, "the creeping fire." He was convinced, he declared, that Christianity, Judaism, Buddhism, and the other religions of the earth were all made by God, though at core absolutely different from each other. Also he believed in Christ, the singing Immanuel, in the Holy Ghost "the perilous maddening flower," and in all institutions that were the result of reading the word of Christ; also that the hope for the union of Christians was his special inheritance, since he and other of his people were pupils of Alexander Campbell; also he believed in the Mass, the Eucharist, the Virgin Mary. He took for his brother the Lord Buddha, and for his friend the founder of Christian Science, and for his master Saint Francis. "I believe that beggary is the noblest occupation of man; I believe in the hospitality of my fellow human, for it has never failed me."

This was scarcely true, as the diaries have shown; but it was no great stretch of credulity to believe in hospitality. That would be like doubting the reality of a silver dollar offered one by the right kind of Christian. However, here was a creed which might have placated all the pious of Springfield; but there were words further on of serpent import. "I have never seen a miracle. I have never seen any one raised from the dead. I do not want to be raised from the dead. Heaven is no goal for me." Thus he spurned the Divine reward of Jesus who had ascended into heaven "to prepare a place for you." "Vision is better than faith, but experience is better than either. I do not believe in the infallibility of any book, teacher, or church." This was the very doctrine which the village atheist all through Illinois had been preaching for years before Lindsay was born. If Lindsay did not think that it was stamped with the marvellousness of originality, he must have been carrying out his exhibitionism by thus declaring himself. If not, what else? Under the heading "A Confession," he said, "Let me declare that I love money. In the city I have the usual human feeling that I am not getting all the cash my work deserves. I am just as deferential as you, dear reader, to people of wealth, especially if they have used their leisure to acquire culture, or sweet religious merit. I have the usual shrinking from the man whose father did not obtain for him early in life an environment of porcelain bathtub and full dinner pail. . . . In my usual speeches as a Y. M. C. A. man, an anti-saloon man, and a Disciple of Christ I am apt to say the things that don't disturb business." Lindsay was now thirty, now approaching his great year of consecration, as he was in the habit of forecasting his future in the diaries. Such language broadcast in Springfield does not sound like Emerson at thirty-four years of age, delivering his oration on the American scholar, nor like the same Emerson at thirty-five addressing the divinity class of Cambridge by which he put himself beyond the pale of orthodoxy and its pecuniary rewards. Yet Lindsay imperilled his wordly chances as much as Emerson did; not by courage and wisdom and direct speaking, but by this catchpenny trumpery through whose rag-picking stuff the head of the serpent could be seen, just under the nest of the dove.

It was not necessary for Lindsay in so many words to say that he loved money. His warfare against money was a way by which to get it. The Philistine may be æsthetically dull; but the Midas gift gives him peculiar powers for reading human hearts where self-interest and money are lodged. Hence the commands in this number of the *War Bulletin* to

enter the great offices and shut the desk lids, and cut the
telephone wires, and throw the keys to the skyscrapers in
the river, and break up the cities, could do nothing but
throw alarm into Springfield. And if Lindsay had been an
alien and had come to Springfield with such a message he
would have been deported under the then recent law against
anarchy, which was passed as a precaution against the as-
sassination of another man as great and good as William
McKinley. This is true despite the fact that Lindsay could
have been exculpated by reference to words of Christian
socialism, in which he declared that it was better to die
seeing angels than to live on iron streets playing checkers
with dollars. Also he was not advocating force; but if people will not leave business, let a few of "us start forth, carrying neither purse nor scrip." To which Springfield said,
no doubt, "Very well, start as soon as you want to." "Let us
be healing the sick imaginations, cleansing the leprous minds,
raising dead aspirations, casting out the devils of money-
lust." To which Springfield said, perhaps: "Physician heal
thyself." "Let us meditate upon the abstinences of those
monks of the Highway: Buddha, Christ, and St. Francis.
Hospitality is the most sacred thing in the world." It is
also the most perfect system under which some can write
poetry, carry on moral crusades, and stand all day under
the falls of Tallulah, and the rest of the people can plow
corn and have supper ready when the water gets cold and
the warm bed allures the mind tired from thinking about
the salvation of the world.

America, "waste not your precious youth in industry.
. . . All you who raise grain are petty imitation wheat kings.
Your little souls are full of the venom of covetousness. You
are subscribers to the business axioms that make this a land
of death. If any man has a dollar in his pocket let him
throw it away, lest it transform him into spiritual garbage."
Yes, for if he throw it away a son of Johnny Appleseed or

Coxey will come along, and find it, and give thanks to God and eat. "Oh, farmers, so jealous of your grain, give all your time to fields of cloud and air. There the harvests are plenteous and the laborers few." There one will find no laborers but knights of the road, whose labor is walking. "The man with a house painted and fields in order is in danger of hell fire. It means he has not taken all his time to worship the Christ of beauty, and his free grace, he has not gathered his children by the fireside to carve something lovely that has not the damning touch of machinery upon it, to look into some wonderful new doctrine or old tradition, to tell an antique story or sing a homely song."

What had become of Ruskin and Carlyle while Lindsay was thus vaporing? He would have done well now to have read *Before a Crucifix*, and taken a large dose of Nietzsche.

Ah, yes, he was a Catholic too, with all the rest of it. "The church of Rome belongs to me. I do not belong to her. I do not go in by Peter's Gate. I am the thief that climbs over the wall." And so with a fantastic tale of "The Boats of the Prophets," this number ended. "Having had an invisible world made visible to me, I cannot but counsel others to seek for the like." All the while Doctor Mohawk was driving about the country by day and by night dispensing pills and earning the money by which the Lindsay house was maintained. He had no time to seek for an invisible world, even as the busy Springfield people had no time for that venture. Every one of them was discharging the social responsibility of feeding himself and those dependent upon him.

War Bulletin Number Five was issued during the Thanksgiving season of 1909. It contained a defense of the Y. M. C. A. and a sketch entitled "How the Ice Man Danced," the story of an afternoon spent in a bar room in New York, when an ice man happy from drink capered about upon a sawdust floor. The argument was that the saloon did little to help the poor on feast days. The sketch was not without graphic merit.

At Christmas time 1909 Lindsay abandoned war and issued the *Sangamon County Peace Advocate*, which was advertised as "free as bread and butter in a hospitable house." It was devoted entirely to verses, and contained "Springfield Magical," otherwise, "the city of my discontent"; also "The Shield of Lucifer," "The Song of the Sturdy Snails," and apostrophes to the seasons as various sweethearts.

In this year also Lindsay issued in pamphlet form a poem entitled "The Heroes of Time," the whole written in praise of Lincoln, the centenary of whose birth was celebrated that year in Springfield with great ceremony, the occasion being one for an admirable oration by Senator Dolliver of Iowa, and one by Bryan as well conceived. Foreign celebrities came to Springfield for the day. Lindsay's poem was declared by himself to be upon the dominating personalities of history, and was sponsored as publisher by the Educational Department of the Y. M. C. A. of Springfield. This is the poem which after several revisions became "Litany of the Heroes" in his *Collected Poems*, which contained tributes to Napoleon, Darwin, Emerson, Roosevelt and Wilson, who were not celebrated in "The Heroes of Time." But in 1923 and 1925, as well as back in 1909 Lindsay was praying, "God help us to be brave," "God make us all divine," "God send the regicide," "God make us wizard kings." There is perhaps no better illustration in all of Lindsay's work of material shaped and modelled, blended and re-drawn with infinite patience which failed more conspicuously to materialize out of his imagination. All through his diaries we have seen Lindsay meditating upon the heroes, and asking for strength to be brave and wise as they were. But the total result was unjustified by the labor and thought spent to produce this panegyric, which is oratorical at best. The poem is not, and never in any form was, a success; and thus we pass it by for good.

In 1909, true to his promise already noted, Lindsay published *The Tramp's Excuse and Other Poems* in a pamphlet of seventy-five pages, with illustrations by himself. A word may be given to his preface to this production, in which he revealed that "The Battle" written in 1897 was his first poem. In 1901 while at the Art Institute in Chicago he wrote "Star of My Heart"; and he had written "The Tree of Laughing Bells" by the time he called upon Robert Henri in New York, as also, it will be remembered, he peddled this poem on his tramp from Tampa to Richmond, Kentucky, in 1906. Let us refer again to this preface. "In September 1906," he wrote, "on the boat returning from Europe, about two o'clock in the morning I was awakened by the overwhelming vision of Christ as a Shepherd, singing on a hill. The first three stanzas of the poem 'I Heard Immanuel Singing,' were half formed in my mind before I woke, and I said aloud, 'I have found my God.' I felt at the time that this experience had more right to authority over me than any previous picture in the air. It came with terrible power. It came after years of struggle between the Hebraism and Hellenism of my universe, and set that struggle forever at rest. It shows how after Christ sets up the moral order he sings a requiem for all the beauty destroyed by the Judgment Day. Then he begins to live the pure Art Life."

These words make it clear that Lindsay had no power of self-analysis, for there never was any struggle of moment in Lindsay's nature between Hebraism and Hellenism. He was bred a Campbellite, and a Campbellite he remained; for he was the type of mind which has the Campbellite diathesis. He even lacked that disposition of lovely paganism which has made the figure of Christ out of the carpenter of Nazareth. He had doubts, to be sure, about Jesus historical and other, but the Hebrew culture with its moralizing, and its millenniums, its prophets and its asceticisms, its oriental and extravagant imagery, its repetends and its hypnotic eloquence—this culture suited Lindsay's genius and appropriated it, all despite doctrinal doubts, the worship of Buddha and other heroes. Apollo, the god of fate with avenging arrows, the god of poetical creation, the leader of all the Muses, the founder of towns and civil institutions, the Sun god whence all life comes—this god was beyond the understanding of Lindsay. On the contrary he could comprehend a mendicant, a wizard, a wandering preacher, a hater of the rich, a foe of Rome, and a trampler of the cities in the name of apocalyptic wrath. He didn't choose Hebraism so much as Hebraism chose him, which first hypnotized him and then bade him follow. He was a susceptible subject.

We may note for one reason or another the poems of this *The Tramp's Excuse*, but mostly because those considered here were later put into books, and into his *Collected Poems*. "Star of My Heart" is a poem to Jesus and has great tenderness, and a certain music. "The Faces That Pass" was written in *vers libre*, and seems to have been discarded by Lindsay. "I am on my knees to woman because she is mysterious. . . . O, woman, to you I build myriad unseen altars." This was not a frequent mood for Lindsay. We conclude that there must have been "a maiden honest and fine," perhaps found on the tramp through the South, or through New Jersey, at any rate there is a poem here so entitled. The same material was worked over in "The Beggar's Valentine," also in this pamphlet of 1909, and later incorporated in the volume *General Booth*, and in his *Collected Poems*. It remains one of his tenderest and sweetest songs, having the additional touching value of being the poem in which Lindsay very truly envisioned himself as "I am the pilgrim boy, lame but hunting the shrine," words of tragic loveliness,

[209]

wrung from his heart by suffering, and blind looking at the mystery of himself and life. "Written to the Most Beautiful Woman in the World," he also saved from this sheaf, that woman being, however, "the truth beyond the moon." "The Beggar Monk" might have been written over, and then saved. It faintly imitated the metrics of Tennyson's "Merlin," and had the vows, "you may drive me to hunger, but never to shame. You may rob me of love, but my love shall be virgin. I will not buy kisses, nor wrong a sweet woman." In fact he lived this creed; and thus he was left to women already wronged, who did not consider themselves wronged, or capable of being wronged. These did not want Lindsay, because of his aloofness, and pontifical manner. He could be a boy, or even a child, with the moon or crickets, but not with women.

It is interesting to note how many of the poems in this pamphlet of 1909, entitled *The Tramp's Excuse,* were preserved by Lindsay, and made a part of his permanent contribution. From "A Prayer to All the Dead Among My Own People," he selected the second stanza, but it is the finer of the two stanzas; and the following list shows what was gleaned by Lindsay from this first publication, which deserves in any sense to be called a book. Lindsay carried forward into his *Collected Poems* the following from *The Tramp's Excuse:* "The Humble Bumble Bee," "The Moon Worms," "The Rose of Midnight," "The Censer Moon," "The Soul of a Spider," "The Soul of a Butterfly," "Ghosts in Love," "To the Young Men of Illinois," "A Prayer in the Jungles of Heaven," "What Mister Moon Said to Me," re-entitled in *The Collected Poems,* "The Beggar Speaks."

In both the Booth volume and *Collected Poems* Lindsay republished these poems: "How a Little Girl Sang," "Drunkards in the Street," "Sweet Briars of the Stairways," "The Potatoes' Dance," "Why I Voted the Socialist Ticket." Lastly, "The Queen of Bubbles," which was printed first in *The New York Critic* in 1904, and was Lindsay's first appearance in a metropolitan magazine.

To end this cataloguing Lindsay published in one of his two first volumes, and later in his *Collected Poems*, the following: "How a Little Girl Sang," "On the Road to Nowhere," "Song of the Garden Toad," "Fairy Bridal Hymn," "The Sorceress," "On the Building of Springfield," "At Mass," "The Alchemist's Petition," "My Lady's Disdain," printed in *The Congo and Other Poems* as "The Proud Mysterious Cat," "Parvenu," "Spider and Ghost of a Fly," "Crickets on a Strike," "I Heard Immanuel Singing," and "The Cup of Paint." This last poem was the one which Lindsay tried to sell or give away on Tenth Avenue, Broadway, and the East Side in New York. It was written while he was studying art in Chicago, and after a visit to Sam T. Jack's salacious variety theatre, in protest of such exhibitions. Thus, in 1909, Lindsay had found many of the strings that he was thereafter to touch with variations, or with better skill, as the case happened to be. "The Congo," "The Santa Fe Trail," "The Chinese Nightingale," and some others to be particularly considered in their place remained for later inspiration and vision.

We may consider for a moment the illustrations which Lindsay made a part of *The Tramp's Excuse*, nearly all of which, if not quite all, were carried forward into his *Collected Poems*. One is the figure of a woman in a small hat, dressed in a skirt which swirls about her. She is carrying a bouquet, and is designated as "my goddess of the road." There is a decorated page with the poem entitled "Indian Summer," lettered amid flying leaves and wreaths of smoke; there is another one depicting a strange but not horrifying man holding a glass from which the souls of rats are flying up. This is an illustration of the poem "Drink for Sale," the poem itself having a decorated page. "The Spider and the Ghost of the Fly" is also a lettered and decorated page. The spider is shown as a woman wearing an apron, which may be taken to symbolize the malefic influence of sexual love. The hands are impossibly drawn; the face might have been drawn by any schoolboy. "The Humble Bumble Bee" is also given a decorated page, with Lindsay's own lettering. The reader will remember the skill with which Lindsay drew flowers and insects in high school. Here the bee is sufficiently accurate. "The Soul of a Spider" is represented with imaginative characterization. Lindsay never excelled this drawing by way of penetrating into the secret nature of a living thing, or the idea of one. It is truly striking and has a sullen concentration in the eyes that makes one stare. The soul of the butterfly does not successfully extract the insect's secret. "The Sorceress" has a decorated page, the principal feature of which is the figure of a woman, whose hair seems to be dressed for a ball or a party. Her skirt is blowing about her, showing very unshapely ankles and legs. She is in a décolleté bodice, which leaves free a towering neck thick enough to be a part of her torso. In her hands is a Spencerian scroll, which is revolving and spinning off into daisy-like figures. Her back is turned on some one or something. In the poem she is asked, "is Aladdin's Lamp hidden anywhere?" A row of exclamation marks above her head, halo fashion, and the phlegmatic stare of her eyes would deny the verity of the answer she is supposed to make, that the lamp may be found by following the thistledown. However this may be, the picture is another demonstration of Lindsay's inability to draw the human face. His *Collected Poems* contain many attempts to do so, and the whole matter may be ended by asking the reader to look at the faces in the illustration of the poem entitled "The Village Improvement Parade." In the preface to this volume Lindsay repeatedly referred to this picture, and to the one entitled the Map of the Universe, asking that readers study them, and when they came to hear him lecture to look at them as he spoke. For example, he wanted to be judged for what he did before he began to tour the country, which was after 1913; so he solicited readers to look at The Village Improvement Parade. The reader is invited to solve this *non sequitur*, if he can. Further, he was teaching, he was going to teach on these tours the Monroe-Henderson *Anthology*—hence look at "The Village Improvement Parade"! In Springfield he had had a Swedenborgian association; so look at The Village Improvement Parade and The Map of the Universe. There was a mystic Springfield, and the Springfield hieroglyphic was akin to The Village Improvement Parade, and to The Map of the Universe. Hence, ponder these drawings! We shall come to the matter of hieroglyphics, and the Egyptian esotericism which haunted Lindsay's imagination. For the present it is pertinent to clear up The Map of the Universe, so that hereafter discussions relating to it, or in which it is in any way involved, will be as clear as the subject admits of its being.

The Map of the Universe began to take form as early as Lindsay's student days in the Chase School in New York, some years before 1909. In the first place one night Lindsay saw the prophets in a corner of his room pass by clothed in gorgeous apparel. At another time he saw them in the same garb in front of an elm tree. He first wrote a story about them, but not to be subdued by the apparition, he clothed these holy men in penitential robes. The universe did not suit him, so he built one all his own, and put it in a book called *Where Is Aladdin's Lamp?* destroyed long before this year of 1909. But The Map of the Universe, he has told us, is the stage of the lost drama of that book. "Do not despise this, my little Mystery Play, all that is left of six wonderful months of eating of the flower of the Holy Ghost." And now for the explication of the Map: The throne mountains were once the dwelling place of the Trinity, but the illustration represents these mountains as grown desolate, save for the vine of the Amaranth, or in other words, the flower of the Holy Ghost, which grows about the mountain throne, and which bears luminous, inflaming honey flowers. The ancient men eat this flower only; and around the mountains are the boats of the prophets, who are prophesying a New Universe. On the plateau below the mountains are the Jungles of Heaven. It will be well to remember the location of these jungles, and what they signify, because Lindsay later in poems repeatedly referred to the Jungles of Heaven. He often walked in them in all serious wonder and sorrow. These jungles then are that part of heaven empty of souls, it is a region of fallen palaces, rotted harps, broken crowns, and swords of rusted gold. It is a kind of purgatory. The angels are the missionaries of the Universe, who constantly go forth to the stars to be crucified, and to be forsaken of God. Their blood, when shed by miraculous transmutation, enters the wine jars carried by the prophets in their boats; and as the wine is poured forth it creates a purple mist in the paths of men, and thus becomes the Gleam, the cloud of glory, Wordsworth's light that never was on sea or land; and then changes to sound and becomes the still, small voice. Lindsay, in his explanatory comment of this map, as here condensed, declared that some day this wine would be poured down, and hell would be redeemed by its flood. "This is just, because it was by a leaping of the flame from the Harp of the great singer Lucifer that the angels fell in love with suffering, and went forth to the stars to be forsaken of God. Thus was Lucifer King of the Universe the moment before he was cursed with eternal silence and sealed in his tomb."

"Beneath the walls of heaven is the soul of the Butterfly, which is the soul of the earth redeemed, and on the edge of hell is the soul of the Giant Spider, who is Mammon. East of the Universe is the Palace of Eve, whence come the perfect brides; west of the Universe is the Star of Laughing

Bells. . . . One bell will quench all memory, all hope, all borrowed sorrow. . . . Aladdin's Lamp sleeps somewhere in the treasure pits of the Jungles of Heaven, with which the New Universe can be built, and all the cities of the wise. The Genii of the Lamp can be commanded to carry the Laughing Bells to every soul, and thus redeem them all. The angels and prophets declare that the New Universe comes by the power of the Wine of God, that is the blood of the crucified angels, which is turned to wine, as already detailed." However that may be, Lindsay declared in this exegesis that after the Millennium Immanuel would sing.

Here is a picture as wild and incoherent as any given in Revelation, the Koran, or the Mormon Bible; and it is a compound of these, together with the Arabian Nights. It is to be observed that the world is to be redeemed by the blood of the angels, and thus the sacrificial lamb of the barbarous Hebrews undergoes a poetical transubstantiation; but also Aladdin's Lamp will play its part in that redemption. Wine-blood and magic will perform the miracle; or literally stated, self-sacrifice and holy living, and dying for good causes coupled with poetry and the arts will save men from falling from the outlying parts of the universe, or the walls of heaven into the jungles of annihilation. We venture at the risk of being wrong, to indulge in this interpretation. The Map of the Universe in the hands of Blake would have been a terrifying thing, touched with many sublimities; it scarcely would have fallen into the baroque proportions which in many particulars Lindsay made of it, with the boats of the prophets scattered about the flame of Amaranth like so many flies crowding for honey, and the palace of Eve represented as rudely as an ancient cromlech. The gulf of silence looks like a couple of quoits with concentric rings in them, and The River Called Hate swirls and curves like two strokes of a Spencerian pen. The upper lefthand corner of the draw- ing is so shaded as to look like a smudge of soft coal smoke on any day in Springfield; while the soul of the butterfly is a small piece of taxidermy stuck on the great wall below the Jungles of Heaven. Altogether this is rather a map of Lindsay's mind, his theology, and theodicy, and cosmology, than of any rationalized conception of the world of mind and matter in which we live. As a venture into eschatology all rational souls will prefer the simplicity and the beauty of the Islands of the Blest, of which the blind poet of Chios sang in a way to win the hearts of artists and lovers to the end of time. If Lindsay as a man of thirty, or earlier, had drawn this map and then later abandoned it, it well might be treasured as the imagining of a poet who became distinctive and nobly lyrical. But the case is quite different. It meanders by reference and allusion through his prefaces and poems to the end. It was indeed a part of his self-made mythology and celestial machinery as long as he lived. In the pamphlet the Map is followed by a poem entitled "A Prayer in the Jungles of Heaven," which is, indeed, worthy of Blake, and for religious fervor, of Cowper. This poem was re-entitled "Heart of God," when incorporated in "General William Booth Enters Into Heaven"; and under that title it found its way into his *Collected Poems*.

Finally, the last poem in this pamphlet is, "I Heard Immanuel Singing," which was republished in *The Congo and Other Poems,* and finally in the *Collected Poems*. Of its kind, Lindsay never did anything more simply musical, more penetrated with that Bible feeling and imagery which, having entered into the mind of the whole Occident through centuries of teaching, and reading, and preaching, responds so quickly and powerfully to its authentic echoes. The judgment that the Bible is the greatest book of time comes out of a judgment made by us who cannot lift ourselves above the hereditary and educational saturation of this book. It is well to remember that a civilization and culture greater than any since its day lived and spoke and dreamed and rejoiced by Homer, through him and through the Greek tragic writers. The Map of the Universe is distinguished neither by beauty nor sublimity, by tragedy nor terror, nor by apocalyptic imagination; it is a drawing, rather literary than pictorial, in which Campbellite theological hypotheses were depicted. The poem on Immanuel proves that Lindsay, who first chose his eye as the organ of creativeness, and who was not fond of music, and who confessed that his understanding of the science of verse was very limited, still turned out to have an ear for the sweet concord of words. Later he wrote of the American heroes and the American scene as it was reflected upon the retina of his imagination; but all along, one sphere of his success was in that species of poetry in which a kind of madness was the engine of miraculous achievement. In this manner of expression his power of lyricism turned the yellow flame of his megalomania into the lavender and blue radiation of flowers of flame.

We may finish with the year 1909 by referring to a fragmentary diary of that year, dated November 21. "I am a preacher," he began, "and I ought to preach till I drop. Vanity and ambition and self-service are the sources of all my misery. Let me abate these if I can." This diary contains his expense accounts while travelling about the Springfield neighborhood, probably making speeches against the saloon. He had been to Boston in August of this year under the Parker Bureau. We find here that he planned poems on the "Millennium," "The Revel in Heaven," "A Prayer to the Dead," "I Want to Go Wandering." He also outlined a lecture on "The Peddler of Dreams," with sub-titles like "The Pack of Curious," "The Day When Magicians Were Kings, Not Peddlers," "Verses on Rameses, Rembrandt, Coleridge, Blake, Beardsley, and Poe." A first draft of his poem "The Wizard of the Street" is contained in this diary; also the sketch of an amatory tribute, beginning with the words, "I send you a passionate rose, speaking of desperate hunger." Here, also, are notes for a study of Utopias. He planned to read Plato's *Republic*, Saint Augustine's *City of God*, Campanelli's *City of the Sun*, Bellamy's *Looking Backward*, Morris's *News From Nowhere*, Howells's *Letters From Altruia*, Wells's *New Worlds for Old*; and he might write a book "Adventures in Utopia, by N. V. Lindsay." At this time he was reading many plays. He was still praying for the city of the Perfect. "God send me a city better than Paris, yet of this earth, where I may swim in a sea of beauty." Evidently Springfield was not that place. He had made a plate about this time with the lettering for "Crickets on a Strike," with a decorative border of crickets. From this plate he had printed leaflets "issued to the citizens of Springfield gratis," as he said later, and "received with profound suspicion about the same days as the War Bulletins." "What war was going on then? The one between me and my fellow Babbitts." This was his private notation under this decorated poem, which he included in a reprinting of *The Village Magazine* in 1925. Lindsay was now approaching a national fame, and at this time he was incurring a Springfield hostility that he had clearly provoked. However, it is difficult to see anything irritating in the "Cricket's Strike," except that staid, practical people, priding themselves on their common sense, might be annoyed by something which they considered foolish and worthless.

The first issue of *The Village Magazine* came out in 1910, and contained many of the poems which he had already published in *The Tramp's Excuse*. But it also was embellished with such drawings as Contents of an Ink Bottle, and The Village Improvement Parade, which, for figures and their postures and action, and for delineation of the human face are more atrocious than words can express. Seven hundred copies of this *Village Magazine* were printed and then placed by Lindsay on the parlor tables of the rural workers of the Anti-Saloon League of Illinois, when he was making speeches at the crossroad churches. *The Village Magazine* was a very dreary failure. It did not, like Hubbard's *Philistine,* have literary material skillfully served; it had no intelligible appeal to the local reader. But in New York Edward J. Wheeler, then the editor of *Current Literature,* spoke some words of encouragement for this strange effort, which came to Lindsay to refresh him in one of the "dullest hours of my life." Because of the fact that Lindsay's drawings for the poem "The Soul of the City Receives the Gift of the Holy Spirit" were reproduced in the reprint of *The Village Magazine* in 1925 they are referred to briefly here, though made in 1913. That gift was made visible to the eye by censers swinging over Lincoln's home, and over his monument; over the Church of the Immaculate Conception, over the Presbyterian Church and the Church of the Disciples, over the Old Courthouse and the State Capitol, over the Old High School Building, and the Horticultural Building at the State Fair Grounds, which may be taken to mean a generous and impartial blessing all around. The drawings might have been made from the hanging lamps of mosques in Cairo. Again he presented The Map of the Universe, and announced that it was used for the frontispiece of his *Collected Poems,* issued in 1925; and that it was the basis of *The Golden Book of Springfield,* to which we shall come in its place. This reprint of *The Village Magazine,* which was made in 1925, contains all this matter, brought over from previous years; and being considered here, need not again be specially reviewed.

Lindsay's diary for 1911 was devoted to his itineraries making speeches, to his expense accounts here and there to the nearby towns, to the collections which he received. There are a few scrawls of germinating poems; otherwise the record has no interest. And so we come to the year 1912, and the walk West through Kansas. The magical year was arriving, the year when he would be thirty-three years of age,

[219]

and out of which would come the poem "General William Booth Enters Into Heaven," which made him famous. It is a poem not so good as some he had written before; but it is more unique, more arresting.

CHAPTER XII

FROM a notebook kept by Lindsay in 1912 we find that he had the following plan for writing poems: "Write poems to conform to popular tunes in the outline of their melody, like 'A hot time,' 'After the Ball,' etc., but with a silk finish. When we consider that one-half the popular songs rhyme moon and spoon we need not fear wearing out the theme of the moon as an adjunct of desire. There ought to be poems on astrology, palmistry, the almanac, the zodiac and spheres." "Nellie Was a Lady," and "Massa's in de Cold, Cold Ground," would be good models, he thought, for such poems. This book contains many suggestions for moon poems, and some to the sun. On one page there is this significant stanza:

"I thank my God to-day
That He has slain desire;
That no path that I tread
Is forked with torturing fire.
The road has cooled my blood,
The road he led me in."

Occasionally now he was contributing poems to *The State Register* of Springfield, whose venerable editor, H. W. Clendenin, was one of the faithful Jeffersonians of Illinois, and a man whose sympathies were broad enough to cover with charity any vagary that Lindsay ever entertained. He could see through the fumes of Lindsay's dampened ignition the bright flame of an ardent and virtuous heart.

The Panama Canal at this time was nearing completion.

Lindsay noted: "The completion of the Panama Canal, the meeting of the waters of Asia and the West, and allied events, mean the making of new songs and arts the world over," a very Whitman utterance. As with Whitman, Lindsay was full of proclamations and programs; and perhaps such things pave the way for better days. If not, then they fill us with daydreams which mitigate the dreariness of life's disappointments and give us inspirations which lead at times to occasional amelioriations. This notation was the germination of Lindsay's poem "The Wedding of the Lotus and the Rose," which Franklin K. Lane, Secretary of the Interior in President Wilson's cabinet, distributed to both houses of Congress on the opening day of the Panama Exposition. It is a good enough poem for an occasion, but does not rise to the vision which Lindsay had when he made the note just referred to. The illustrations to the poem are in Lindsay's very worst manner. The completion of the canal deserved a celebration like the opera "Aïda," or like the "Persians" of Æschylus, if indeed it was a joining of the East and West in any such mystic sense as Lindsay imagined it to be. Lindsay may have been familiar with the address of that Vivekananda to the Congress of Religions at the Columbian Exposition, which electrified the audience. He was supposed to have brought about his own death in 1903 on the Fourth of July to symbolize the union of the Occident and the Orient.

In the spring of 1912 Lindsay had evidently modified his bellicose attitude, which was so strident in the War Bulletins, for he issued an eleven-paged magazine, eight inches by eleven, printed on a kind of rag paper, in bold type, with woodcut initial letters for the beginning of the articles. He called this publication *Vision, A Quarterly Journal of Æsthetic Appreciation of Life*. The first article was entitled, "The New Localism, An Illustrated Essay for the Village Statesman." The sub-head was "We Are Face to

Face with Centralization." But he was not afraid, for the impending centralization could be opposed with New Localism. Lindsay's political thinking remained puerile to the end of his days, so that his *Litany of Washington Street*, a prose work published in 1929, excites wonder that it could have found a publisher. The point need not be argued, it is only necessary to say that in 1912 centralization was not a thing about to come to pass, just then being faced. It had made itself guns and bayonets out of the shackles stricken from the slaves; and in 1912, with commerce and the railroads controlled at Washington by bureaus, with the tariff in the hands of its beneficiaries, with an imperial army occupying far dependencies, with the States struck down in their sovereign powers, with banks and money-owning presses which could make contemptible any one who tried to recall or revive the old liberties, centralization was an accomplished fact. Republican orators were declaring that Hamilton's hour had come at last. However, what was Lindsay going to do about centralization?

He had been to a picnic at Liberty, Adams County, held by the members of three churches. Lindsay had attended this and had been reminded by what he saw that the mail-order house and the metropolitan newspaper were in evidence, first by the eatables served, and next by the fact that those newspapers had been used to wrap sandwiches and the like. So while these picnickers were subservient to powers afar, yet they were together in communal recreations which made for the New Localism; and the New Localism was a matter of outlook. Outlook! The saloon and industrialism went hand-in-hand; but the outgoing saloon meant that agriculture reigned. Hence, get rid of the saloon. "In brief the New States' Rights is social, not political, an opportunity, not a legal system. It is based on a Renaissance of so many commission cities, dry villages, and school-centered country communities. This view of the state is the basis, not the consummation of the New Localism." Also, "The devout dry town will establish the noble equivalent of the Oberammergau Passion Play, not necessarily a Bible drama, but a lofty and soul cleansing morality." Also, "Every little place will soon have its special calendar of out door festivals. The country High School, here and there, will produce not only its rhymer, but its poet, its orchestra of real composers, its own succession of sages, painters, Sibyls, its corn-field song, its festival insignia." Also, "not only will there be changes like these, but in all its passions and pursuits of the higher man, from novel writing to schools of philosophy, the best of our towns will bear the fruit called genius." Also, "many a stopping place will have its endowed ceramics and carvings, its special spice for the imagination, its peculiar proverb, its own type of men." Also, "The New Localism will bring among its principal benefits what might be described as the Democratic Fine Arts, will bring an exquisite sensibility and powerful beauty making faculty among common men." As to the Constitution of American art, "It will of course be unwritten. In many ways it will assume a parallel between itself and the political constitution. It will declare that bad taste is mob law, and good public taste is democracy. . . . Æsthetically speaking we are a mob on the prairie, and a despotism in cultured circles. The creative power represented by the Art Institute, Chicago, or the International Studio, or the Cathedral of St. John, Morningside Heights, or the Metropolitan Museum, fertilizing and helpful within a certain pale, but is European. The taste of the most radical, America-worshipping painters in New York is European." The principle of Swedenborgian correspondence underlay many of Lindsay's prophecies and arguments; and so "The Lincoln rail and the McKinley front porch were Constitutional necessities. The constitution of American art will develop similar phenomenon among our faithful citizens." Finally, "Art student with the divine call

Vachel Lindsay in 1912.

—Go to Rome, Munich, Mecca, Benares, Nikko or Kamakura, if you must, for Beauty's sake; but bring back all
your inspiration to help us here."

The logic of some of this program may be impugned; but
none can deny that these words came from a heart that
loved his country, and his fellow men, and would fain have
done something to brighten the Philistine dullness of rural
America, from which he had suffered in his hoped-for
Springfield. But after all Bacon's *New Atlantis* must have
seemed wildly visionary to the hard-headed thinkers of his
time. On the other hand, Lindsay's various bulletins advocating social changes and protesting against conditions may
well suggest to ardent radicals to come that few men of
thirty know what to do about the complex difficulties of
government and the despotic machinations of money. In
later life such idealists nearly always discard much of what
they have thus prematurely advanced for the good of mankind. They come, indeed, very much to the position that
their seniors occupied when such bulletins were scattered in
a tough and sagacious world; and so arriving there can
smile at their vanished dreams, and the wounds received in
their rejection as well.

Accompanying this discussion of the New Localism and
the future of suburban America were illustrations of the
poem "The Village Improvement Parade," of which enough
has been said. *The Vision* also contained the poem, "The
Hearth Eternal," which has already been considered, when
speaking of Lindsay's mother. The last article in *The Vision*
is entitled "On the Soap Box." In this Lindsay said, "Every
artist in America is necessarily in sympathy with the radicals, yet there is hardly a reformer but despises the artist."
Lindsay had found this out to his sorrow, as Whitman did.
It is observable that Lindsay was shooting forth climbers
out of a Whitman root in many of these calls to his country-
men. "Democratic Vistas" seems to be the original stalk of

much of these preachments in *The Vision*, but finer in structure, and in some particulars more in detail than a good deal of Whitman. It must be remarked that Lindsay's poems conceal the Whitman derivation, if any there be at all. Perhaps the most that can be said for a kinship between Whitman's and Lindsay's poetry is that the later singer was sustained in courage by the older in a championship of democracy, originality, and Americanism. After being so sustained and emboldened he chose his own themes and his own manner, both of which were as unique as Whitman's.

There was not much in *The Vision* to placate the hostility of Springfield against Lindsay, or to arouse its indifference to his activities. We do not wish to stress too much the unhappiness of these years from 1909 to 1912. It is generally said that Lindsay had a hard time of it in this period. In consequence he took to the road again; and he could not have done a wiser thing. On Wednesday, the 29th of May, 1912, he walked out of Springfield, having California as his destination.

He resolved as a rule for the tramp, "I am looking for the honey in labor, not the thorns. I shall work just long enough each time to get the spiritual honey, not the bitterness. I want to dive as deep in labor as I can without striking sorrow." For this trip he made an oilcloth case to protect the book he carried in it from rain. The book, about eight inches by eleven, was bound in substantial black boards. He carried this book to entertain the farmers on the way, and its contents show the intellectual and æsthetic standards at which Lindsay had arrived at this time. On the inside of the front cover was pasted one of the sheets on which was printed the "Gospel of Beauty," with its prologue: "I come to you penniless and afoot to bring a message. I am starting a new religious idea." This idea had no conflicts with any church creed. He was founding the church of beauty. "The church of beauty has two sides:

The love of beauty and the love of God." He was also bringing the gospel of the New Localism, for the making of democratic neighborhoods. There the children should become
devout gardeners, or architects, or teachers of dancing in
the Greek spirit, or novelists, or poets, or wood-carvers, or
dramatists, or actors, or singers. "They should believe in
every possible application to art theory of the thoughts of
the Declaration of Independence, and Lincoln's Gettysburg
address." They should wander over America, and then return to their own neighborhoods with hearts filled with the
righteousness of God." "Their reason for living should be
that joy in beauty which no wounds can take away, and that
joy in the love of God which no crucifixion can end." On the
page opposite the "Gospel of Beauty" so pasted was a reproduction of Rudolf Marschall's picture of Jesus leading a
flock of sheep. The next page contained pictures of rooms in
Ruskin's house at Brantwood. Then followed pages on
which printed slips of his poems already published were
pasted. Then a picture of Ruskin's bust, made in his seventies. Then four pages from some magazine in which he had
published some of his adventures while walking from Tampa
to Richmond, Kentucky. Then a large reproduction of
Ruskin's watercolor of the Castello Vecchio. Then a copy
of *The Village Magazine* of 1910, containing the inevitable
"Village Improvement Parade," also such poems as, "On
Reading Omar Kháyyám," "The Cornfields," "The Empty
Boats," illustrated; "The Candle Moon," "The Moon
Worms," "The Rose of Midnight," "The Censer Moon,"
"What Mister Moon Said to Me," "The Shield of Lucifer,"
"Genesis," "The Wizard in the Street," "The Storm
Flower," "Contents of an Ink Bottle," "The Potatoes'
Dance," "Crickets on a Strike," "The Wizard Wind," "The
Illinois Village," "On the Building of Springfield," "What
the Great City Said," "The Airship of the Mind," "The
Milkweed," "The Sunflower and the Robin," "Concerning

the Acorns on the Cover and Through the Book." This issue of *The Village Magazine* had a drawing of the Taj Mahal done by Lindsay in 1906.

The black-board folder also contained a copy of *The Peace Advocate* dated Christmas, 1909, already considered; a picture of the colossal statue to Black Hawk set up on the Rock River near Oregon, Illinois; also the cover of another issue of *The Village Magazine*, with sheets inserted on which were pasted a picture of a bust of Poe, an article clipped from some magazine, entitled "Rules of the Road," in which Lindsay as the author set forth his principles of tramping: Keep away from cities; ask for dinner about a quarter after eleven; travel alone; be neat, deliberate, chaste and civil; preach the gospel of beauty, etc. One of the pages had pasted upon it a sheet with etched heads of Whistler, large and small. Then followed pages pasted with reproductions of Whistler's Nocturne and La Vielle Aux Loques.

Then followed the covers of *Vision* in which were inserted, pasted on sheets, pictures of an Egyptian temple, the Parthenon, the Pantheon at Rome, the Mosque of Saint Sophia, the Taj Mahal, the leaning tower of Pisa, Notre Dame, Paris; Saint Peter's at Rome, Trinity Church, New York; Lincoln's home in Springfield, Lincoln's law office in the same place, the Springfield Courthouse. Then followed in the folder a copy of *The Vision* pasted over with the following: a picture of Assisi, of Saint Francis by De Monvel, an avenue of trees at Yásnaya Polyana, the entrance to the park of Yásnaya Polyana, the mansion house, Tolstoy as he was in 1857, as he was in 1862 and 1876 and 1887, and as he was when Bryan visited him in 1906, when they were photographed together. Finally, a picture of Tolstoy in his workroom from the painting by Ryepin, and on the inside of the back cover, a picture of one of the idols of Buddha. All through these pages so pasted with pictures were various poems which had been printed in leaflets and clipped out to make this scrapbook for the journey to California. Obviously, space has been taken here to give the reader a full idea of what Lindsay was carrying with him, because it shows the heart and mind which had matured in him to this time, and the spirit with which he undertook this long tramp. But this was not all. He had had printed for distribution along the way a pamphlet of sixteen pages, six inches by nine, entitled *Rhymes to Be Traded for Bread,* which contained forty-four poems in all. A list of the principal ones may be given to show what Lindsay had done up to this time. They are the following: "The Wizard Wind," "The King of Yellow Butterflies," "Love and Law," "An Apology for the Bottle Volcanic," "Queen Mab in the Village," "The Dandelion," "The Hearth Eternal," "The Soul of a Butterfly," "Here's to the Spirit of Fire," "Look You, I'll Go Pray," "Heart of God," printed in *The Tramp's Excuse,* as we have seen, under the title "A Prayer in the Jungles of Heaven"; "The Perfect Marriage," "The Leaden Eyed," "The Eagle That Is Forgotten," "The Trap," "A Prayer to All the Dead Among My Own People," and "On the Road to Nowhere." The whole list need not be given; but many of the poems of *The Tramp's Excuse* were put in this later leaflet, and an inspection of Lindsay's *Collected Poems* will inform the reader how many were carried forward to that final volume. Thus with this sheaf of poems, and the leaflet called *The Gospel of Beauty,* and the large black-bound folder of miscellaneous material Lindsay set forth. By this time he had had considerable experience in dealing with people approached for hospitality, and how to entertain adults and children, and how to awaken interest in his poems and his message.

The first entry in the diary of this tramp placed Lindsay twenty miles from Jacksonville and twelve miles from Springfield. What hour of this day of May 29 it was cannot be told. Jacksonville is almost due west from Springfield,

and its county and that of Scott are in a tier of counties of
the same latitude. A family of some distinction entertained
him formally in Scott County. On Thursday night he was
at Valley City, on the Illinois River, something around thirty
miles from Springfield. Here in a general store, which was
also the postoffice, he wrote a letter to "My Dear Penelope,"
in which he tells her that yesterday in Jacksonville he left a
copy of "The Village Improvement Parade" with the newspapers there, and was given the promise that they would
read it. He wrote her that at Exeter in Scott County a
tenant farmer gave him a "grand meal," and provided him
with a place to sleep. "Emerson's Law of Compensation
works on the road," was his journal comment. In the little
town of New London he heard wonderful singing in a Catholic church. He was headed now for Hannibal, Missouri,
across Pike County, Illinois, and found the country rolling
and grove-filled. June the 3d at noon he had fare with a
farmer who knew Kipling and admired him. That night he
slept in a hotel at Sadonia having had bad luck all day
begging old women to be allowed to sleep in their barns,
and being refused. In the hotel he had told the landlord that
he was walking across the country and was dead broke, but
wanted a bed. The landlord cheerfully complied with the
request. The next morning he had two glasses of buttermilk for breakfast and set forth. This day he found what he
called a "wild rose bird," with "twenty different systems of
sound." It turned out to be the Rachel Jane, which he celebrated with such success in "The Santa Fé Trail." At the
village of East Lake he was entertained by a sage, and slept
on sacks amid the chickens and the ducks. The sage was a
stationary engineer, a shrewd old man, who told Lindsay
that he was born in the spring, and that his birthmark was
between his hip and his knee; hence Lindsay's legs not feet
got tired. In Mexico, Missouri, about sixty miles west of
the Mississippi River, Lindsay witnessed a Catholic wedding,

which interested him greatly, while the admonition of the
priest to the couple won his approval. That evening he applied for hospitality at a big stock farm, and was refused.
He repaired to a Negro cabin, where he was received, and
ate supper with the Negro and his wife. They were greatly
interested in his Lincoln material contained in the black-
bound book. A great evening ensued, as Lindsay characterized it. The Negro told Lindsay that the "wild rose bird"
which he had heard was called the Rachel Jane; and Lindsay decided to write a poem about it. Leaving this friendly
roof he walked hard for Jefferson City. A mile north of the
Missouri River he left the bluffs and descended into a beautiful valley. Having no money to pay his toll across the bridge
he left his packet for security; and in town got letters and
stamps with which to return and settle his toll. He sold
twenty-five cents worth of stamps and used the money with
which to get lodging at a hotel—but without supper. The
next day for breakfast he had doughnuts which he got by
giving two copies of *The Rhymes to Be Traded for Bread.*
On Friday, June 7, he ate with a farmhand who lived in a
log house. That night he asked for lodging at a crossroads
store without avail. Later, calling at the house of the priest
of this locality, he was informed that the priest was not at
home. Lindsay waited, and later the priest came, but approached the house the back way. When he entered he told
Lindsay that he had company, and gave him a quarter. He
got the night clerk's bed at the hotel. He reached California,
Missouri, about thirty miles west of Jefferson City, where
he received an excellent meal, but had no supper; and for
breakfast the next day only one dry cooky, for which he paid
with *The Rhymes.* At Clarksburg, ten miles or so from
California, he was tenderly cared for, as he phrased it, by the
"most pitiful of women," whom Lindsay dared not offer any
compensation. "I was just a dumb, humble, fumbling tramp
in her presence." At this place there was a Baptist revival,

and a local infidel making himself heard. Going forward Lindsay noted the sunflowers, and made pictures of them in his diary; he named the verbenas, sheep's tea, Indian Paint, wild mustard, morning-glories, larkspur, buttonweed, and brown-eyed Susans on the way to Springfield, Missouri, where they grew profusely in the hedges. Lindsay had a very delicate eye for certain phases of nature, though he never became a nature poet. Those who have travelled through Missouri in June, along the Missouri River, where orchards abound, or around Springfield, where the upland strikes the Ozarks, will appreciate what Lindsay felt at this season of the year, in youth and strength, as he walked and meditated poems.

On Sunday evening, June 9, he reached Otterville, sixteen miles east of Sedalia, where he obtained permission to rest in the livery stable. He was very tired, and slept profoundly, though bedded only on horse blankets. The next morning he got a piece of bread without butter for a copy of *The Rhymes.* He reached Sedalia at noon the next day, and called on a newspaper editor, but was frostily received. He then went to a restaurant, behind which was a saloon where he read "The Trap," and the Altgeld poem to a politician, a doctor, and the saloonkeeper, and found them all hearty companions. He then went on, and after a while stopped in the woods to write up his diary. Seven miles west of Sedalia he had a good evening reading his verses to a hospitable family, where there were interesting young girls. "And now I have learned to stick to the proposition of being a rhymer, and make a better single impression than I did on the ——," mentioning a family met with on the trip through the South in 1906.

In Warrensburg he again slept in a livery stable. On the morning of the 12th he got a ride of a few miles with some "exceedingly frosty" men. The diary reveals that the idea of *The Sangamon County Book* came into his mind, "colored and decorated to the limit," to be given away to the farmers there. He planned to write Penelope about it. On the 13th he made twenty-five miles, mostly by hopping rides. His scrapbook, already designated as the black-bound book, made a very unfavorable impression upon a family to whom he showed it. By this time he had not had a bath since he left Jefferson City, and no clean change of underwear since he walked out of Springfield, Illinois. One mile east of the Kansas line he remarked strange flowers, and sketched them; and then turning into a yard was well received by elderly people who gave him buttered pancakes, for which he hoed corn all morning. On the 15th he was speeding toward Emporia, and eating wild strawberries by the way. At Spring Hill, Kansas, he disposed of his *Rhymes* to a good-natured woman; but nevertheless, hoed weeds in the orchard for an hour to pay for his dinner. Sunday noon, June 16, he was attacked by a vicious dog as he entered a yard, and bitten in the heel, though not through the leather of his shoe. The woman of the house gave him a grudging slice of bread. The dog shook up his nerves badly. He rode into Pomona, Kansas, on a handcar, and also into Wellsville, where he noticed the Mexican houses, and began to see Mexicans by the railroad. The rain descended upon him now, and he ran to a shack nearby where he found some Mexicans huddled about a stove. One of them offered Lindsay cigarette tobacco. "Sorry to decline," says the diary. He got dried out here and indulged in picturesque talk with the Mexicans. They gave him out of their dinner buckets, one of the men surrendered his dessert to Lindsay. Then Lindsay started on, walking in the rain till seven that night, after which he went without supper, and slept in a damp blanket. This was at Neosho Rapids. He had cheese and crackers the next morning for breakfast, and walking on reached Emporia without further rain. There he called at the office of *The Gazette*. "Frosty reception at *Gazette*. Interviewed, not received." Here, however, some friends of his mother, from the days of her European travel, received Lindsay very kindly, giving him dinner, supper, and breakfast. He took a bath here, and washed his clothing, wrote to Penelope and rested. He decided now that he would join his father and mother, and Penelope in their camp in Colorado; but first he would work for some farmers for a month.

He got a ride to Saffordsville, a few miles from Emporia, and there that night slept on the floor of a livery stable, but with clean horse blankets under him. Ten miles from Emporia he saw with delight The New Santa Fé Trail. The diary here notes the features of the landscape, the absence of hedges, the houses standing distantly apart, with trees crowded about them. He noted here: "Thoreau and Ruskin I dreamed of last night. My visit to Prof —— [referring to his hosts in Emporia] just begins to stir the literary bug again. And then I want to get Thoreau for other than literary reasons. And then I have foolish thoughts of truck-gardening in Trinidad on papa's patch of land there. And then I am anxious to get to the Colorado camp."

On June 20 he split kindling for his breakfast. That afternoon in Strong City he tried to get work on an alfalfa farm and failed, and went on to Cottonwood. Here he traded *The Rhymes* for an enormous breakfast at the hotel. He then took to the Santa Fé Trail. We quote here from the diary: "There should be a poem on the future called, Written in a Kansas Graveyard. I have just passed one. The endless suggestion of memorial futurity, when this yard shall be fit to be the subject of Gray's Elegy, an ode on the death of Wellington, as it were, though now but a grim raw exhibit of certain private griefs. The feeling of the inevitable dignity of the years to come, and the towering of these little evergreens and these cypress trees that shall one day be cypress indeed. The New Santa Fé Trail going by, now nothing but a well dragged mud road, auto trail, then to assume the dignity and the granite setting of a Roman highway. To the East the little scattering county seat, with courthouse and ambitious college on the hill, some day wisdom and statesmanship gray shall be there."

At Elmdale he found a charming hotel, and a perfect audience for his poems, perfect attention on the part of some youths, and hearty approval. Lindsay recited "The Proud Farmer," and "The Building of Springfield." At Clements, fifty miles west of Emporia, he was reciting "The Proud Farmer" at the hotel there, when a guest at the table left in disgust. "Performance a flat failure." That night Lindsay slept in a livery stable again. The next day he dug in a garden and cut weeds all afternon for three meals, which he ate ravenously, and was still hungry. He then caught a ride of twenty-five miles. On the 25th he stayed with a Mennonite family, and was engaged as a harvest hand. He worked here several days shocking wheat. He was almost sunstruck during this work, and had to have water poured over his head. He was working for $1.75 a day. The table was rather Germanic, he observed, but everything else delightful. There were family prayers, and much singing. On Sunday he walked to church with these people. Lindsay was going to stay through the threshing time, but the old Mennonite decided he would not need Lindsay for that. Lindsay was accordingly paid off, receiving $7.87. He did not recite anything in this household. "I felt I was a man of sin, the subject of silent prayer, and deep solicitude." After breakfast, therefore, Lindsay walked on to Newton, where he bought stamps, a felt hat costing $3, some guaranteed corduroys at $2.75. Then he went to the cobbler's and had his shoes repaired for ninety cents. After some other expenditures he had thirty-five cents left, and spent twenty-five cents for lodging at the hotel. The next money he got he resolved should be spent for blue ties, in order to be more presentable. On July 3 he had dinner with the harvest hands of a bearded Dutchman, who had two savage dogs. This was in the sunflower part of Kansas, and he was near to Hutchinson. The diary here notes many new flowers which he was seeing, orchids and the like. He was drawing pictures of some of the most singular of them, and dreaming of a book to be called *The Golden Book of Village Improvement*, to excel *The Village Magazine*, to be printed in Los Angeles, and paid for by some kind of work. At Sterling he slept in a livery stable again. At Raymond he recited for his dinner; at Ellinwood he traded recitations for supper; and then slept in the stable office.

He reached Great Bend Friday, July 5, and there got his mail. There were letters from his family saying that they would start for the West on the 10th, and would make the return trip to Springfield the middle of August. While he was reading his mail he was hired by a farmer who came along to shock wheat. His name was Russell, who had a tenant by the name of Weaver. Without breakfast that morning Lindsay started to work. Lindsay took his meals at Weaver's house, where the food was better than at the house of the Mennonite. The reaper broke down, and Lindsay was treated to a fine streak of profanity on the part of Weaver. Lindsay was consigned with many apologies to the haymow to sleep. Saturday night came and Weaver wanted Lindsay to stay on to help put up alfalfa. Lindsay at first consented; then he remembered what he had written his people about meeting them in Colorado. While Lindsay was writing letters on Sunday, Weaver and his helpers undertook to break a bronco, stimulating themselves with whiskey betimes to forward the work. These men beat the bronco cruelly without accomplishing anything. So it was here that Lindsay got material for his poem "The Bronco That Would Not Be Broken." That was Lindsay too. He saw himself in this contumacious animal. Lindsay shocked wheat and put up alfalfa here for several days, and did odd work, like wiping the dishes for the housewife. For his work he drew $12.50, sent $10 to his mother, bought two gaudy neckties, and put up at a hotel at Great Bend. He was played out with his hard work. He went on now and reached Kinsley where he traded *The Rhymes* for a sandwich. At Offerle a man treated him to ice cream. He then slept in a livery stable. "Have been thinking all afternoon about *The Golden Book of Springfield*. I want it to be four times as impressive as *The Village Magazine*." On the 14th he was walking in level country beside the Trail. Here the diary contains a graphic picture of Spearville as he approached it, and saw its many windmills, all standing on a fine hill. At one restaurant in Spearville Lindsay had a sandwich for *The Rhymes*, ice cream at another, and a full meal at a boarding house, where *The Rhymes* were taken "in exactly the right spirit." Here Lindsay was hired at $2.50 a day for the harvest field, and walked two miles in the dark to the house, finding it the abode of a German Catholic family.

The next morning Lindsay was set to work mixing concrete for the building of a tenant house, on which he labored until two harvesters struck for $3 a day, and did not get it. So Lindsay was transferred to the harvest field. The barley was slick and fishy, the oats green and heavy. This was the country then of Russian wheat, with the Russian thistle as an accompaniment. Lindsay was contemplating now amid his labors an exhaustive reply to Thoreau, and would call the book *Fifty Years After Walden*, or *Walden and Sangamon County*, or *Walden and Utopia*, or *Ruskin vs. Thoreau*. His diary now is figured with drawings of thistles and dragons. He would write a poem on the seven dragons of art: the butterfly, censer, brazier, whiff of foam, etc. While working for this German Catholic he was associated with a laborer who on occasion had been an officer at the local field meets. Lindsay recited to him Swinburne's

"When the Hounds of Spring," much to the latter's delight, who wanted to learn it himself. "He is most pornographically minded," observed Lindsay, "and sings and tells more material of that kind than any I ever knew. He is a Baptist preacher and insurance man in the winter time. Great character for a story. A spontaneous, sensitive rascal, and full of fine feeling." With the German Catholic Lindsay walked to mass, and had quite a conversation. On Sunday, July 21, he made this entry: "An idea in books. *The Golden Book of the United States* to parallel *The Golden Book of Springfield*. A rhyme about every corner of the United States, and the Gospel of Beauty argument in rhyme as much as possible. Illustrate both books at the same time, making them twin books. Rhymes on Florida moss, Georgia violin, a New Jersey orchard in the spring, New Jersey hills in the morning, A California orange grove, A Washington apple orchard etc. The San Francisco exposition. Their decorations through the books from censers to dragons." Behold how Lindsay's heart was set on producing a beautiful book of verses and drawings! How the dream of doing so filled his heart with happy meditations!

On Monday the 22d he was on the road again with fifteen dollars in his pocket for his week's work for the German Catholic. At Dodge City he bought some articles of clothing, and had dinner at the Santa Fé Station in "bang up style," and sent $10.50 to his mother. Then he read Thoreau in the public library all afternoon. "Am still dull from work, yet hungry for a place to write for 6 months; yet I am eager for San Francisco. And then I feel just like harvesting again." He was on the Santa Fé trail again amid a forest of sunflowers. He was walking along the Arkansas River, a rather dried-up stream at this season. He reached Cimarron at two in the afternoon of July 23, with ten cents in his pocket with which he bought fig cakes. Offering *The Rhymes* to a druggist for an ice cream he was emphatically turned down; so he proceeded to the town of Ingalls, about ten miles on, where he managed to dispose of *The Rhymes* for a sandwich. Here he could have got work on an irrigation ditch; but he was in a hurry now to reach Colorado. He slept in a livery stable in Cimarron. By sunrise the next morning he was on the Santa Fé Trail again. He encountered a workman riding a motorcycle who offered him work on the ditch, but Lindsay refused. At Charleston, about twenty miles west of Cimarron, Lindsay had breakfast with a couple, a man with locomotor ataxia, and a wife who waited constantly upon her invalid husband. Lindsay offered to recite, but the man's nerves forbade. Lindsay therefore cut weeds and cleaned up the front yard. This put the housewife in excellent humor. She gave him a large piece of pie and sent him on his way rejoicing. "Pierceville to Garden City is the real stuff. Trail turns N.W. from railroad, and there is nothing but the wide road and the shadows of the telegraph poles. Neither tree, beast nor farm. Sun hot as the devil, but a good wind. Kansas as she used to be. Suddenly a wheat field. A new kind of cat tail or timothy wild flower. How is this for a rule: travel as a troubadour, work in any one place as a manual laborer. Then travel as a troubadour, and Franciscan again." He got an auto ride into Garden City, where at a store he bought a copy of the August *American* and found himself celebrated in it in an article by a certain mysterious O. V. R. He then was fortunate enough to get a ride clear to Lakin, a distance of perhaps thirty miles. All the country here was a garden, due to irrigation, "most beautiful to see."

On Thursday morning, July 25, he split kindling for breakfast at a house just outside Lakin, and preached the Gospel of Beauty. He then went on, passing windmills and irrigated patches. For dinner that day he preached the Gospel again; then he proceeded and climbed a range of hills into Kendall, where he found no hospitality. Going on, rain drove him into a house, where he preached the Gospel

to the occupant for breakfast. He left Syracuse behind him
and at noon on July 26 he did manual work for a fine dinner,
which was served to him under a tree, and consisted of
chicken and other edibles. Farther on he was asked to work
in the alfalfa field, but declined and hoed beets for food.
The next day he was at Granada, Colorado, where he received a meal for *The Rhymes*, and was not asked to work.
The food, however, was not much. At Grote Station, some
miles west of Granada, he stayed first in the basement of a
block house, and was eaten by ants; and so he went to the
station, where he sat up all night with the train despatcher.
Leaving Granada, he encountered a large band of gypsies
in five wagons. The women hailed him and wanted to know
what he had for sale. They were gaily dressed and spangled.
He got a ride with a man who turned out to be a fanatical
Socialist, and so got to Lamar. There he had dinner in a
house with no screens and full of flies. The corn bread,
however, was good. Cars repeatedly passed him in the afternoon without offering him a ride. Finally two Jews came
along who had a bag of gold and a dog in the rear of the
car. That afternoon of July 28 it rained heavily; but Lindsay walked on, reaching Hasty, seventeen miles east of Las
Animas, at about seven in the evening. He slept that night
on wet alfalfa, in a roofless barn, wrapped in canvas. He
found a couple here from Terre Haute, Indiana, who gave
him meals. He resumed his way and walked within six
miles of Las Animas, when he got a ride, and arrived at
that place with its houseless stretch of street on the north
side of the Arkansas River, and its hospital for consump-
tives. At Las Animas he slept in a filthy harness closet of a
livery stable. He had a chance now to work for $1.25 a day,
but refused. As he went on, he began to see little mesas on
the horizon.

He pressed on now to La Junta, a distance of twenty miles
from Las Animas, and arrived there before dinnertime on

July 30. Here he split kindling for a meal. Here he became acquainted with a doctor who advised him to read George Borrow. The doctor was a Bull Moose and a reformer, and read Lindsay's poems through from beginning to end. The fare here was of the best, consisting of chicken and fresh vegetables from the garden. Going on, Lindsay met some Springfield acquaintances at Rocky Ford, who gave him a party, the first that he had had since he left home. Lindsay, at this point, stated his position on the labor question, "that labor by the week is noble and exhilarating and illuminating; but by the year, 12 hours a day too hard. But my special job is to celebrate the exhilaration. The other fellow can take the long hours. I am looking for the honey in labor, not the thorns."

He arrived at Orchard Park in the pitch dark of night, and at a hotel recited verses to the children he found there around a table. They adored "The Owl Moon." So here he had bed and breakfast. He thought now that he would write 100 poems on the moon, and we find numerous scrawls of their beginning which he made on the backs of envelopes and the like. He copied off "The Owl Moon" for the landlady of the hotel, and started for Avondale, which was about ten miles from Pueblo. He reached Pueblo after many circuitous windings through its surburbs, and washed up at the hotel. Then he repaired to a residence, where he was given dinner without paying for it in work or otherwise. Not tarrying in Pueblo, he travelled along a convict-made road, and reached Wigwam at night, August 2, where he stayed with a hospitable man. During the evening Lindsay recited verses to the best of attention from the men of the ranch, who were called in for the occasion by ringing a bell.

Saturday morning, August 3, Lindsay walked ten miles and rode fifteen, thus arriving at Colorado Springs at eleven. Here he called upon a young lady acquaintance and they took a walk after dinner up the slope of the mountains. "The views were lovely," commented the poet, "I kept thinking of when papa first took me through that region when I was a little boy."

On Sunday, August 4, Lindsay started for Denver, a distance of sixty miles and more from Colorado Springs. The young lady undertook to walk a little way with him. They arrived at a small station and, finding there was no train, returned to Pueblo, but not till after a long wait, during which Lindsay wrote many moon poems. That night Lindsay walked to Manitou, a distance of ten miles perhaps, and became chilled.

On August 5 he made seventy-six miles into Denver, forty by auto, six by horse, and the rest afoot. That night he slept on the cement floor of a garage. On the edge of Denver the next day he hoed weeds for breakfast. Starting forth, he reached Golden at eleven, and cut grass for a meal for a Wisconsin couple, "husband pretending business, but plainly an invalid." He gave Lindsay twenty cents for supper. Lindsay was hurrying now with all possible speed. He reached an open shed five miles from Idaho Springs at dark, and slept there, warmed by a comfort loaned him by a boy. The next morning he walked on to Idaho Springs, and was given breakfast by a Swedish woman. "The Springs quite a crisp, tiny village. All the way up the cañon, mining enterprises."

He slept an hour on the station bench at Dupont. Having a bad heel from a bite or from an abrasion, and the altitude being high, Lindsay was now experiencing exhaustion. He reached Empire Station at 12:30, and found from something said by the station agent, that —— had come four days before. This may have been that Penelope to whom he had been writing along the way. At any rate, Lindsay now met his father going to Guinellar. The family had arrived in Colorado from Springfield for a summer's camping. Lindsay went on and found his mother and Penelope (so we shall call her) up the cañon, gathering strawberries. It was now August 7, and Lindsay had been on the road since May 29. That afternoon Lindsay had strawberry shortcake, and a walk up Mad Creek with Penelope, and another lady. He planned to write a matter-of-fact poem on the moving picture, while having the first walk and talk of any length with Penelope. He found his father's and mother's camp most elaborately worked out, most orderly and comfortable. The long tramp had made him long for a week of inertia and luxury.

On Friday, August 9, Lindsay rose in prime condition, and dressed in his father's trousers, having washed out his own corduroys the day before. "The whole camp quite merry, and the sun shining." He washed the breakfast dishes. Penelope went into the mountains to draw; and two other members of the party explored Green Lake and climbed to the battlefield of the gods. Lindsay's foot troubled him, and he resolved to keep in camp until it was well. There are no entries in the diary now until August 18, when Lindsay noted that he walked the cañon all day with Penelope. These nine days were full of miracle and ecstasy for Lindsay. It was the 19th that Penelope went to Denver. "I was sad without ——," says the diary.

Lindsay became the center of interest in the camp. He drove with Penelope and others for miles and miles into the hills, seeing the glacial lakes, and through cañons where Lindsay cupped his mouth and shouted for Debs until the echoes rolled around the granite heights. On one occasion the party climbed Mount Flora, where Lindsay found extraordinary violets, and then ascending higher gathered snow with which he pelted the less adventurous spirits. One day a terrible storm came upon them, with rain and darkness and keen lightning, which kept flashing upon the steep descent, and showing the way. Lindsay matched his voice against the roar of the thunder, singing, "The old time religion is good enough for me." Another day they were caught in a storm and repaired to a cabin where a woman was frying doughnuts, despite the leaking roof. Lindsay and the rest sat upon the broken chairs and ate doughnuts, which Lindsay relished enormously. Sometimes they went high up in the hills, and scanned the beautiful valleys below them. On these occasions Lindsay was telling the company about his plan to write poems to the rhythms of the old gospel hymns. We have seen how steadily he kept this experiment in mind, as well as his idea of writing poems in the rhythms of the popular songs of the day. This was far indeed from trying to capture the harmonies of Swinburne, or Poe, or Coleridge, or Blake. The gospel hymns came out of immediate religious experience. The popular songs out of the very heart of America. He was truly on a new path to contemplate such prosodies. One day in the hills Lindsay was singing, "Are you washed in the blood of the Lamb?" The first poem to make his name known was thus germinating in his mind. Over and over he sang this old song there in the picturesque ways of Colorado in this August of 1912. He was wont, too, to recite for the group his poem, "The Wedding of the Lotus and the Rose," which is written in such simple meter, but with delicate intonations. The ranch neighbors came to the Lindsay camp and told thrilling stories of old prospectors, of strikes into rich veins of gold and silver. If Lindsay had been a student of character he would have found this material rich for portraiture. He used some of it for lyrical narrative, just as he put his memory of the Santa Fé Trail into a scherzo of wonderful power and music.

Penelope went her way, as we have said; and Lindsay, amid his poetical plans and meditations turned, as he did many times before, to the problem of practical existence. He resolved now to go to Denver, and somehow there to print his poems, and to live comfortably and out of debt. On the 20th another member of the party went to Denver, and Lind-

say sent a note by her to Penelope, and that night worked
on his moon poems. On the 22d the party broke camp,
Lindsay nailed boxes, and then took the train to Denver,
where he put up at a hotel, and then saw some moving pictures. On the 22d Lindsay's father and mother left Denver
for Springfield. "Put them on the train," says the diary,
"Papa paid for my bed over night at the hotel, and gave me
a dollar. This was more than I let him do for me when I
started out from Springfield. Spent most of my dollar that
night at Elitch's Gardens. Felt very sorry to leave papa and
mama, and never felt so fond of them." On the 24th he
walked out of Denver for Colorado Springs. "Terribly low
in spirits from leaving my family and lady."

About seven miles out he met with a gardener who hired
him for $2 to thin beets in the afternoon, but also to
be compensated by food the next day, which was Sunday.
That Saturday night he lost his moon poems, and was
greatly distressed. His consolation was the fact that the
September number of *The American Magazine* contained his
"The Proud Farmer," and "The Gospel of Beauty." Thus,
eight years after his appearance in a New York magazine
he was publishing in another. At Littleton, Colorado, about
ten miles south of Denver, he spent a number of days thinning beets, and weeding onions. He confided thus to his
diary: "I am so full of writing projects I can hardly wait
to get home to work them out, and I am so homesick once or
twice a day I am in actual danger of going home." He was
surely weakening now, and at last abandoned the road; but
for some days yet on he went working at odd jobs for food,
eating with Mexicans, and having some rough experiences,
particularly with filthy houses, and infested beds. He
reached Trinidad, September 2, where he had friends who
gave him a room. Here he wrote poems for several days in a
good spare room. From here he forwarded nineteen poems
to *The American Magazine*, the editor having refused to be

interested in letters reporting his tramping experiences. In
the library here he read Ruskin, and at night went to the
park, where he saw dancing. He paid his way by chopping
kindling; and finally he received $5 from home, with which
he had his shoes soled and paid a dentist bill, and bought
stamps and candy. On the 5th he left Trinidad with much
new verse in his mind, not yet written. At Raton, New
Mexico, he slept in a livery stable, and was reflecting that
he had 1138 miles more to walk before reaching Los Angeles;
but he was told now by a man he met that the walk across
the desert would be the best part of the way, because section
houses where he could sleep were not more than fifteen miles
apart. So on he went, refusing a job at $1.25 a day for
driving a garbage wagon, which would be an all winter's
employment. At French, New Mexico, he slept in a concrete
livery after having undergone the misery of a terrible
dust storm, and with no supper. The next morning he split
kindling for the reward of breakfast, which was a good one.
On the afternoon of the 10th he reached Springer, and
canvassed the town for dinner in vain. But he met a Spanish
beauty there who told him that her husband would help him
out, which he did with twenty cents. Lindsay bought ten
cents' worth of fig cakes, five cents' worth of cheese, and five
cents' worth of peaches. In spite of loss of sleep, and no
rides, and writing up his diary, Lindsay made twenty miles
on the 11th, and that day arrived at Colmar at dark. He
was hospitably treated here. On the 12th he came to
Wagon Mound, a place about forty miles north of Las
Vegas. He was drenched from the rain. Here he approached
the head of the Commercial Club for work, but got nothing,
and that night slept in a bed bitten to sleeplessness by bugs.
Awakening the next morning he decided to ride to Los
Angeles, and write after working there a while. So he went
to the station to telegraph home for money. The telegraph
agent taunted Lindsay with having lost his nerve. Lindsay

replied, "this is not my brand of nerve." Let us take the change of resolution as Lindsay set it down in his diary: "My reasons for losing my nerve were as follows: (1) In northern New Mexico I outlined a dozen poems on the sun. I was impatient to write them out at leisure at my next stopping place. Los Angeles was the next stopping place. (2) The country was very much like that in which I had been walking for a month and a half, only poorer. (3) Was thinking about home a good deal. (4) The stations were growing poorer and farther apart. Walking lost most of its taste of adventure, was too much routine. (5) The same things were happening every day. (6) Ahead of me was 1000 miles, mainly desert. To cross it afoot would be merely a stunt like walking on one's hands for a wager. I am not out to do a stunt, and I allow myself to lose my nerve whenever I please, knowing I shall get it again in good time. My business is writing and preaching the Gospel of Beauty each day as I see fit, and not doing the thing that bores me, merely to be consistent."

And so the money arrived from Doctor Lindsay, $40 it was, and on September 15, Lindsay stepped from a Santa Fé train and stood amid the scenes of Los Angeles. He was not a great while here, for a little later he appeared at Mills College, of which he wrote in 1926, "Surely there is something of the hand of fate in my connection with Mills College." Here he was taken in by Professor E. Olan James and his hospitable wife, who together with their children took care of him for a month, before he had the nerve to go home, as he later confessed. The instructor loaned him a pair of pants in which to make an appearance while he took Mrs. James to the Art Gallery. Years after this Lindsay returned here to recite, duly dressed in evening attire for the formal occasion, and had for a hostess little Miss Elizabeth Conner, who became his wife in 1925. Before he came to Professor James's house as the termination of his tramp, he had written "General William Booth Enters Into Heaven." It was one of the consummations of years of meditation upon American themes, done in the tone of the gospel hymns. So much, at least, Lindsay had made out of the tramp. What he derived in other ways may in part be discovered by reading the Proclamations which he published in *Farm and Fireside*, and which end the book *Adventures While Preaching the Gospel of Beauty*. But these Proclamations are for the most part admonitions to the city dwellers to seek the country. They are also prophecies of new religions and new arts in the Lindsay vein, with which the reader is now fully acquainted.

For some reason not given by Lindsay, the narrative concerning this trip West, as published in *Adventures While Preaching the Gospel of Beauty*, ends with his arrival at Pueblo, on August 1. For the rest in the book he added a flourish of moon poems, written at about the time he was in Colorado. The book contains nothing of his joining the camp of his father and mother at Idaho Falls, nothing of Penelope, nothing of the joyous days by the glacier lakes, and through the cañons; and nothing of his travels onward through New Mexico after the camp broke; and nothing of his abandoning the hike, telegraphing for money, and going by train to Los Angeles. Likewise, he gave no hint of his sojourn with Professor James at Mills College, either in his diary, or in *The Adventures*. Lindsay, however, had written the General Booth poem, and so much he could count to the incidents of the long walk. But he could have produced this in Springfield without ever venturing as far as the Sangamon River. Why did Lindsay indulge in such supressions? It seems evident that he felt apologetic about abandoning a plan which he had adopted with such deliberation. He was loath to publish that the way of the road, the privations of Saint Francis, and the delights of the mendicant were not so romantic as they seem when reading *The Adventures*. However, what did he get from this trip, not as analysis of the story of it may show, but what he concluded himself that he got from it? Extracts from a diary begun in 1912 and containing notes into 1913 will give us the information.

CHAPTER XIII

THE truth is that Lindsay was almost cursed with restlessness, a longing and a disquietude of spirit that were to a degree pathological. He was an all-sufficient specimen of the genus Americanus, by which to know and to judge the stock as a whole, not in all particulars, but in many salient aspects. The restless spirit of migrations may be justified by political or economic pressures, or by the prospects of free land, which took the early Americans over the Appalachians, and made them settle California and the New Northwest. That is one thing; but the restlessness that takes men from settled habitations to a wandering about the country, and to the adoption in succession of different places of residence is a deeper symptom of soul disturbance and lack of equilibrium. Granted that Springfield was not golden, yet neither was Ayr free of unhappy circumstances, nor London, nor Brooklyn. Whitman had his days of travel as a young man, but he came back to his place, not because he had to, but because it was his place. Lindsay finally got as far away from Springfield as Spokane, and for a time was fascinated with the country, and took it forever as his own. It was characteristic of him to burst into flames and to see visions and to make great resolutions. The fire always subsided in him, and then he returned to his basic form. So he came back to Springfield at last as tired out with his exile as he was fatigued in New Mexico where he took the train for Los Angeles.

All of this is only another way of saying that his strength was not sufficient for the ardor of his spirit. He planned, and dreamed and made notes of hosts of things to do which he never accomplished. That is true of all men, doubtless. In his case it was the more conspicuous, because he used such prodigious energy for cultural and literary and artistic works which never materialized. Simply stated, he gave out. Goethe did not have time to use the vast spiritual foundation which he laid for himself; Lindsay did not have the strength, the permanence of vision. But at the last his fire settled into a certain phase of steady flame of a quality truly American. Perhaps if there is one thing that can be fixed upon as essentially American, manifesting itself equally in Iowa and in New Hampshire, it is the religious spirit; and if there is a Union of the States, a union in disunion such as binds a family by blood ties which cannot be shaken off and is even more powerful in domestic strife, it is this matter of religion. America was peopled by all the nonconformist stocks of England, France, and Germany, thus leaving England to the established Church, and France and Germany in chief to Catholicism. America started as an evangelical culture, all despite the deism of Washington, Franklin, and Jefferson. Lindsay was immersed in this culture; and in this sense he was wholly American. He became the voice of his culture, and being so, perhaps was the most national poet that America thus far has had. There is no other culture so ubiquitous and so deeply ingrained in the people as this religious culture, of which to sing, from which to rise and of which to prophesy.

What, then, were Lindsay's valuations of the tramp through the West? We find in this diary of 1912–13 that he planned to walk back to Springfield. He even made note of resolutions to govern him along the way. He would keep no diary, he would carry no printed matter, he would work when possible, he would have no letters from home, he would recite poems when it came about in a natural way, "including Booth"; he would be a plain beggar, explaining himself as little as possible, he would receive no money from home; his main object would be to get home as soon as possible; but his real reason for walking back would be "to finish this trip with some kind of beggar's and mendicant's honor, dignity, and self respect, having begun it." On this walk Saint Francis would be his master, not Ruskin. His expectation would be "to find and eat and endure the bitterest core of beggary. Having reached home, never to beg again." All this, and yet we find him at the home of Professor James at Mills College, and perhaps by money sent from Doctor Lindsay, travelling by train back to Springfield. This entry in his diary, dated Springfield, January 23, 1913, discloses what he thought of the tramp West, and as usual shows him still full of plans, theories, and resolutions.

"Thinking this morning," he began, "it seems to me that if I go on the road again it should be first of all as a monastic discipline, with the getting of all the manual labor I can stand, work myself to death if necesary, with the motto victory or death written across the sky. I see that only by such a grim determination will I ever win my way upon the road, and break up through the crust of society. I ought to have my book on Springfield written and started and all literary and advertising impulses suppressed. I should write to no one but my people, and work with an open mind with all previous ideas set aside as much as possible. . . . The trouble with my previous trips was that they were made too external. The only part of me that was open minded was my imagination. I was willing to put down impartially what I saw, but I was not willing to live up to each hour completely for its own sake, as I should have stayed and worked for the market gardener south of Denver. There is where I lost out. I had reasonable work and a kind family, but I had too big a notion of what I was going to do when I left the place, instead of sticking it out."

"I expected on this last trip a complete physical renovation, plus literary material and a certain public assertion of principles. The next one I should expect a complete spiritual overturning, to last me through my life thereafter, as well as a physical one. I should expect spiritual self-mastery, and light every man I meet and every day, and every piece of work sufficient unto itself. And while not too confident of victory, and feeling I may perhaps be driven back to town at last, or dragged back by my literary faculty, I should be considering the possible permanence of my work, and discharging myself from old privileges, try to build them up step by step on a solid basis. Also it seems to me that I ought to hope not to walk far, I ought to conquer all mere restlessness, I ought to assume that the third or fourth farm where I work will be the right one, and expect to settle into a permanent member of that community, if possible, and take the same medicine as they do, not asking any special privileges whatever, or holding before my eyes any dream of escape, and the place ought to be near enough to Springfield to be holding some sort of organic relation to it. . . . Also I ought not to expect the least thing idyllic in the life, and be reconciled to the routine, to expect to find my main pleasure in the business of being physically weary, and the business of digging up and discovering my reserve physical strength that I did not know I had, and discovered in the harvest field. This all I might view as my social ambition."

"Sometimes I think I would like to preach in some country church on Sunday, like Grandpa Frazee. Possibly my circuit should be to become a retired farmer at fifty, like other retired farmers, having at first become a farmer and won sufficient place economically to have a right to retire. However this be, work should be my motto as I go on the road next time, and an absolutely sincere and open mind and soul that follows the event as it unfolds. If I put my soul and body without reserve into the hands of the Lord my part will be done. Then let them lead or kill or cure me as they will."

As it happened all this ideologic list of resolutions, which were so written out because they were not sufficiently concrete to himself when carried in mind, and were not remembered and adhered to even when written out, were superflous now. There is everything here of spiritual architectonics, except those which related to intellectual discipline by which he might have deepened and broadened his capacity as a poet, if that had been possible. And yet in a few weeks now he was to become sensationally famous as a poet. His future was soon to be determined, even beyond his own will, having gone so far in the way of preparing himself to be a poet, and having done nothing to be anything else. For the poet's mind was now full grown. The stalks were all forth which were later to produce all the different variety of blossoms of which his nature and its fibre and sap were capable. Before taking up a discussion of his literary works it will finish this review of the growth of the poet's mind to list what he had been reading along the years to this time, in addition to what has been given of his studies and reading at school and while preparing to be an artist.

Lindsay learned to read in very early childhood by spelling out Grimm's stories to the household cook, and from childhood onward he read Grimm and Hans Andersen. He was wont to say more than half in earnest that the paternity of "The Chinese Nightingale" was in one of Andersen's stories. But in Grimm, too, there are speaking birds, frogs, and other animals. The raven which croaked Nevermore in Poe's poem may have had some creative influence on Lindsay. Without repeating what has been hitherto listed, these books may be set down as those which Lindsay pondered in childhood, and early boyhood: *A History of Japan in Monosyllables; The Boy's Own Book*, being a history of science, art, and crafts; *Heroes of Chivalry*, including the Cid and others; McGuffey's *Readers; Tom Sawyer* and *Huckleberry Finn; Uncle Tom's Cabin;* Poe's Poems; Milton's *Paradise*

Lost; Artemus Ward's books of humor; Lowell's Poems and *Biglow Papers*, and Swift's *Gulliver's Travels.*

In his young manhood Lindsay read Hudson's *Law of Psychic Phenomena*, all of Shakespeare many times; all of Kipling and O. Henry, Swinburne, Keats, Lanier; the poems of Morris and Rossetti; many histories of art, as we have already said in part; Sabatier's *Life of Saint Francis;* Tolstoy *in toto;* the Scriptures of the Hindus; the Koran; the Bible, with particular regard to Revelation; the *Analects of Confucius;* Carlyle's *French Revolution,* already mentioned; Pater's *The Renaissance;* the plays of Ibsen, Shaw, and Rostand; Stanley's *Darkest Africa; The Book of the Dead,* and Breasted's work on Egypt; Ferrero's *The Women of the Cæsars; Don Quixote;* Bryce's *American Commonwealth;* James's *Varieties of Religious Experience;* the state papers of Jefferson; Howells's *The Rise of Silas Lapham;* Meredith's *The Ordeal of Richard Feverel;* Lewis's *Main Street,* and Wells's novels, short stories, and *History of the World.* This list brings Lindsay to about thirty-one years of age. All the while he was an omnivorous reader of magazines, and other miscellaneous literature. This list which has been furnished by an authentic source is marked by surprising omissions. There is no *Piers Plowman* here, no *Shepherd's Calendar,* no Chaucer, no Elizabethan drama, no Sir Thomas Malory, no Marco Polo, no Sir John Mandeville, no Bacon's *New Atlantis,* no Sir Thomas More, no Thomas à Kempis, no Sir Thomas Browne's *Urn Burial,* no Pascal, no Plato, no philosophy of any sort; no Boccaccio, nor Rabelais, nor Rousseau; no Calderon, Dante, *Faust,* no *Niebelungen Lied,* no Homer, or any of the Greek dramatists; no Virgil, Horace, or Lucretius. He saw much of nature around Springfield and on his tramps, yet he did not turn to Bion, Moschus, and Theocritus, nor to the *Eclogues* and *Georgics* of Virgil, nor to Wordsworth, nor to Spenser. He might have read, one would think, Tasso's *Jerusalem De-*

livered, and perhaps Petrarch's *Sonnets*. And how did he miss Shelley, an ardent humanist and radical like himself, and Whitman and Emerson not in casual hours but as a matter of daily communion? His poetical reading was nothing like so extensive as Whitman's in the days of the latter's preparation for song. Later, after Lindsay became a master, he turned to Browning. Ibsen was not for him, but rather *Prometheus Bound;* and the severe classicism of Landor was farther from his metier than the odes of Shelley and his songs of liberty. Yet after all he was really compelled to do everything for himself; and if most poets have done so, many, if not most of them, have lived under more emancipating, more cultured conditions. He might have arrived sooner and used more of his genius and the material he accumulated if he had had some directing friend.

Lindsay's favorite poets were Tennyson, not Browning, Swinburne, not Arnold, and Lanier and Poe. *Paradise Lost* had a peculiar fascination for him to the last; and he read *Hamlet* unendingly. He preferred Longfellow to Whitman, until he arrived at the maturity of his political thinking, and then he hoped the time would come when the names of Washington, Jefferson, Lincoln, and Whitman would be those linked together by America in the hagiology of chief spirits. He awoke at last to the realization that Whitman lived the political faith which he himself most deeply cherished, that Whitman was a Jeffersonian, and without Jefferson one could not understand Whitman. All this may be found in Lindsay's *Litany of Washington Street*, published in 1929. This badly-written and unimportant book is nevertheless immensely revealing of Lindsay's political passions out of which so much of his poetry produced long previously to the date of this book proceeded. Somehow, considering Lindsay's excessive Americanism it seems a blindness, a separation from his spiritual place, that he did not find Whitman at the very first and cling to him constantly through life. Nothing in Lindsay's reading indicates that he derived any of the articles or his creed of life or writing from Whitman; and yet the two men shared many beliefs together. Let us listen to Whitman: "To love the earth and sun and the animals, despise riches, give alms to everyone that asks, stand up for the stupid and the crazy, devote your income and labors to others, hate tyrants, argue not concerning God, have patience and indulgence toward people, take off your hat to nothing known or unknown, or to any man or number of men; go freely with powerful, uneducated persons, and with young men and with mothers of families, dismiss whatever insults your own soul, and your flesh shall be a great poem." To this might be added Whitman's resolution to "map out, fashion, form and knit and sing the ideal American, to project the future, and to depend on the future for an audience." He saw the necessity of doing this in the absence of the boundlessly rich material, the characters and the history which Shakespeare found ready-made to his hand. Lindsay in a comparable disadvantage would invent his own classical allusions, and choose American characters for his songs. In so many ways Lindsay was related to Whitman; but the relation was like that of a gifted son who does not resemble his father, while using modified, and some respects finer, gifts to an entirely different end. We even find that Lindsay often spoke of dressing with formal elegance. Whitman, until he found himself, affected a certain nattiness of dress. Both men were enormous egotists, individualists, with a tendency toward the wild and woolly. Whitman ached with sex, and so did Lindsay. One took America for his love and thus sublimated; the other poured out his heart to Mystical Springfield, to religion, Christ, Buddha, and the heroes, and thus consumed emotional energies which conceivably might have taken a Byronic direction. Lindsay did not go with powerful uneducated persons; but all the while he stood convicted, feeling his father tugging at him to cultivate masculine interests. It might have been better for him if he could have heeded his father's call. Perhaps Lindsay had more cardinal ideas than Whitman; but up to a certain point their ideas were almost identical. They shared a like physiological experience. Whitman and Lindsay were both natural celibates; both were old men at fifty. Both were victims of the Civil War, and both idolators of Lincoln. Whitman ruined his health during his hospital experience, and suffered morally from the despotic tightening of the country when the war was over. Lindsay embraced the era of that war despite the influence of his grandfather Lindsay, and despite all his Jeffersonian adherences. He sang the country which was changed by that war, and which was changing fast about him as he was reaching his majority, and changing faster later. The remarkable thing is that when American literature was so much tinged with satire as the result of rebellion against the consequences of the war, he remained a bard of love and hope. But at last it was the forces, the culture created by the war which did most to destroy him. Without historical perceptions, and unconscious of the meaning of the war, and unmindful of who it was that waged it, and to what end, he celebrated its central figure, Lincoln, as if Lincoln were the chief figure of the pioneers, and the fellow of the Virginia heroes. History was never more misvalued; nor great song more compelled to rest upon itself without assistance from the truth.

CHAPTER XIV

WITH the acclaim which came to Lindsay on the publication of the General Booth poem, Lindsay stepped from the obscurity of a dreamer and agitator, a writer of verse for *The Register*, and a queer character tramping about the country, and returning to Springfield to warn it against the wrath to come, he stepped from all this into the spotlight that stares like the eye of Polyphemus upon the bewildered soul that has courted attention from the giant public, and at last has it to the full. In 1904 he had published "The Queen of Bubbles" in *The New York Critic*, in 1905 in the same magazine an illustrated poem entitled "At Noon on Easter Day"; in 1911 in *The Outlook* he had published "Incense." In the fall of 1912 he had appeared in two or three New York publications. The magazine *Poetry, a Magazine of Verse*, started in the fall of 1912, had the distinction of presenting the Booth poem.

The Booth poem was the first extravagant flower of all that sowing and tilling which Lindsay had done for years, and of which we have now given the history. Lindsay having become a celebrity, and needing no more to think of cartooning, or painting, or anything except the matter of financing himself, began to produce poems and books of prose. In 1913, not many months after the appearance of the Booth poem, he published a volume of verse with the title *General William Booth Enters Into Heaven and Other Poems*. It contained 60 poems and had 119 pages. The poems were those which he had traded for bread through Kansas, and which he had put into the pamphlet *The*

Tramp's Excuse. When Lindsay's poetry is discussed this volume will be considered. For the present his prose will engage our attention. Between 1914 and 1929 he published five books of prose, and while they are valuable to literary history because it was he who wrote them, they have little intrinsic worth.

Nothing more need be said touching the contents of *A Handy Guide for Beggars,* or *Adventures While Preaching the Gospel of Beauty.* These books were put together out of material as rich as any that came to the hand of Goldsmith, or Bayard Taylor, or conceivably to Johnny Appleseed; but with that material as a whole Lindsay did not know what to do. As we have seen he strove many years to acquire a prose style of sharpness and condensation. But expansive and diffuse as the style of these books is for the most part, and in spite of the fact that in places he rose to eloquence in them, the matter of style, of the use of words in prose as an instrument of expression is not the salient fault of these books. That fault is obviously that he did not make use of his material. The physical and psychological characteristics of Lindsay growing out of his frail childhood and his never vigorous manhood made their marks on everything he did, and left these books as but suggestions of what they might have been. He dreamed and planned prodigiously, so much so that the ejaculation of his thoughts often went thin. We shall find that this happened with many of his poems, and that only a few of them comparatively came out full panoplied and armed from head to foot. The history of the Doniphan-Frazee-Hamilton families, referred to at the beginning of this book, shows the Frazee blood in particular to be that of articulate, public-spirited, reformer type of people, fond of publicity and given to writing, speaking, holding office, and attaining prominence of one sort or another. Lindsay's veins surged with this blood. To a degree he quieted it, channelled it, and truly he made it sing. But the point now is that these first prose books left unused and unconverted daily happenings that in the hands of Dickens, not to mention Marco Polo, and other famous travellers, would have been a chronicle of the first import. Even Walt Whitman, who wrote too frequently with a slack hand, has given fuller report of his experiences in the camps and hospitals of the Civil War than Lindsay has told us in these books of the really significant events of these tramps. One cannot imagine Dreiser failing to give a full account of the abandonment of the walk to California, the visit to Professor James at Mills College, the return home to Springfield. He would have done this, and thrown in a minute exposition of all his reasons and his mental states. He would not have cared if such a revelation cancelled the picture of himself as a happy mendicant who went resolutely to the end with the journey to which he had set his face. Fortunate is the man who doesn't get tired of his task, or see his vision fade, or lose faith in what he first passionately believed, or come at last to think that there is no use to what he tried to do. Did Lindsay see that there was nothing but futility in preaching "The Gospel of Beauty"? We may think that he did arrive at such a conclusion, at least in respect to doing it as a mendicant hard put to it, while sleeping in livery stables, and being denied food, and having so many deaf ears turned to his message. Lindsay was certainly influenced by these circumstances. With all his faith he had borne in upon him the inevitable fact that the crowd sees all along nothing in life but food and physical operations. Their religion is to be saved from hell. Magical Springfields produce no food, and improve no defecations. One of Lindsay's tragedies was that he was never to know the truth about anything, for the reason that he scarcely knew the facts about anything, at least unobscured by his vaporings and coruscations. One must have the facts to extract the truth. He must have seen himself in the rôle of Johnny Appleseed, who didn't know whether his orchards would grow or not, as Lindsay could not know to what extent the seed of beauty scattered in Kansas and elsewhere would thrive. Was the seed really good, or was it sterile, or would it sprout amid rocks and thorns, and where human buzzards would eat it and make nothing of it? Lindsay's poems prove that at times he reached depths of soul darkness that match any into which Dante or Shelley descended. He saw the carrion birds wheeling around his head. "I Went Down Into the Desert" is one of these tragic utterances. The best that Lindsay could hope for was that orchards would grow here and there from scattering "The Gospel of Beauty," but that they might be overtaken by scale or sapped by water sprouts or choked by willows or sycamores. This is the final result of preaching "The Gospel of Beauty": scattering unprevised seed while sleeping in livery barns. And this is all that need be said about those two books of prose.

The Art of the Moving Picture, which Lindsay published in 1922, is characterized by his unusual mixed categories and incongruous analyses, in a word by his inherent incapacity to reason and to think. His motive in writing it was sufficiently laudable. He wanted this new form of amusement to serve the people rather than the avaricious vulgarians into whose hands it had fallen. In dividing for the purpose of his discussion all pictures into action pictures, intimate pictures and splendor pictures, it is clear that his classifications overlapped, and did not separate the really different kinds of photoplays. He called an action picture one set in the open. But is not the film of "The Letter" or the "Doll's House" an action picture? He called intimate pictures those which deal with restrained moods, having an interior for a setting. But does not "The Letter" have an interior setting while dealing with anything but a restrained mood? Why compare as he did such pictures to the art of Rembrandt? He may have been thinking of the aphorism of Simonides, that painting is dumb poetry, and poetry is speaking painting. If so, no less the principle underlies any one of the classes of pictures which he delineated. Lindsay had no doubt the desire to establish a relation between the photoplay and the fine arts, a really academic conceit. It goes without saying that the photoplay becomes a fine art when it becomes such. The relation is there though hidden by melodrama and meretricious falsity, a tautology that unfolds with the statement of the Lindsay doctrine. Finally the splendor pictures are of the outdoors, of mountains and the like, and thus is architecture in motion, or frozen music made fluid. It is difficult to see that these suggestions will ever influence the makers of photoplays. They are a dull crowd, but they knew this much before Lindsay told them. Lindsay would give magic to the photoplay; but that can be done by dealing with truth and reality.

Lindsay advocated the puppet show as an adjunct to the photoplay, and nothing better could be devised to keep it trivial. It was natural for him to do this, because a puppet show is an analogue of the poem games, of which we shall speak later. Finally he would have the photoplay utilize the hieroglyphic. Lindsay wasted many precious hours over this theme of hieroglyphics, and in his later years studied Roeder's *Egyptian Grammar*, and drew the Egyptian pictographs by the scores of pages. Yet an hieroglyph is but the symbol of a thing. An eye is represented by the picture of an eye, a linen-band by a curved line, a wall-top by a lunette figure, a pond by a parallelogram crossed with two diagonal lines, and the like. Suppose Chicago could be hieroglyphed by an outline of Old Fort Dearborn, or New York by an outline of the Woolworth Tower, how much farther would the photoplay be toward a real art? Why not have the thing itself dramatically interpreted instead of such symbols?

Then at last Lindsay wrote that the picture theatre would be a substitute of the saloon, as if wine and beer with food, and spirits for a stimulant could ever be surrendered for the chance of looking at photoplays, however decorated with hieroglyphs. These suggestions and preachments may be a further chapter in "The Gospel of Beauty," as Lindsay intended them to be. He was engaged in a salutary work when trying to reclaim the photoplay from the banal themes, the sensational pornography which had captured it; and that may come to pass when economic pressure compels a rehabilitation of the art. When that time arrives Lindsay may be given credit for being a pioneer in its formation; but he will stand as one who called for this progress, not one who showed how it could be attained.

Lindsay once said to me that my literary paternity was the science of law, and his that of art, a judgment characterized by his usual mixed ætiology. If it be true is his work governed by the principles of pictures, and mine by the logic of legal thinking? Goethe was a lawyer, and so were Scott and Lowell; and Byron read Blackstone with delight; but they studied many other things as well. And Lindsay at Hiram College had a course in commercial law, and one in torts and one in contracts, and stood well in them as we have seen. The point need not be pressed. In considering his prose book, *The Litany of Washington Street*, however, it is pertinent to say that he might have produced something more significant, and to be plain, something even more rational if he had known a little of law and constitutional history. It would have shown him that Washington, Jefferson, Hamilton, Madison, Jackson, and Lincoln cannot be understood or portrayed without knowing thoroughly that they were the products of political philosophy and of constitutional legalism. They were this as well as sons of Locke and Rousseau and Voltaire, and the Greek worthies. No amount of imaginative frenzy, no amount of symbolization upon the basis of any possible reality can make these fathers of the Republic anything else than creatures of the spirit of Athens and strangers to the spirit of Jerusalem. These men were products of Greek thought. If Lindsay had portrayed them in that capacity with genuine passion for their intellectual heredity he would have presented them in their actual character, not in that which his own kind of evangelism and religiosity in general set them before us for reverence. It results that Lindsay's prose book, *The Litany of Washington Street,* published in 1929, is almost the most fantastic thing that he ever wrote, and of no conceivable value. He called it a Gilbert Stuart kind of book. Washington is summed as "The Great Red Indian White Chief." Jefferson, Hamilton and Jackson and Lincoln are treated in similar fictile fashion. The book is obscure, verbose and slovenly, and contains no thought. It has the one merit of proving Lindsay's ardent Americanism, his desire to call the country back to its primal vision. To this end he did more in the poem "The Virginians Are Coming Again" than in many times the number of pages of this book. For in poetry it did not matter so much if he got off the earth at times when swept up by his own inspiration. Here in prose he cut the figure of a riant Romeo walking Broadway with the eye shadows unwashed from his face, yet dressed in the costume of the street.

Although *The Golden Book of Springfield,* published in 1920, is an incoherent performance and a disastrous descent from the long dreams of Magical Springfield, it must receive more attention than the other prose books. The Mormon Bible, the ravings of the book of Revelation cannot match this book for frenetical and moon-struck visions and adventures. But here again we must take account of Lindsay's impulse. "In the works of man as in those of nature, it is really the motives which chiefly merit attention," is one of Goethe's aphorisms; and we have to consider that Lindsay was not the first to dream of a Utopia, and to give it impracticable embodiment. If he didn't read Plato's *Republic,* or More's *Utopia,* he knew Morris's *News From Nowhere,* and he was familiar with the works of Henry George, the speeches of Debs, and the experiment at New Harmony, Indiana, under Owen. And as the theme of Magical Springfield recurs often in the poems to be later considered, it will be well to define as clearly as possible what was in Lindsay's mind and heart with respect to the regeneration of his city and his country; and then to show what he did when he came to giving a picture of his city to be. To this end let us not take Morris's *News from Nowhere,* nor More's *Utopia,* nor Bellamy's *Looking Backward* as test systems of Lindsay's ideal state. Let us take Plato's *Republic,* which is profounder and more imaginative than Bacon's *New Atlantis,* as well as very much more detailed and of larger survey. In doing this we shall not show that Lindsay derived his Magical Springfield from Plato, and by no means did he write *The Golden Book of Springfield* with Plato's work as a model, for he did nothing of the sort; and if he had he would have produced a much more significant work. But already we have canvassed Lindsay's dreams about his city and about America; and it will give dignity to Lindsay's day dreams, to many of his poems, and to the goodness of spirit which was his, to see how his preliminary drawings of the city, and his specific ideas here and there concerning it were not unworthy of Plato. After doing this we shall regretfully give a synopsis of *The Golden Book of Springfield,* and wonder what impotence it was that overtook his hand, if it was not that from that recurrent lowered vitality to which we have already alluded; from that weakness which resulted from the magnitude of the dream, leaving no strength to execute the plan. Shelley said in his youth that whatever the poet conceived he could render into words. Nothing falser was ever uttered respecting the poet's art. No one demonstrates the unsoundness of that judgment better than Lindsay.

Lindsay knew well enough that the America and the

Springfield which he would reshape were not places of a common blood, common religious center, nor, outside of baseball, a gathering for a game or games in which all the people participated. When he entitled one section of his *Collected Poems* "Orations, College War Cries and Olympic Games" he was trying to amalgamate a vast and loosely articulated nation into a spiritual whole, to which appeals could be made which would touch all nerves simultaneously and evoke the one exact cultural response. Plato had Greece whose people were unified by games and song and language. His hope was to shape men and a new state by an irresistible influence of art. That was Lindsay's proselytism from beginning to end. All of Lindsay's advocacy of dancing, of chanting and singing, of the new theatre, of appropriate music for the theatre, meant in the Plato sense the building of the soul to the strains of music. His celebration of the heroes from those early days of writing was out of a vision of the philosopher as ruler, the Marcus Aurelius, or the Saint Louis. Those who cannot share in Lindsay's ideas about prohibition, chastity and the ascetic life may be reminded that Lindsay did not practise these principles himself, and hold them forth for the government of Springfield the magical out of a narrow morality. He was looking toward a high ideal of life, and was willing to make physical sacrifices to attain it. So Pythagoras advised the practice of these austerities in order to tune the ear to the music of the spheres, the harmony of the universe. The soul came from heaven, said Pythagoras, and said Wordsworth, and to get it back there after performing a mission of goodness on earth it was necessary that the gross part of the flesh should be subdued by capturing the music of the spheres. This is not the creed of business men, war men, and materialists; it must be that of high souls, leaders of cities and nations bearing the crucifixion of lifting men to the wisest and highest activities, and the happiest life, meaning by that the life of deepest satisfactions. With Plato deriving in these things from Pythagoras the whole life of a citizen was an education in music, and thus, and thus only, could the Perfect City be brought into being. This is Lindsay's doctrine, and the essential core of The Gospel of Beauty. We get it from his diary, his pamphlets and booklets, his scrap book carried West in 1912, and from many poems. It is regrettable that he did not put it into philosophic form in *The Golden Book of Springfield*.

As compared with Greece, and with the possibilities of Plato's plan for the Perfect State or city, America has lacked a god fitted to harmonize the whole country. Lindsay believed that Christ was the God who should rule the spiritual realm, and we have seen that part of his diary where he recorded that Hebraism had triumphed in his soul. But no one can say that Christ has been a mollifying influence reducing all elements to one substance. He has rather been a syncretic deity who has kept the sword drawn and the zealot full of wrath and slaughter. He has been far from that Dorian Apollo, the god of order, of music and of beauty, who presided over the philosophy of Pythagoras and was selected to rule Plato's city of the Perfect. There are many centrifugal forces in America proceeding from a variety of churches; and Lindsay's restlessness and wandering are centrifugal; they are characteristically American, they are in part the result of lacking a calm god like the Dorian Apollo. Nevertheless Lindsay held to his "Gospel of Beauty," and tried to make Christ its king. Nothing better describes Lindsay's soul pilgrimage, and his message to his fellows than those words of the Mantinean Sibyl in the Symposium when discussing the doctrine of love. "For the doctrine of love," she said, "or of being conducted therein by another, —beginning from these beautiful objects here below ever to be going up higher, with that other beauty in view; using them as steps of a ladder; mounting from the love of

one fair person to the love of two; and from the love of
two to the love of all; and from the love of beautiful persons to the love of beautiful employments, and from the love
of beautiful employments to the love of beautiful kinds of
knowledge; till he passes from degrees of knowledge to that
knowledge which is the knowledge of nothing less save the
absolute Beauty itself, and knows it at length as in itself
it really is. At this moment of life, dear Socrates, said the
Mantinean Sibyl, if at any moment man truly lives, be-
holding the absolute Beauty, it will appear beyond the comparison of gold, or raiment," or beautiful persons as creatures of flesh. This too was what Lindsay was often trying
to say; and this is the creed of democracy. Of this passion
he would beget virtue, the mystic child, "born of this mystic
intellectual commerce or connubium of the imaginative reason with ideal beauty; and reared it will become dear to
God, and if any man may be immortal he will be."

Like Plato, too, Lindsay was a lover, and by love would
have power over the city and its life. With Plato, lovers
were the cornerstone of the ideal state. Whitman sang of
comrades having arms of love about each other all over this
land of America. Lindsay would have his magical Springfield a place where the citizens did not strive, did not hate,
did not cheat, destroy, practise any injustice, where they
had communion with fields and trees, and beautiful architecture and rhythmic dancing and song. So Heracleitus
would have had it; so would Rousseau have had it. When
Lindsay chanted of Saint Francis he was celebrating peace
and love; when he worshipped Buddha he was calling America to war upon all manner of destroying lusts. If one would
see Lindsay as a lover, as a prophet of the future America,
as a gatherer of those to make the Perfect City, he may do
so by reading the poem "These Are the Young," to be
found in *Going to the Stars*, published in 1926. A new mob,
speaking an alien tongue, alien to the old and the cynical,

passes by like Olympian white butterflies of flame. They are calling "brother," "sister" to each other. They are a separate race, a chosen people. They are the young! The poignancy of this poem lies in the fact that Lindsay no longer felt himself young, and he perhaps imagined his dreams and songs unintelligible to the new race taking the field of life, yet how he loved these athletes and riders of horses! Lindsay not only had the madness of the poet, but what Plato called "the enthusiasm of the ideas," the fourth form of madness, "wherein when any one, seeing the beauty that is here below, and having a reminiscence of the true, feels, or finds his wings fluttering upward in his eagerness to soar above, but unable like a bird looking towards the sky, heedless of things below he is charged with unsoundness of mind."

These butterflies of flame, full of a holy grace, these young are singing too! So did the boys and girls sing in the Lacedæmonian schools, and learn everything by heart so to sing it, and thus put their beauty and strength to the service of divine Hellas. These are the young! So should they do for the glory of America. The Greeks danced, so should they dance in Lindsay's Magical Springfield; and themes should be danced, as they were long ago in theatres scooped out of the hills, and finished with blocks of stone. We have seen that one of Lindsay's earliest poems, one which he took with him on the tramp West in 1912, and incorporated in the Booth volume of 1913 was the one entitled "On the Building of Springfield." It was not to be built large, but by countless generations of souls. Every citizen was to be joined to it as to a church; and in the city music should grow and beauty be unchained; and science, machinery, and trade made slaves of the city, and deposed from their materialistic rulerships. In this city no man should rule who held his money dear. Parks should be laid out with Phidian ornament; songs should be sung having the virility and the richness of the Elizabethan times. The western glory thus should rise; and if it does not the cities were doomed. Men on the desert dream of water, and men in prison dream of green fields. And many have been the gifted youth in Illinois who dreamed these Lindsay dreams, but never sang them. They were crushed by materialism, they were broken by Philistine persecution, they were suffocated by the fat Prairie, and hunted down by the factory spirit which swelled the purses of slaughterhouse men, steel men, brokers and bankers, who made Chicago a soul possessed by torturing devils, whether those of the wronged Indians of long ago, or of the revenging souls of men, women, and children who were used and broken for profits, as hogs at the packing houses were utilized for commerce down to the bristles on their tails. Lindsay endured the crucifixion which he called "the usual Middle West crucifixion of the artist," but instead of turning satirist he sang of Mystic and Magical Springfield, the city to be. It should not be rich and populous, as Plato's city of the Perfect was not to be; but it should be morally strong, it should be beautiful in spirit. In those years between 1909 and 1912, when Lindsay returned from New York, having made no success there that was visible to Springfield, it was easy enough to point to him as a kind of fool; and America as a whole could share in the Springfield estimation of him. But let them remember the dreams of Plato, of Bacon, and of many bearers of civilization for the benefit of the common man. This depreciation of Lindsay was helped by the fact that he did entertain many "medicinable lies," as Plato calls them, particularly with reference to the heroes; and he had Whitman's fine dreams like inventing for America classical allusions of her own, and of making for America her own mythology which passed the understanding of sensible people.

Lindsay said of himself that he had a limited understanding of rhythm, and it may be true that he did not know a spondee from a trochee, or a line of hexameter from one of pentameter. At least, if he didn't, that ignorance did not impugn his inner ear which was rhythmical in the highest and most original sense. He was a bard, a builder by Amphion power. He might have written as Plato did, "is not education in music of the greatest importance, because more than anything else, rhythm and harmony make their way down into the utmost part of the soul, and take hold upon it with the utmost force, bringing with them rightness of form, and rendering its form right, if one be correctly trained; if not the opposite? . . . Yes, he answered, it seems to me that for reasons such as these their education should be in music." Lindsay's drawings, bad as some of them are, even his vine-like Spencerian scrolls, speak of rhythm; the grotesque "The Village Improvement Parade" has rhythm; music is at the bottom of his poetry, and informs all his ethical fervors. Lindsay had a fine conscience of art; he needed to be cut and carved, to be tightened by some astringent discipline which would have taken away his jungle luxuriance. He needed to master facts, and to polish his jewels with that mastery.

The matter of hieroglyphics runs so much through Lindsay's thinking that we encounter it everywhere in his prose. It crops out as already mentioned in *The Art of the Moving Picture;* it is referred to many times in the prefaces to his *Collected Poems*, and it threads its occult way in *The Golden Book of Springfield.* He wrote that his pictures of the censers might stand for a conjugation of the verb, "To have vision." And like Plato, whose intellectual absorptions emptied his purse, Lindsay went broke more than once printing his drawings of magical Springfield and his hieroglyphics. Lindsay's eye, which was really lacking in penetration in many particulars, as for faces for example, and for reading men as men, was not helped by the welter of confusion which was about him in Springfield and in America. He could well say that the American mind had become an overgrown forest of unorganized pictures, and that the whole world showed a like state by its grotesque and unsynthesized political cartooning. It was natural, therefore, that he wanted to fetch forth the essential nature of the American mind, of America, of Springfield, of many things by hieroglyphs which would settle his vision as to their nature, while it fixed their character in an art form. He wanted to get a hieroglyph of the United States. He had Swedenborg's passion for making everything stand externally for some inner nature, as a horse as the embodiment of the spirit of duty; a bee as the embodiment of industry and the like, down to apple trees, weeds, and all living things. So when he was repelling the charge that he was a jazz poet he could go so far as to say that "The Wedding of the Lotus and the Rose" was not a jazz poem, that is not a scherzo, a joke in rhythm; but that it was a hieroglyph essentially, a symbol in words of a union of East and West. And so it was that he could see California in the likeness of a whale, North and South Dakota as a blanket, and Illinois as an ear of corn. His imaginative mind ran always to symbols, figures, pictures and resemblances, and with a Swedenborgian faculty he strove to bind together the whole visible scene of life by some unifying tie or principle. He announced that his business was not jazzing, but that Springfield and vision seeing, and adventure and hieroglyphs were his business. He might have left others to say this evident thing for him. The word jazz was affixed to him and his work, out of that American smartness which must have a nickname for every prominent person, and by those epiphytes of New York's Knickerbockerdom who have never produced anything from the days of Nathaniel Parker Willis to the present hour. He had tried to express the United States in cartoons and could not do it; but he could see Johnny Appleseed as a Swedenborgian, and a hiero-

[273]

glyph; he could see the faces of audiences as hieroglyphs. When he went touring he took Mystic Springfield with him. He wanted it torn down and rebuilt according to the visions that might have appeared to an Egyptian. The hieroglyph to him was a minute cell of thought, the alphabet with which might be spelled the sentences of the new vision of Springfield and America. With the hieroglyph he was fighting business America, and materialistic Chicago, which he would have given some pictorial exponent signifying slaughter, cruelty and blood, a Hittite fierceness having its great modern capital, an Aztec City of Mexico with its stone pyres and its knives of obsidian and its human sacrifices. The Map of the Universe and Mystic Springfield oriented out of that Swedenborg, Single Tax group in Springfield, of which we have already spoken.

Thus the poetical and ethical passion of Plato were both his in these visions, and they are not to be too lightly treated, not even when they are lost in the jungles of meaningless imagery in *The Golden Book of Springfield*. Lindsay said that America will take long to ripen; he did not think that The Village Improvement Parade would bring quickly the city of the Perfect. "That flower town shall come," is the final word of his expectation. He knew by singing of the walls of China that America might not stand forever, as Rome did not stand. All his celebration of Virginia and Jefferson and democracy was opposed to the European ideas, greeds and feudal principles, which never belonged in this new soil, and which our best minds have tried to root out and keep from spreading. Lindsay knew that these exotic growths would likely destroy America at last, as even now they have obscured the American vision. Business knows no state lines. It is that international thing which has no patriotism, and no care for man at large except to turn him to dollars. But it is like Midas with ass's ears, whose identity cannot be buried, but of whom every roadway weed whispers in infamous words. All of this is the background of *The Golden Book of Springfield*. It must be reviewed as one of Lindsay's prose books, with whatever profit as the result.

CHAPTER XV

AN analytical index containing only proper names, real or fictional, and principal subjects, such as cities, famous buildings, famous books and the like, mounts to 404 themes, or reference matters which Lindsay wove into the 329 pages of *The Golden Book of Springfield*. It is a form of story-telling for which Lindsay had little or no talent. He could handle enough of fiction or history for the purposes of a chant, a lyric; but in this book he undertook what Morris and Bellamy had done in their way, with the result that it is neither good sociology nor good prophecy. There may be seeds in it which will make Amaranth orchards sometime, as it may have been that some of the seed scattered by Johnny Appleseed produced some of the fine orchards of Michigan and the Middle West. Lindsay did not have great invention, not for story-telling anyway; he could not draw character; however, this book must be accepted as his attempt to sketch a new state. All radicals have these dreams. Lindsay had them in great measure; and we must take this book for what it is worth, and it is worth just what any literary curiosity is worth. It is difficult to condense this book; it is even hard to keep track of all the tendrils, and shoots which issue from the larger vines, and which in turn stem from the main trunk. All of these are tangled and impleached. They run this way and that. They run over and under. They deceive the hand that would thread them along, by curving about, or ending; and suddenly one finds that he is following a different vine altogether. They are like a grape vine which has grown for years up and around an old house, and over its roof, and above its windows. They are the Jungles of Heaven, this *Golden Book of Springfield.* To condense this story within readable limits, yet not to slight it, is not an easy task. But the result is measurably as follows:

David Carson was the Campbellite pastor in Springfield, whose plea was that all professing Christians should call themselves Christians, and that all of them should be united as one church under that name. In the pastor's study was a picture of Alexander Campbell, which was an heirloom as rare to Southerners as old spinning wheels and old Bibles were to Plymouth Rock and Manhattan Island. Also in Carson's home were bound volumes of Campbell's *Christian Baptist and Millennial Harbinger.* We are made by these reverences to forget that Campbell opposed the emancipation of the Negro, and that he predicted the Second Advent in 1866.

A Prognosticators' Club about to be formed was the fictional device of the apocalypse soon to happen. Somewhere near was Anne Morrison, a descendant of Johnny Appleseed, the latter having been always honored by Campbellites and Swedenborgians. Lindsay interpolated here that Johnny Appleseed "was three times deserving the laurels of Thoreau, and nearly every worth while crown of Whitman." Another likely member of the club was at hand in the person of Eloise Terry, a rich woman, who took a decent part in politics and social settlement work. Lindsay all the while is the interlocutor of this fantasy, but he is also Saint Scribe an objective character; and as the reader passes from 1918 to 2018, and from room to room with the wings of the Golden Book, where characters change through rebirth, he would do well to concentrate his wits in order not to be bewildered by the maze. Carson, therefore, and Lindsay sent out invitations for the formation of the Prognosticators' Club. John Fletcher joined. He was a doubter of high position, a money man, yet religious. In brief he was a Republican. The next member was Clara Horton, who is perhaps Lindsay's public school teacher in this disguise. The next was Gregory Webster, an artist, once familiar with the boulevards of Paris. The next was Nathan Levi, the son of a Jewish rabbi. Then followed Margaret Evans, a Christian Science reader; and after her a prophet preaching hell, once a Y. M. C. A. physical director, perhaps a satire upon some of the men in this institution whom Lindsay encountered South or in New Jersey. Then came Ruth Everett who was a welfare worker in France in the World War.

When the club assembled, the first vision of the future was seen by Carson, the pastor, who by the time of the Mystic Year of 2018 had been re-born three or four times. At that idyllic period he was a Catholic priest, and was known as Saint Friend, the giver of bread. He presided over the new Cathedral, as fine as Notre Dame, which was called Saint Peter and Saint Paul, and stood at the corner of 6th and Reynolds Streets, Springfield. Carson thus vaticinated, and as he did so the other members of the club fell into heavenly visions. They saw a book of air, gleaming with spiritual gold, which came flying through the walls. It was a book of homilies addressed to New Springfield; for suddenly the time was now 2018, the Mystic Year, and Springfield stood transformed. Then Anne Morrison, the florist, told how the Book was revealed to her.

First she saw the days of Johnny Appleseed returned, for in this Mystic Year Springfield had fully developed the Great Amaranth Apple Orchards, from seeds given by Hunter Kelly, one of the founders of Newtown, Calhoun, or Springfield, as the first chapter of this book recounts. Now he who ate of the Amaranth Apple was filled with love of eternal beauty, and Springfield had taken it as its symbol. In 2018 one of the teachings in Springfield was Democracy, of which the symbol was the Golden Rain Tree, brought from New Harmony, Indiana. By 2018 Anne Morrison, through

[278]

re-births, had become Roxana Grey, and as such she saw an outdoor statue of Johnny Appleseed, to which she walked and by which she stood on the great day of the Mystic Year. Suddenly she was aware of an egg-shaped, rose-colored boulder in the front yard of the governor; and as she was looking at it, a bolt from the clear sky struck it, and the Golden Book came forth, and soared to the Shrine of Flowers. Then she lost track of the Book; and the next day she found it on her altar, with its wings gone, but lying open to be read. So now she read the Book, whose doctrines were those of flowers. But the margins had many texts from Swedenborg, from the Old and New Testament, from Adam Smith, Karl Marx, Henry George, together with wise sayings by two local characters: Joseph Bartholdi Michael of the blacksmith tradition, and Black Hawk Boone, lately of Cairo, Illinois. The visions of Joseph Smith at Cumorah Hill do not surpass these, nor those which quickly follow. For now the Book floated in and out of rooms, and every time it returned it presented a more difficult teaching, as though a work by Henry George were changed into one by Swedenborg.

One after one the members of the Prognosticators' Club were re-born in their fancies into the year 2018. The Book went into edition after edition, and was circulated among the scholars and artists of Europe and Asia by the grace of their colleagues who were attending the World's Fair of the University of Springfield.

Gregory Webster, the old artist, once a war man, had become a pacifist in 2018; but for wishing to recall the days of the Czar and Carnegie's Hague Tribunal, he was sent to the World Government Prison in Springfield. Nathan Levi had become Rabbi Terence Ezekiel, a rank heretic, who was for the photoplay, and crossed swords with Saint Friend, who opposed it, at the Cathedral. To Rabbi Ezekiel's synagogue came wise of all the world; and Ezekiel Oaks were planted all around the world to symbolize his rule. In 2018, at the beginning of service in the synagogue the Golden Book floated in, as genii, giants, and the like were made to perform in *The Arabian Nights.* It had six wings now, like some of the beasts of Revelation, woven, however, of moonbeams. It settled on the desk and, opening, showed prophecies of the soul of Springfield. The Rabbi now saw Lindsay, or perhaps it was only the interlocutor of the tale, sitting in the audience. But now the Christian Scientist, once Margaret Evans, and now Rachel Madison, declared that she had seen this person in the Christian Scientist congregation. Is she right? For she declared that the Book was not a Golden Book, but was made of silver. Whatever it was the air was now full of music as the Book appeared, just where is not clear, whether in church or in the room where the prognosticators were seeing visions. The Book now had six wings like celestial swans.

Mary Timmons, a Negress, now joined the group. She saw the Book, but she insisted it was nothing but the Bible, opened at the Beatitudes. She had seen it in her church when the congregation was singing "Swing Low, Sweet Chariot." The scene now changes.

Gwendolyn Charles, a club member, was directing in 2018, on All Saints Day, a motion picture. Her high-toned enterprises, like grand opera, ran at a loss. The picture was the story of Hunter Kelly, and of his devotion to Johnny Appleseed. Kelly had died several times during a century, and every year the devil had dug Kelly up and showed him Springfield. Every time Kelly had said, "Take me back to my torture. The city is not yet started." Finally, in 2019, he was willing to trust the town to go on, because the citizens were then eating the Apple Amaranth. Having made this discovery Kelly built himself a cell in heaven out of broken fragments of forgotten palaces in far jungles. There he wrote the Golden Book. By day he lived the life of Saint

Scribe, that is Lindsay, who became the teacher of Saint Friend. John Fletcher, the doubter, had been re-born as Mayor Sims. He saw the Golden Book rejected. Malcontents arose, strikers rioted, and were shot down—yet it is 2018. Finally, only one copy of the Book was extant; but it was full of sedition, it was tabooed, and was passed around surreptitiously in Springfield. At last it was dropped into an abandoned coal shaft; and having no wings now sank.

Joseph Bartholdi Michael, of blacksmith tradition, had a father who made the Avanel blade, longer than the largest cavalry sword. He shoed horses and ideas, and hammered souls into shape on the anvil. He had been a student under Percy Mackaye and others, and had established a pageantry calendar which the City Commissioners had adopted. In the Mystic Year the cottages of the blacksmith clan were all over Springfield, each having a flag decorated with six anvils and six hammers.

Black Hawk Boone had the following vision: While Michael was shoeing a white pony the Book flew in the shop and settled in the arms of Avanel, who turned out later to be Saint Scribe's companion in many saunters about New Springfield. The Book now contained a new chapter for the World Government, "based on the life and teachings of Springfield's deathless citizen, Abraham Lincoln." Now this work of Lindsay's becomes more settled narrative. The story is started. Lindsay enters the scene as Saint Scribe. He has died, but hears through the grave a galloping and shrieking. He comes to life and goes to the public square, where he buys a copy of *The Register* and sees that the year is 2018. It is Avanel who has awakened him, and they start out together for a walk. Lindsay finds the shops the same, the advertisements the same, the same Springfield in every way, though he is endowed with new powers. He wears several bodies by turns. First he kneels before the image of the Virgin in Saint Peter and Saint Paul; an hour later he is City Hall stenographer for Slick Slack Kopensky, the mayor. **Later** he clerks for a justice of the peace. Meanwhile he cowers in the presence of Avanel, who is supercilious and curt. Avanel's story, her ancestry and alliances and occupations are too numerous to mention here. In truth, Lindsay has just returned from art study in New York, and is being received as a kind of bore. No less he starts art classes. And so he goes about with Avanel, looking at the ancestral flags in front of the houses, and at the International Government flag displayed everywhere. They go finally to the Sunset Towers, and there climb the Truth Tower, and look over the Lincoln Memorial Park. The new architecture of the city has been done by a Thibetan boy. Here in one of these towers Lindsay and Avanel, on another occasion, have dinner, and look over the city and the cottages, which are dominated by a complex rhythm and are of violet hue. Some have gilded roofs and cupolas. Springfield now extends over the whole country, and has many groves where the titan Amaranth Apple vines rise on trellises high above all other trees. There are also many parks, some named after members of the iota subscripts of literary New York of 1914–20, perhaps as a placatory oblation. The Negro districts have beautiful, flamboyant jungle houses.

The Golden Book now recounts political fights of the same tenor as those that happen at the present time. The women vote, to be sure; but they are also in all occupations, from locksmiths to billposters, and cat doctors, and what not. Black Hawk Boone is running for mayor, and New Harmony sends recruits to him, but perhaps not voters. For Springfield has become a city after the New Harmony model. The fight goes on. The political machinery includes the city hall dragnet with drug stores, coffee houses, and dance halls. The one source of all political corruption, the saloon, has been ended. Lindsay is glad that in a former life he was a member of the Anti-Saloon League. Coca Cola, Bevo, with mysterious elaborations of coffee and tea and spiced drinks from the jungles of South America prevail; and the soda fountains riot in prosperity. The old bookstore remains, the same magazines are on the counters, the automobile horns are deafening in the streets. Wild Singaporian music pours from places in front of which are Asiatic lanterns. There are Yellow Dance Halls, all under a syndicate which is manned by Kusko, a coffee-house man, running a place in particular called The Hall of Velaska. He sells knockout coffee. All in all, the politics is as bad as it is reputed to be under Tammany. Lindsay goes from place to place, visiting The Opium Fish, The Spanish Gypsy, The Whing Whang Tree, The Mock Duck, and other places where "they unroll the beautiful ensnaring legends of the Malay peninsula."

Days pass, all recorded in diary fashion. Lindsay or Saint Scribe goes about with Avanel, who frowns upon him. However, she tells him that there are three orders connected with the cathedral: one is the Order of the Blessed Bread of the More Liberal Observance; one is the Order of the Blessed Bread of the Strict Observance; the third is the Order of the Pilgrimage, founded by Saint Scribe of the Shrines, by Lindsay, in a word. Then Lindsay and Avanel make the rounds of the ice cream parlors, and visit the place of Najim, run by a Syrian. A question has arisen concerning the lease for aeroplanes, and there is controversy over the matter of uniform rents for their use. After a hard contest between the political factions of the New City, all are given equal rights in the air, as Avanel who has now grown kinder and become the interlocutor's love rejoices at sunset with Saint Friend over the great consummation. But this is followed by an anti-Singapore panic, too tedious to describe. Something more comprehensible can be given.

Avanel and her lover, that is, this interlocutor, dine by the gates of the Inner Wall. They have visited Lincoln's monument, the first shrine of Saint Scribe, the grave of Hunter Kelly. At table, Avanel breaks the bread of Saint Friend, and quotes from the Gospel of Saint Luke. The bells all over the city begin to ring. Avanel says, "The trouble with this breaking of bread is that it is a pledge to break our bodies. I do not want to break mine yet for a long time." Her companion then indulges the hope that the body of Christ, the whole human race, will be raised from the dead.

Through the sermons of Saint Friend, the Yellow Dance Halls are voted out. An incident now is the visit of the interlocutor with the old artist to the Hall of Velaska, where they see the portrait of Mara of Singapore, and a fairy fashion plate of a gown to be worn by an exceedingly wealthy bumblebee; also a picture of the devil making candy, one of the sewing-machine of fate, and the like. Later, he and the old artist have an evening together, and go to a lunchroom, where the talk is about the Yellow Halls, and of Kusko who owns them all and uses them, as Slick Slack Kopensky and Mayor Sims want him to do. The talk at the tables is loud.

A strange episode now ensues. Surot Hurdenburg, who took the pledge of the lordship of Christ and swore to support the Constitution of the World Government, is lynched; yet Springfield goes on with the delights of summer; June brides march, and the towers are gorgeous from nightfall till midnight. But Avanel and her lover are ensnared by devil's gold, and the Utopia wobbles along. Later, this narrator, this lover, who had a sense of being an Anglo-Saxon, feels that he has turned Malay in this year of 2018. He is a slave in the house of the Man from Singapore. But as a Malay he witnessed the conversion of Kopensky to the Cocaine Buddha. After this he is taken by the Thibetan Boy beyond the North Star where he is shown the true Buddha.

Then follow the lynching of Black Hawk Boone and the

mysterious stabbing of Kopensky. Three months pass, and no one is punished for these atrocities. But the Golden Book comes down to Avanel, who is mourning for the sad state of Springfield. This gives her courage; and she leads her people against Singapore, that wicked nation which has declared war on the World Flag. Seven years after Saint Friend tells his vision as it came to him when the Book first appeared; and Avanel goes forth and sows the thistle of dreams, the Apple Amaranth seeds, the acorns of Ezekiel, the seed of the Golden Rain Tree; and new visions are thereby bred. Avanel and her lover prepare to found schools of young prophets. Hunter Kelly tells of the tomorrows of Illinois, and of saints to be born in the image of Johnny Appleseed and Abraham Lincoln. After this Avanel and her lover rise in a boat through the air, following the Amaranth Vine, and trace its branches through the Jungles of Heaven. They then defy the devil's gold, and find the empty sack of Johnny Appleseed. And suddenly the teller of this story finds himself back in the Springfield of 1920, and Avanel is one hundred years away.

This is *The Golden Book of Springfield* which came out of such long years of meditation, and so many entries in diaries, as we have already related. Allegories are good in so far as real things are aptly symbolized, and by that process made to gain in imaginative wonder, and be made more significant by figurative interpretation. As Lindsay could not think straight in prose, and was unequipped for a sociological study like this, it was inevitable that he could not imagine and choose fitting and correct symbols, and accurately apply them. A discussion of his poetry will prove vastly more fruitful.

CHAPTER XVI

THE estate of poetry in America was especially feeble when Lindsay published his General Booth poem. Whitman had been dead more than twenty years, and no one had come along to carry forward his ideas of an American art. During the latter part of his life, and after his death, poetry was in the hands of those who made poetry a matter of fancy work and embroidery. The magazines were controlled by such poetasters. The days were those of manikins. Moody had given great promise and some performance; Markham's heart was right, and on occasions his voice had volume and always sincerity; but on the whole from Whitman's day to Lindsay's, stars of different magnitude emerged and then winked out or went dim; while such men as Stoddard, Aldrich, Stedman, composing a party of influence in the field of poetry, had died, leaving no inheritance. Riley was living on, but as an invalid after 1910. This, in brief, was the condition of the poetical street when Booth came along beating his drum and shouting, "Are you washed in the blood of the Lamb?"

Lindsay, as we have seen, had been in New York for about five years, from 1904 to about 1909; and by making the rounds of the magazines he knew what their editors wanted in the way of poetry, if they wanted anything, which was unlikely. During these years Gilder was the editor of *The Century;* and, being himself a writer of respectable verse, may be accredited with an interest in the art. The difference between him and Lindsay may be clearly seen by comparing his little poems on Bethlehem and the like with Lindsay's

"Dear Heart of God," with its welling, crying passion for peace. There is no rhetoric in it. It is all heart's blood. But Lindsay was born with a personality, with character. Faith and vision were in his blood. He was never like a poetaster looking for something to write about, and working with virtuosity on his technique. It was in his nature to make war upon the whole tone, temper and morale of post-Civil War America; and there was a good deal more of his heart south of Mason and Dixon's line than north of it. He had fought to live the life of happiness, what John Cowper Powys has called the ichthyosaurus life in which a sensuality concerned with beauty, truth, and reality floods the soul with peace and satisfaction. We have seen, too, from his diaries that his ideas of poetry concerned themselves with catching the American voice, taking it out of hymns and popular songs, but somehow capturing it.

The time in which Lindsay emerged with his Booth poem was exactly like the time of which Goethe wrote in 1831, in description of German letters. "At present," he said, "everything runs in technical grooves, and the critical gentlemen begin to wrangle whether in a rhyme an S should correspond with an S, and not with Sz. If I were young and reckless enough I would purposely offend all such technical caprices: I would use alliteration, assonance, false rhyme, just according to my own will and convenience; but at the same time I would attend to the main thing, and endeavor to say so many good things that every one would be attracted to read and remember them."

Lindsay did not indulge in many radicalisms, such as false rhyme and assonance; but in manner and subject matter he was as radical as the German master wished to be if he had been young again. We must remember, too, as bearing upon Lindsay's keeping to his own path, that by 1913 very importunate schools of poetry were flourishing in France, where one of the chief innovators was Paul Fort, who printed his "Many Things" on the page as prose, though it possessed rhythmic swing, and intricate rhyming, and other verse decorations. By this time Reedy's *Mirror* in Saint Louis was publishing translations of the *vers libre* experiments of Europe; but there is no evidence that they impinged upon Lindsay's attention. In a certain delicacy and fairy fancy there is some kinship between Maeterlinck and Lindsay, but Maeterlinck had nothing to teach Lindsay. Neither had Rémy de Gourmont, André Gide, or Stéphane Mallarmé. Parnassians, Symbolists, and Radicals passed Lindsay by without notice from him. He was not interested in theories of sensuous flow, in presenting images for their own sake, in inducing hypnotic conditions by repetitious rhythms, in refinements, in exoticisms, in neo-romanticism, druidism, dadaism, paroxysm, or vitalism. His interest, his passion was America, the American heroes, American democracy, beauty, and religion; and in finding the soul of the U. S. A. and giving it voice. So on the one hand he was oblivious of the dead corpse of poetry lying about him mesmerically squeaking for culture, technique, and form; and on the other hand he did not hear the raging schools quickly arising around him. He exercised his original freedom by writing the Booth poem, and later "The Kallyope Yell," and "The Santa Fé Trail." From the beginning poetry with Lindsay was not technique, not fine writing, not culture, but it was courage, faith, vision, great belief in American democracy. From the first he saw life with the exuberance of Whitman and nothing less, and with the imagination of Coleridge plus Joseph Smith, plus Jakob Boehme, and plus Swedenborg. Like all the genuine poets he knew that nature was vastly greater than any inner check.

At the time that Lindsay became famous a new sort of dance music, which had been growing up for more than a decade, was coming to full tide. Negro comic songs and tunes like "All Coons Look Alike to Me," "Ain't Goin' to

Weep No More," "Take Your Clothes and Go," "Just Because She Made Dem Goo-Goo Eyes," and many others that swept over America, had led to dance music like "The Merry Whirl," "Hello, Frisco," and "The Alabama Jubilee," "That Lovin' Rag," and many others. Before this time a catchy time piece called "Too Much Mustard" had come over from France with a fast one-step; and then there were "The Bunny Hug," "The Rag," "The Lame Duck," "The Drag," "The Tango," all modifications of the one-step. All this meant that formal dances like the waltz and the polka were giving way to any extemporaneous step in which people with music in their feet could express it to music which was equally spontaneous and unconventional. There was great dancing over the world just before the World War, just as the American Indians go on the war dance before they start after their enemies. This freedom in dancing and in dance music was a contemporaneous phenomenon of Lindsay's poems. Long before this time he had been brooding upon a way to put his own themes into the voice of his time. That voice turned out to be the hymns of the pioneers, but perhaps not so distinctively as the syncopated music which came along, and carried aloft his first successful poems. Lindsay resented the epithet of jazz; but Beethoven nearly a hundred years before him had put in the scherzo of the B-flat quartet (No. 6) the exciting accentuations, the pauses, and the silences which Lindsay blew into his humorous and many-voiced lines. These Beethoven artifices, however, are much more conspicuous in "The Santa Fé Trail," and some other poems to be considered, than in the Booth poem.

The Booth poem captured America. *The Review of Reviews* called it glorious and touching, and both poignant in conception and expression, and the despair of imitation. "It is perhaps the most remarkable poem of a decade," were other words of this tribute. William Dean Howells was at the time the veteran contributing editor of *Harper's Maga-*

zine, and he wrote, "it is a sensible relief to turn from our uncertainty about these 'songs' [referring to one of the usual books of verse of the day] which do not really sing, to Mr. Nicholas Vachel Lindsay's book, where the songs begin their music with the cymbal clash and bass drum boom of that fine brave poem, 'General William Booth Enters Into Heaven,' that makes the heart leap; and the little volume abounds in meters and rhymes that thrill and gladden one. Here is no shredding of prose, but much of oaten stop and pastoral song, such as arises amid the hum of the Kansas harvest fields, and fills the empyrean from the expanses of the whole great West." Later, but in the wake of the acclaim which came to Lindsay through other books, John Masefield wrote, "It has been possible to say of every other American poet of this day that he was kindred to some American or English poet; but no one knows the parentage of Lindsay. He sings America, but not in the White-man's key; he turns sometimes to gnomic and mystical chants, but they are aloft in a different space from that which Emerson's muse visited. Sometimes he has the repetend in a way that reminds one of Poe; but the repetend is a matter of manner only, it is not one of substance; and the haunts of Poe's and Lindsay's imaginations are as far apart from each other as those of any two poets in the world. . . . He sings of America as lustily as Whitman did, but it is a different America, and a more refined liberty . . . his utterance has been transmuted by the strange genius which is his, which speaks not its sources and inspirations, but Lindsay himself." These are judicious words, and all true.

A glance at the Booth poem will show how subtly and intimately its quantities and accents voice the vigorous psychology of Lindsay, how they communicate the intonations of his speech and his laugh, his cries of rejoicing, his modulated reverences; how they pulse and rise and fall with the very breath of the man, as he breathed in the flesh; how they express his physical and, what is more a matter of genius, his spiritual diaphragm. He spoke loudly and laughed loudly; he walked firmly, planting his first step down with the emphasis of spasmodically released energy. The Booth poem is written so. Take the first line:

"Booth led boldly with his big bass drum."

The first foot is a molossus, that is, one of three long syllables. Syncopation is achieved by the use of pyrrhics, that is, feet composed of two short syllables. He interspersed trochees for swing and vigor, and anapests for running, romping, racing, banging drum effects, and for marching time. They are what Coleridge called the swift anapests which throng, "with a leap and a bound." Lindsay's genius dictated this fine onomatopœia. He did not by any rationale of verse say to himself that the drum speaks in the molossus, in spondees, and that people marching plant a foot down firmly and then lift the other one; nor that Salvationists hurrying to the corner go half leaping and bounding. He had in his mind the idea, the picture of the Salvation Army; his internal ear did the rest. It was a stroke of genius which no culture, no thinking, no discipline in verse, could ever have attained, or ever can attain. The very title of the poem is a miracle of inspiration, as very many of his titles are, such as "The Golden Whales of California," "The Congo," "Old, Old, Old, Old Andrew Jackson," and many others. Often after capturing his theme and its substance in marvellous titles of this sort, the execution of the poem failed him. He broke its wings in its capture, which is another way of saying that a man's strength can well give out. Lindsay went as far as an American could go in solving the difficulty of an American classical allusion, in this and many other poems. If the East cannot be interested in log cabins, in Jackson, in Bryan, in the prairies, even in Honest Old Abe, except as a mask with which to conceal money plots by wearing it at banquets and in patriotic parades, still all America knows and knew the Salvation Army, and it is as understandable to the cities over the land as the dances and revelry were with which the Corybantes celebrated the rites of Cebele in ancient Phrygia. When correct and formal writers have the field correctness and formality may be the only virtues; but when a Lindsay comes along intelligent judges join with Goethe and Havelock Ellis in favor of originality and feeling which are strong enough to make the reader forget the words in admiration for the substance. G. K. Chesterton said that Lindsay's Pegasus was a real horse.

Lindsay published in all eight volumes of verse, beginning with the Booth book and ending with *Every Soul Is a Circus*, published in 1929. This list does not take in his *Collected Poems*, brought out in one volume first in 1923, and in a revised form in 1925; nor a volume of *Selected Poems* published in 1931; nor a book made up of his Johnny Appleseed poems, and bearing the title *Johnny Appleseed*, published in 1930; nor the *Daniel Jazz* published in England in 1920, which included poems previously issued in America. *The Collected Poems* contained all his verse, except that of the volumes entitled *Going to the Sun* (1923) ; *Going to the Stars* (1926) ; *The Candle in the Cabin* (1926) ; and *Every Soul Is a Circus* (1929). He divided the *Collected Poems* into eleven sections, entitling them "Moon Poems," "Politics," "Songs Based on American Hieroglyphics," and so forth. It is needless to name all the titles of the eleven sections. The point now is that all the poems he wrote down to the last can be grouped under those heads which he made in 1923; and in considering his work as a whole, we shall proceed by that classification, though not in the order that he adopted.

Some attention must be paid before beginning a study

of Lindsay's poems to those matters in his various prefaces, which have not already been touched upon. These prefaces are very long, and contain much irrelevant observation, and much illogical reasoning. He was very proud, for one thing, that his poems could be danced; and yet he said that all poetry is first and last for the inner ear, which is absolutely true. Havelock Ellis, in that inspiring book called *The Dance of Life*, wrote that, "If we are indifferent to the art of dancing, we have failed to understand, not merely the supreme manifestation of physical life, but also the supreme symbol of spiritual life." This is profoundly true; yet it does not follow that poems should be danced. Where "virtue is deep and silent" there is music, and where there is fine ceremony there is music, too. These are Confucian tenets, and of great import. The turning from right to left while chanting the choruses of the Greek tragic writers is a part of the dignified drama of those works; and if those choruses were spoken without action they would degenerate to oratory. But it must be remembered that such dancing is for the eye, even as script is for the eye; and by this process the eye and the ear are wedded. All is rhythm. Now, after Lindsay said that poetry is for the inner ear, he appealed to his readers to judge his verse by his thoughts of painting, and not to judge it phonetically. One feels that he was here dodging the designation of jazz. But nothing can be clearer than that the sound of his verse is better than the visual qualities, which partake sometimes of his awkward drawings. In the preface to *The Candle in the Cabin* will be found his theories about the Spencerian system of handwriting as a principle of a school of art. And he went on there to say that the arabesques of the Arabs were evolved from scripts and texts of the Koran; and that the painting of the Chinese and Japanese came from the brush work of their languages. Likewise, he insisted that their architecture rose from their ideograms. But all this being true its application

[293]

is remote to Lindsay's poetry. Like many poets, like psychics who perform mystical tricks, like Plato's poet, who wrote what he did not understand himself, Lindsay did not have a keen critical perspective upon himself. Whenever he tried to expound his art theories, or his mechanics of verse, he was lost. Thus, when he said that "The Song of Lucifer" contained such rhythm as he understood, he failed to take into account that that poem was written in iambics as the dominant foot, while many of his poems ran characteristically to trochees and to anapests, to the molossus, and the pyrrhic.

During the revival of poetry in America, from about 1914 to about 1920, when many of the prominent poets of that period, as well as realistic novelists like Dreiser and Lewis, were depicting America, and trying to define its spirit and character, this one or the other one of those writers was selected as the best interpreter of the country, and the most faithful historian of its nature. But here, to determine a question like this we are led into the domain of metaphysics, we have to consider that eyes differ, and that any report is out of some particular eye. Fidelity may be settled upon finally by a sort of consensus of the best minds, just as the comparative excellence of literary works is adjudged at last. But, as bearing upon Lindsay's theories of the art of poetry, and as to whether he saw the country aright, and gave it reliable expression, a few words out of Aristotle will help the solution. For just as Lindsay saw the external world as no one else saw it, one might say that his calliope singing of America, and his chants of Springfield and other things were out of space and out of time, and bore no relation to any existing fact or thing.

That may be true altogether or in part only. But in the *Poetics* we are told that tragedy does not imitate life, but a conception of life, which avoids the disastrous reasoning of Plato that as poetry is an imitation of things, which are

[294]

themselves the external manifestation of ideas, the art of poetry is exercised in copying appearances; and the result is thus twice removed from the actuality. Thus defined, the art of poetry, according to Plato, is vicious and unworthy of a man of intellect. Plato had many sons, and along the way of the years they have derided Dante, and Blake, and Keats, and Poe; and in America they classified Lindsay with a species of strabismus and madness. But if poetry reflects nature and men, and is unnecessary, since nature and men may be had at first hand, yet what is it that does the reflecting? It must be the energy and the inspiration of the poet which give forth the imitation of themselves in appropriate and harmonious language. Imagination, with which Lindsay was greatly endowed, is the impelling influence of poetry. Lindsay's objects of imitation were not the Kansas wheat fields by which the touring cars were passing at sun up, but his conception of them, his reflect of the pageant which the actual procession created in his imagination. This pageant to Lindsay was more than the human events which externally composed it; and thus it was natural for Lindsay to seek symbols always and to try for hieroglyphics with which to body forth his internal vision. As Lindsay was a lyrical and not a dramatic poet, he experienced emotional moments which were more to him than the events which caused them; and when he was successful in capturing his own ecstasy concerning them he communicated that ecstasy to his readers; though sometimes his readers could not see the moment or the thing as he saw it. All his moral poems were expressions of his mental life at its highest and purest points; while in such poems he was especially the man, for as Longinus said, "Style is the man." Probably Lindsay knew nothing of Aristotle's *Poetics*, or Horace's *Ars Poetica;* and yet by adopting free and sometimes oratorical forms he was justified by Aristotle, who was the first critic to discard the artificial distinction drawn by fastidious metricists between poetry and prose. For prose forms can perform the imitation of heightened conceptions. Poetry can be written as prose, and prose as poetry. Lindsay needed no Wordsworthian example to use, as he did, the language employed by men, as he knew them. The poems on Bryan and others are proof of this fact.

In his formative years, when taking tramps over the country, Lindsay formulated his æsthetic creed, and the poems he wrote then and afterward were an expression of adherence to that creed. Lindsay did not seek primarily polish and culture and technique; he sought first the perfection of his own mind and nature; and thus he was worlds apart from those artists who do more for themselves than nature has done for them by giving them birth. The latter are often very successful in repainting the descent from the cross, or working over themes frequently interpreted before. Lindsay had an organic, internal development, and his poems came forth as naturally at last as the flower follows the growth of the stalk and the formation of the bud. We have already adverted to some articles of Lindsay's æsthetic and moral creed. The whole of it can be found in his *Collected Poems*, and *The Gospel of Beauty* in its diffusion over years and pages contains the material from which it can be condensed. One tenet of it is "Ugliness is a kind of misgovernment"; another is "Bad public taste is mob law," and another is, "A bad designer is to that extent a bad citizen," another is, "a well considered poverty may be exquisite." He favored all things that bring men together in sympathy, and therefore he was against the possessive instinct, and at war with materialistic America. *The Gospel of Beauty* produces no sanguine contests because the more who adopt the Gospel the greater satisfaction there is to all. Its æsthetic takes the hand of morality; and thus Lindsay had, like Shelley, moral courage and passion, as well as adoration of the beautiful. He found the good and the beautiful to be but two names for the same thing; and his poems make this clear. He was so much artist that Puritan morality, which manifests itself in controlling other people, slipped away from him through the good offices of the beautiful, and because of his Jeffersonian faith, which was rock-ribbed. Lindsay's vows of poverty, his prayers and his shrine hunting, have little of self-salvation in them. They were rather activities for the salvation of men; and when he contemplated turning a Franciscan, or some other kind of monk, the idea back of it was the bringing in of Magical Springfield, the City of the Perfect; the new America; the return of the Virginians. He was supremely the artist in the sense that he was a racial fashioner, he was a poet because he was a maker with this lofty and transcendent inspiration.

All these things considered, Lindsay's Map of the Universe gains in significance. It has a certain philosophy, for it poses the matter of evil and suffering, it pictures Mammon as the spider, and beauty as the butterfly, and the tomb of Lucifer, who was cursed by the angels for singing too well. Heaven has become a jungle empty of souls, for the angels as missionaries of the Universe have gone to the stars to be crucified, and to be forsaken of God, and to pour forth blood wherewith the dream of men may be made. "The map has dominated all my verses since 1904," wrote Lindsay. This is Lindsay's really profound pessimism, his analysis of the sorry scheme into which human beings are born, and the demi-gorgon rulership to which his soul submitted and sacrificed itself. His adhesion to the Campbellite faith may not have been out of harmony with this pessimism of sin and punishment; it is hardly consonant with it from an eschatological standpoint. Lindsay declared that Buddha was to him "the supreme personality of history," which put Jesus in second place.

So we find in Lindsay's poems, such as "Poems Speaking of Buddha, Prince Siddartha," that he divined with his master that the nature of evil is unsatisfied desires, and that the overcoming of evil consists in the suppression of desire, and that salvation consists in Nirvana, which is annihilation, or absorption into the divine. Lindsay's inherent celibacy took its root in these conceptions of life and man.

Lindsay wrote a number of religious poems, to many of which we have already paid some attention. We may refer briefly here to his rather long poem on Alexander Campbell which came out of Lindsay's heart, because he was fainting with love. "Why do I faint with love?" is one of its lines. Unlike Emerson, who looked back at the church with respect, but with gladness that he was a new man for having left it, and discarded it, Lindsay held to the faith of Grandfather Frazee, and of his mother. Lindsay, like Channing, was possessed of the idea of forming a superior race of men; but not as Channing tried to do it by being a direct son of Rousseau. Lindsay, like Alcott, would have brought back another Athens, but he imagined somehow that Alexander Campbell was one of the influences through which that might be done. Here we find the Lindsay complex and inconsistency, as we find something of the sort in all men, as in Newton who was very devout, as in Kepler who believed the earth might be an animal, as in Faraday who was an elder in the Sandemanian Church; and there are many other remarkable examples of the philosophical and mystical mixture in the minds of great men. Lindsay following Campbell interpreted nature, at least when following him, in a way that hid nature. He interpreted nature through the mysticism and asceticism of Buddha and through the redemption and sacrifice processes of Christianity. He never had the pantheism of Rousseau or Wordsworth. In contrast with Lindsay's religious attitude that of Emerson gives Lindsay's the clearest outline and identity. "I read my communion," wrote Emerson, "in every cipher of nature, and know that I was made for another office, a professor of the joyous

Lindsay's drawing, "A Map of the Universe," made in 1909 and later published in *The Golden Book of Springfield.*

science, a detector and delineator of occult harmonies, and unpublished beauties, a herald of civility, nobility, learning and wisdom; an affirmer of the one law, yet as one who should affirm it in music and dancing." This was Lindsay, too, who affirmed much in life by music and dancing; but he felt compelled to take Alexander Campbell with him while he carried out his mission. It was a lesser incongruity to introduce into this poem, as he did, parrots and princes, according to his formula for childhood and moon poems, drawn from the dreams of innocence, than it was to hold to Campbell while celebrating a freedom of spirit which was so alien to the Campbell mind. After Lindsay's first vogue abated, after he was no longer a curiosity and a new wonder to the sophisticated centers, he was smiled at satirically for his piety; but the matter of a man's religion, seeing that we know nothing of ultimate things, and little of things near at hand, would best be left to the man himself. Many people, poets included, may not see God as Lindsay saw him, may not indeed see him at all; and yet if Lindsay is to be criticized for his vision of God, and of Immanuel, a great mind like Goethe's shall not escape; and his "Prœmium to God and the World" may be set aside, and its words:

"Im Namen dessen, der Sich selbst erschuf!
Von Ewigkeit in schaffendem Beruf,"

set down as bad theology, and worse philosophy.

It is an easy passage from Lindsay's religious poems to his love poems, which are in fact unlike those of any other poet. Lindsay never had a mawkish period, as so many poets have had; he never had a Eulalie who "upturns her violet eye"; he never in verse committed himself to the melancholy of amorousness; and on the other hand he never wrote poems of exquisite passion like Keats and Shelley. There was in his love poems the chastity of deep seriousness, a

[299]

seriousness tinged by fate, by life's strange dream and the suffering heart of mortality. Such a poem is "Two Easter Stanzas," in which Lindsay lamented the death of one, which was deadly and a tremendous wrong. So he would set this blunder wrong by seeking faith amid the lilies and the candlelight. The second part of this poem has one of Lindsay's miraculous titles. It is: "We Meet at the Judgment Seat and I Fear Not." We may make a partial list of the love poems, such as those to "Gloriana," "To a Golden Haired Girl in Louisiana," "Kalamazoo," and "The Celestial Circus," where he and his love will leap from the backs of the horses to the cliffs of day and night. Is this not a characteristic Lindsay vision of a reunion in paradise? Other wonderful titles are: "My Lady Is Compared to a Young Tree," and "The Gamblers," where he sings that "all he ever had he gave away." "The Beggar's Valentine," again at this place referred to, is one of the most moving love poems in the language. It is so wholly different from any other, so steeped in the resignation, almost tragic of "The pilgrim boy lame but seeking the shrine." What fitter epitaph could Lindsay have? "The Flower of Mending Wall" has delicate music and imagery. But "Beauty" is a priceless lyric with its moving importunity to all lovers to give the poet kind thoughts. They should read him in their transcendent hours, and while they kiss and pray; they should be the poet's partisans, and build themselves great fireplaces where they might stand in bridal peace and in complete comradeship. Out of the fire should come his soul's gospel. Thus, if he should never have the feast of a wedded life, if he must pay for his foolish search for the shrine with dust and rain and weariness, and passion and hunger, still he would build hearths for the lovers everywhere, while he tramped on along a road more dear after all than love or life or youth.

The Candle in the Cabin, published in 1926, after Lindsay's marriage to Miss Elizabeth Conner, has many love poems, nearly all of them breathing an indefinable pathos, as if human love did not suffice him, while he had yielded to its promises to escape a lowering loneliness, and the fears that thronged from tragic mutabilities. "I love, but Oh, not one of ye," was the cry of Shelley. Lindsay as a God-intoxicated man, was of a mind too disorderly and ill-disciplined, and too like Ruskin, a secondary name in the field of thought, to take love as one of the comforting blessings of life, as Goethe took it with his Christine; for all Lindsay's ideas about sex and self-denial and the suppression of desire first rightfully his by nature and then made second nature by his mother's influence and his religous training, perplexed this marital experience with a sort of sad dubiety, at least this is so if we read aright the elegiac notes of these love songs in *The Candle in the Cabin*. The beauty of "The Hall of Judgment" lies in its evanescent composure; there is faint despair in "The Writhing Imperfect Earth. "The Hour of Fate" cannot be read without a slowing down of one's heart. The bridal couple has returned to the cabin, and they are standing before the fire on the hearth. "It is the hour of fate." They have planned and plotted against sorrow and time, against the gray hairs, and the sod of the grave, and against tears. Now it is the hour of fate! The mighty bridal hour has come; either that or the closing of the gate of love! Yet in another poem in this book entitled "Snow Born Butterflies," love is called the naked glory of the white, eternal, snowy, splendid summits of the year. The locale of these poems is Glacier Park, through which Lindsay tramped with Stephen Graham in 1921, and to which he came as a honeymoon retreat. Lindsay was now forty-seven, and he was beginning to feel the effects of writing, and thinking, and tramping, and hungering. He was beginning to feel himself old. His dreams did not flit before his vision as visibly as they once did, and he was led to sing in an epilogue that

he would have out-built New York and Rome, but now all
that he could do was to bring home one more song.

> "O Thou, who plumed with strong desire
> Wouldst float above the earth, beware!
> A shadow tracks thy flight of fire—
>   Night is coming!"

In this volume, the poem entitled "The Candle in the
Cabin" pursued and tried to capture an imaginative fila-
ment, as he often tried to do the same thing in his drawings;
and in "Why We Do Not Return?" he longed as Shelley
longed for a love that earth cannot give. "Those to whom
love is a secondary thing love more than those to whom it is
primary," said Landor. With Lindsay sexual love was a
secondary thing, and therefore he was a tender and devoted
heart; but like Shelley he was a saddened heart, accepting
a human relationship that he never expected to assume, as
we have seen from his diaries.

Nearly every poem of Lindsay's is an affirmation of his
artistic faith and creed down to the last book he wrote. "The
Hunting Dogs," to be found in *The Candle in the Cabin,*
expressly declares that his passions are America, Beauty,
Song, Religion, Love of Lone Games, the Indian, the Proud
One, the Brother, and God, the Chief that no one names.
"The House of Boone" in the same volume is a celebration
of America. "The Babbitt Jambouree," also contained in this
volume, protests against the wrong done the Indians who
have been turned into a show, after having at first earned
the land. When all these foolish days are done the Indians,
as sons of the soil, will come into their own as sons of Mohawk and Pocahontas. In the preface to the volume *Going
to the Stars*, he wrote that the log cabin meant to him Nancy
Hanks and Andrew Jackson. What can this mean to people
who have neither seen a log cabin nor had ancestors who were
born or lived in one? My grandmother Masters was born in

one near Nashville, Tennessee, and lived in one in her early married life in Illinois. Her grandmother before her was born in a log cabin in North Carolina. As a youth I often sat at the hearth of a log cabin owned by my grandfather and occupied by his tenant-farmer. Before a roaring fire I have heard this farmer, a native of Kentucky, play the fiddle and tell stories of Kentucky, as the numerous children, bright-eyed and healthy, stood about to listen; and as his laughing, vigorous wife, of very sterling worth, finished the domestic work of the day. Kind plenty, humble security, affection, laughter, good will, were all about the circle. Having seen such cabins I know what Lindsay meant when he sang of them, and how truly he spoke when he called them one of America's classical allusions; they are indeed fit to supplant the shepherds of Arcady, and the nymphs of the Vale of Tempe. It was the log cabin that elected Jackson, and brought about one of the only successful protests in American history against the rule of money, stock gambling, and the reign of Poseidon over Demeter. One of the acutest observations of a political nature that Lindsay ever made will be found in his preface to the volume *Going to the Stars*. It is that Jackson having triumphed through the log cabin, the Hamiltonian party, calling themselves Whigs at the time, invented the false pretense of Tippecanoe and Tyler too, of Hard Cider and the Log Cabin. He might have said as well that fence rails were the second slogan of the same party, and that by that they took hold of the government and have largely kept it ever since.

It will be found that Lindsay covered the whole country at last with his creed of America. "The Flower-Fed Buffaloes" laments that the old America is gone, and that it lies low with the Blackfeet and the Pawnees. In Virginia he saw men riding to wisdom and wonder, but also to doom; for Virginia is the wonder and the heartbreak! Virginia, Virginia, of Pocahontas and Powhatan, Rolfe and John

Smith, Jefferson and Poe! And Virginia, the ruin, the ruin of Virginia! But if in far Thibet the poet's dust shall sweep across the desert walls something will whisper the immortal melody of Virginia. America has not yet awakened to the incalculable service which Lindsay did in creating the substance of love among Americans for America. If his songs do not build a Union, and the songs of those seeking to fix for America a distinctive character, such as belongs to it, do not perform this nationalizing labor, then orations like Webster's are nothing, and armies which subdued secession fought in vain. For nothing can make a nation but culture. It cannot be made by force.

Lindsay wrote in all twelve poems with Johnny Appleseed as the subject. "In Praise of Johnny Appleseed," which may be found in his *Collected Poems*, contains three divisions, and is long. The first division is entitled "Over the Appalachian Barricade"; the second is "The Indians Worship Him, But He Hurries On"; the third is "Johnny Appleseed's Old Age." The poem is full of vigor, color, and action. Old Continentals crossed the mountains, as Johnny did, carrying seeds of peaches, pears, cherries, grapes, and apples, "tree souls of precious things." Johnny went his way singing the songs of the Ancient of Days, leaving behind the old settled states, "every shackle gone." Through the forest the unicorn was ramping, the rooster trumpeting. How vibrant, imaginative, and sweeping this poem is may be better seen by comparing it with a poem like Bryant's "The Prairies."

Johnny asked the eagles to guard his planted seed. The Indians stuck holy feathers in his hair. His heart was a wind-blown wheat sheaf and a new-built nest. But on he went, leaving the Indians; on he went to live on roots and bark and to sleep in the trees. The maple's spinning seeds called to his apple's seeds, and the soft fauns stopped to hear his orations.

Then at last when the settlers put up their rafters they asked: "Who gave this fruit?" By this time Johnny was further west, wearing for a helmet an old tin pan, more sane than the helmet of Tamerlane. He was priestly and free! The Indians now overtook Johnny, and passed him, and so did the orchards. Everything that he found wild had become tame, the cats, the ponies, the pigs, canaries. The only real frontier left now was his sunburnt breast. He lifted his hands to the farm-filled skies; and the sun became a broken barrel out of which apples rolled, with an angel in each apple, a state capital, a high school, a college. All America was in each apple. Who will doubt that for the purposes of a new poetry these apples well take the place of those of Hesperides? What rich imagination here; what wealth of figurative language!

Death came on Johnny Appleseed, but dying he saw each state a flower, each petal a park. Then he slept like a "stone washed white," there in his four-poster bed with autumn rains for curtains, and autumn leaves for a quilt. All this allegory in which sowing of seed is the symbol of planting civilization refers to Lindsay himself. Johnny Appleseed is Lindsay. This poem lacks condensation, and because it is so excellent one wishes that somehow its wonderful material and imagery had been given the benefit of the file. With all its faults, however, it remains a remarkable poem, wholly original, and of really great import.

Still Lindsay was not done with this fascinating subject. "Johnny Appleseed Still Further West" is the title of a poem in the volume *Going to the Sun,* published in 1923. With it Lindsay furnished an illustration, badly done, and in which he again demonstrated that he could not draw the human face. The same volume contains "The Apple Barrel of Johnny Appleseed," who is now reading the books of Swedenborg, on the mountain top called *Going to the Sun.* Lindsay makes fine use of this mountain by employing its name as a haunting repetend. The poetical effect is magically musical.

"Bob Taylor's Birthday," a poem on "The Tennessee Orpheus" celebrates a later America than that of the Johnny Appleseed poems. Lindsay liked this poem better than Whitman's "Song of the Broad Axe," but if Whitman's poem is profuse in catalogues and geographies, Lindsay's poem is verbosity gone mad. Whitman's poem contains 260 lines; Lindsay's 402 lines, besides a preface in prose of more than 2500 words. Lindsay called his poem "sky-painting oratory," and there are many blue sky laws against its length and lack of artistry. Emerson put all the ideas contained in these 400 lines in the quatrain:

> "I will have never a noble,
> No lineage counted great;
> Fishers and choppers and ploughmen
> Shall constitute a state."

"Where are the furious wills of the nation?" Lindsay asked. So asked Whitman. All the prophecies of Lindsay in this poem are reminiscent of Whitman; and this poem together with some of the lines in "In Praise of Johnny Appleseed" are of the Whitman quality, whether derived from him or not. "The Trial of the Dead Cleopatra in Her Beautiful and Wonderful Tomb" is somehow classifiable with the Bob Taylor poem, at least on the basis of length and incoherent exuberance. It is maundering and digressive, and as Lindsay said that he wrote it over more than a hundred times it is clear that the material defied his hand. It is original, however; it is unique; it has many of the Lindsay excellencies; but on the whole it is a failure.

Lindsay wrote many poems on Springfield, to which reference has been made along the way. When he was practically in exile from his city he wrote "The Butterfly Citizens" in which he spoke of his town as a star afar.

Springfield as the City of the Perfect haunted him to the last. His social poems, or poems of reproof or satire, or hope are filled with Springfield. "The Soul of the City Receives the Gift of the Holy Spirit" is one of them. Of these "The Drunkard's Funeral" is one of the liveliest, and most telling. It was directed against the saloon. The poem entitled "Sew the Flags Together," with its refrain of "Rise, Rise, Rise," is reminiscent of Shelley's lines; but "Tolstoi Is Plowing Yet" is Lindsay's very own, and quite memorable. "A Curse for Kings" which calls for a hell of a million years for those who start a million souls toward death rather condemns one of Lindsay's heroes who committed what Lindsay called in another poem "the unpardonable sin," by sending "forth rapine in the name of Christ." But we shall not press the point of consistency. If we did we should object to Lindsay who compared Roosevelt to Saul in one poem, and referred to him as the "dude cowboy" in another. Then in the poem "Babylon, Babylon, Babylon the Great" Lindsay made Lincoln a prophet at Cooper Union who threw away his speech, and spoke from inspiration, which did not happen, even if no mention is made of the fact that Lincoln was not a Free Soiler then, nor an emancipationist, but only a champion of Congressional imperialism for keeping slavery out of the territories, as against Congressional imperialism on the part of Jefferson Davis for forcing slavery on the territories. A myth loses its beauty and its goodness which serves only to amuse and befool the populace, while the actual principles of the actual man destroy liberty.

In *Going to the Sun* there is a half successful satire on Boston and New England; and in the same volume a presentable attempt entitled "Babylon's Gardens Are Burning." These later volumes, even *The Golden Whales of California*, published in 1920, give evidence only too frequently of the thinning of the waters of Helicon. *Going to the Stars* is wholly redeemed by the deeply moving poem "These Are the Young," and by "Old, Old, Old, Old Andrew Jackson."

First and last Lindsay wrote more than thirty moon poems. They range all the way from "The Old Horse in the City," which appeared in the Booth volume, down to "The Moon's a Devil Jester," which may be found in *Going to the Sun*. Perhaps the best moon poem in the Booth volume is the one entitled "Beyond the Moon," in which Lindsay declared that he had a lonely goal beyond the moon, and that even beyond heaven and hell he had a goal. These moon poems are either written around what the moon said, or around the conception of the moon by the hyena, the rattlesnake, the clown, the snail king, the snow man, the grandpa mouse, the forester, the ghost of the gambler, the hermit, the tramp, Semiramis. These poems of the moon are the work of fancy, they are ingenious, ornamental, graceful; they are the Spencerian system of penmanship very often applied to words. Thus to call the moon a brass-hooped water keg, open furnace door, a peck of corn, an opening flower, a snowball, a candle glow, a chalice of honey and wine, a sack of gold dust, a monk, the tombstone of the sky, an emery wheel, a censer, to so picture the moon is an exercise of fancy, of the powers of finding similarity between objects, that is all. There are delicate, poetical lines very often in these poems, but on the whole they were but the pastime of the hand which penned "The Santa Fé Trail." One of them, "Three Hours," to be found in the volume *Going to the Stars*, has a Shelleyan music.

Of kin to the moon poems are Lindsay's songs of innocence, as they might be called, or songs of childhood, of fairies. They began with "The Queen of Bubbles," with the history of which the reader is already familiar; and they end with such poems as "The Pansy Wedding," "The Moth and the Unicorn," and others to be found in *Going to the*

Stars. "The Child Heart in the Mountains" may well be placed side by side with Wordsworth's:

"My heart leaps up when I behold
The rainbow in the sky."

Sometimes Lindsay gave vent to his heart hurts, his mind doubts, but never Byronically, never in a way to offend good taste. He was sensitive about opening his heart, and as a result he was wont to dramatize his feelings and his own imperfections. As he called himself the pilgrim boy, lame but hunting the shrine, so he wrote a poem entitled "The Lame Boy and the Fairy," in which he tried to catch in words the rhythm of Chopin's "Berceuse," something impossible to do. Lindsay knew himself to the extent of appreciating the fact that he was a boy, a lame boy, a creature destined to remain a child forever, always to play cross tag and I-spy, and always to meet Little Red Riding Hood on the highway, and to greet Santa Claus there, and Goldilocks. James Whitcomb Riley could invoke these childish figures for the purpose of delighting children; Lindsay invoked them to express himself. Yet "The Lame Boy and the Fairy" has adult sighs of sorrow. For after childhood men shall see silver ships, and singing ships, and the ships of love which shall take them home. In these songs of innocence, as we may call them, Lindsay works his miracle often in the choice of titles, such as "Crickets on a Strike," "The Dangerous Little Boy Fairies," "The Fairy Circus," "The Pansy Wedding," and so on. The spider as eater and the fly as food were obvious phenomena for Lindsay to see and then to draw and write a poem of twelve verses about very early in his career. The only philosophy of that contest in nature is one of food. Lindsay never sang the sexual hostility that destroys insect mates, as Emerson did, who compared the philosopher who throttled his passion for the death of a mother, to "that devil spider that devours her mate scarce freed from her embraces." Such Strindbergian reflections were not for Lindsay, especially not for his songs of innocence.

Among the songs of innocence are such poems as "The Potatoes' Dance" and "The King of Yellow Butterflies," which Lindsay used for what he called poem games. These and all such in his work may be dismissed with the remark that they bear the same relation to poetry, when used in that way, as charades do to the drama, or bell ringing to chamber music. "King Solomon and the Queen of Sheba" was presented by Lindsay as a sort of poem game, but rather it was a dramatization, for the lines were chanted. But we have seen that Lindsay himself said that poetry is for the inner ear. The Higher Vaudeville, as he termed it, of reciting, chanting, or singing poems, makes for loudness, for triviality, for a *tour de force*, and for vulgarization of nuances and delicate tones. In his hands, and though he was a master platform poet, it fell into a stunt, a spectacle, that annoyed him infinitely at last, when to ask him to recite "The Congo" was to fill him with writhing nerves. All this chanting, reciting, and acting is akin to the mixed art of grand opera. It is not poetry. Poetry recited for the sake of reciting it restores no lost art, for there was never any such art to lose; on the contrary it harms and lessens the art of the poems, unless they happen to be oratorical in nature. The best of Shakespeare is more beautiful when it is spoken in a way to touch the inner ear, to accentuate the vibration which the eye gives to the auditory imagination. Lindsay having come along as part orator to begin with, having tried to be a public speaker and even a preacher was easily seduced to chant and to act his poems, but without any benefit to himself except as his income as a lecturer was increased. His art gained nothing by the practice; and at last his rôle as a public performer became tragic with weariness and revulsion for a kind of forensic skill which he had been betrayed into acquiring by his own predilection, and a public response to the boom of his voice and the gymnastic of his acting. At the beginning there was some literary judgment of an ex-cathedra sort which welcomed the return of chanting as a sign of great art restored. That was a silly phase of the hour's intoxication with the new poetry which was significant with poems like "The Chinese Nightingale," and trifling with "The Potatoes' Dance."

We have before remarked that Lindsay never became a poet of nature, although on his long tramps he was much in the presence of mountains and valleys and fields. And yet the poem "In Praise of Johnny Appleseed" has many magical touches of nature; and this may be said for "The Bird Called Curiosity" in the book *Going to the Sun*, which in addition has illustrations by Lindsay of almost Japanese delicacy. By a nature poet one means one who celebrates the soul of the visible world in sublime and comprehensive interpretations. But Lindsay only gave sympathetic and imaginative touches to his observations of flowers and trees and mountains, having gathered his material in Glacial Park and elsewhere. This is true of "The Pheasant Speaks of His Birthdays," in *Going to the Sun*. But true to the Lindsay manner he had to decorate that poem with lollipops, cakes, ices, dragons and toys of childhood, carried into symbols and figures of speech. He hears no voice of an awful unseen power, but the unicorns of sunset ramping are audible to his imagination. However, the reader may compare Lindsay's poem on the dandelion with that of Lowell for the purpose of seeing how a fuller Americanism can surpass a lesser. Turn also to "The Red Eagle Love Song" in *The Candle in the Cabin*, and catch the strength of Whitman as Lindsay lifts up his voice and rejoices; or read "The Angel Sons" in *Going to the Stars* and hear Lindsay exult while singing that he would rather be the Great Sun Mountain, "drinking the cup of dawn," than to be Byron, Christ or Buddha. Or read "The Celestial Trees of Glacier Park," "Jack in the Pulpit," "Geology and Mountain Angels" in *Going to the Stars,* for the purpose of seeing Lindsay's approach to the sublimity of nature. He wrote these poems when his vogue had diminished and that world, which sates its sadistic passion by contemplating the failure and downfall of the great, was saying that Lindsay had run out. These are poems touched with genuine greatness, and while writing them he was in communion with Thoreau, Saint Francis, Blake and Johnny Appleseed. It may have been better if he had stayed with the mountains, and not have returned to Springfield. He might the better have endured that diet of which Emerson sang:

> "The hero is not fed on sweets,
> Daily his own heart he eats."

He might not so soon have become, to quote Emerson again:

> "The much deceived Endymion
> Slips behind a tomb."

And so before coming to Lindsay's principal poems, those that the best judgment has already selected for a permanent place in American and world literature, it may be said of the rest, of all the briefer songs that Lindsay has no crystal lyrics of jewel size like Poe's "To Helen," like Shelley's "Far, Far Away, O Ye Halcyons of Memory," or "O World, O Life, O Time"; like Keats's "In a Drear-Nighted December," like Landor's "Rose Aylmer," like several songs by Shakespeare reduced by astral fire to a few matchless, inevitable lines. Perhaps Lindsay's "Look You, I'll Go Pray" is his nearest approach to this miraculous turning of the heart's carbon into a pure diamond of song.

This poem, however, contains traces of the gross stuff of Lindsay's evangelical preoccupations; and all the sincerity of his passion could not entirely burn it away. In some of the delicate musical poems of minor length in the volumes *Going to the Sun, Going to the Stars, The Candle in the Cabin* and *Every Soul Is a Circus* Lindsay achieved a purity of line and sound that is absent from his famous successes, those upon which his reputation first rested. A more refined taste will choose these rather than poems like "The Congo," and "The Chinese Nightingale," for the purpose of showing his genius in its finest manifestations. And one is almost led to believe that in those later books he was approaching the realization of an art which would have been the work of his genius purged at last of all dross, eccentricity and marring mannerisms.

CHAPTER XVII

JUDGES of any art are likely to differ, and to have good reasons for their opinions as well; but I venture to select as Lindsay's best poems the following: "The Chinese Nightingale," "In Praise of Johnny Appleseed," "The Santa Fé Trail," "The Booker Washington Trilogy," "The Congo," "Poems Speaking of Buddha, Prince Siddartha," "Old, Old, Old, Old Andrew Jackson," "The Virginians Are Coming Again," and "Bryan, Bryan, Bryan, Bryan." Trailing after these as sparks in the wake of their flame I should put: "Rising Wolf," "The Child Heart in the Mountains," "The Hall of Judgment," "The Hour of Fate," "Virginia," "Shantung, or the Empire of China Is Crumbling Down," "I Know All This When Gipsy Fiddles Cry," "The Kallyope Yell," "How Samson Bore Away the Gates of Gaza," "The Village Improvement Parade," "Two Easter Songs," "The Drunkards in the Street," "The Beggar's Valentine," "Look You, I'll Go Pray," "The Golden Whales of California," "I Went Down Into the Desert," "I Heard Immanuel Singing," "In Which Roosevelt Is Compared to Saul," "Three Poems About Mark Twain." This last poem might be put among his best. "I Know All This When Gipsy Fiddles Cry" is one of the few poems in which Lindsay essayed the unrhymed iambic pentameter; and it is thoroughly characterized by his spiritual voice. It is unlike any other blank verse by any other master, and it is highly successful, though more lyrical than dramatic in tone.

Having listed these poems as Lindsay's best and second best I take the responsibility of saying that they constitute the most considerable body of imaginative lyricism that any

American has produced. At once the challenging name of Poe arises. But Poe wrote not to exceed twelve principal poems, and their body is much less than these of Lindsay's. Whatever Poe may have accomplished in art for art's sake, he did little with art for life's sake, and he is no more the spokesman of America than Charles Brockden Brown. One would as well say that Hoffman is the voice of Germany and not Goethe. But is this the test, this matter of voicing a people, a civilization, a culture? Is great poetry that which performs an Amphion work and builds a nation by showing what it is, and what it ought to be? If Homer and Goethe and Shakespeare are great for having played such rôles, as they were among their other marks of greatness, then this test of poetry is sound. Scarcely any of Lindsay's work has the finish, the exquisite music of Poe's; but its diapason is so much more significant. A preoccupation with death, with recurring figures of tombs and worms cannot make the best poetry. It may be taken as one way of reducing the multiverse of life to an inescapable conclusion, saying this is all. Whatever may be sung of democracy, of heroes, of Christ, Apollo, Buddha, or Jefferson, of the greatness of a nation, of the glory of liberty, of love, human and divine, the final thing is death:

> "The play is the tragedy man
> And its hero the Conqueror Worm."

Philosophers and poets are likely to carve out of the shifting air and mist of life's manifest a sphere of interpretation, and say here lies the main interest, here is the place from which the whole landscape of life can be viewed and appraised. Not only that but every poet can make his empire thus created the very substance and meaning of the whole. It is like taking into a phial some of the sea's water, and calling it all that can be said of the sea as to quality and essential substance. But men will not allow life to be summed up in terms of tombs and worms. They will side with Whitman who called such poetry the work of jim-jams. And thus to compare Lindsay's poetical creed which included America, Beauty, Song, Religion, Love of Lone Games, the Indian, the Proud One, the Brother, the Chief that no one names with Poe's play of tragedy with its worm as the hero is to see how greater Lindsay's intellectual and emotional scope was. Furthermore to consider that Poe was concerned, as he declared in essays on poetics, with producing a poetical effect, and that in writing "The Raven" he built up his music with mathematical care, is to see the difference between the integrity of the two men. At the same time it may be true that Lindsay never achieved the musical miracles that Poe did in lines and in whole stanzas, and even poems. But as to that, Lindsay has staves of harmonies that may well compare with the best of any lyric poet though totally different in key and pitch from them all.

Much that has been said of Poe in this connection can be applied to Lanier, who was a much more conscious and skillful metricist than Lindsay; and yet Lanier did not produce melodies as sincere, authentic as Lindsay did, as close to the American heart, and perhaps none more magical than Lindsay, though more complex. If comparisons are to be extended the name of Emerson cannot be ignored. Perhaps Lindsay wrote no poem so quotable, so clinging to the memory as "The Rhodora," so utterly purged of all that is nonessential, and perhaps so profoundly emotional. And perhaps Lindsay has given us no poem so stirring, so close to the roots of national feeling as "The Concord Hymn." All of which makes evident the difficulties of comparing the two men, who are scarcely comparable, except on the broad ground of a distinctive Americanism, where both of them stood four-square. Lindsay, however, was all bard, and Emerson was the philosopher with Pythagorean verses. He really sang infrequently, but when he did he brought down pieces of an infinitely blue sky, shining with gnomic secrets. At his best no brook rippling down a pine-roofed slope, where the sunlight and the shadows flutter, and where the scent of needles and faint wildflowers fill the air of a summer afternoon in New England was ever more purely the voice of the Gleam, the ideas of Plato, or the heart of hieratic beauty.

Lindsay thought that "The Chinese Nightingale" was his best poem, and perhaps of his long poems it is the most finished, the most coherent and balanced to the end. To study it is to note the Lindsay vigor putting the first foot down hard as he did in the Booth poem. Its music may not be so delicate as that of "Kubla Khan," or the "Ancient Mariner," but it is more original. Coleridge took accents from the ballads to be found in Percy's "Reliques"; and he transsubstantiated some of the harmonies of the English odes of an earlier day than his. But where will the intonations of Lindsay's poem he found except in his own voice? Nowhere else are the variations so musically rung on sorrow and love, glory and love, and love and creation as eternal. Life is a loom weaving an illusion, bringing dreams that are good, and dreams like those of the "Ancient Mariner," and dreams of romantic lost loves cushioned upon the velvet violet lining of a study chair, where a black raven has perched on a white bust of the goddess of classic Athens. All is fresh and miraculous with the setting of Lindsay's poem. Its message is not out of any Christian sophistry, namely that "he prayeth best who loveth best"; the small gray bird on the joss carols that love and creation are eternal. The Chinaman Chang declares that his breast with vision is satisfied. True it is that Buddha is Lindsay's highest god, not Christ. In this poem Lindsay touched hands with the young Keats who saw that truth is beauty and beauty truth, and he left Coleridge behind. Listening to

[317]

the small gray bird sing "like a long unwinding silk cocoon," he turned away from the bird that croaked, "nevermore," for love and creation are eternal.

"Shantung, or the Empire of China Is Falling Down" does not deserve to stand with "The Chinese Nightingale," but it is an admirable poem. It puts a lasting stigma on the European and American swine who broke over the walls of the ancient empire to harry the mandarin, and make him leave off his scholar's gown and live like the swine. How great was Confucius, asked Lindsay, who made China and for so long preserved it? He brings into line Alexander and King Arthur, and Napoleon. Where are they? All of them were tempted to destroy China. But a sea girl laughs in her swing like the sleeve of a gown. China does not fall. The Sphinx sees all the western nations spent, and wolves, Christians, and false custodians rioting on the shore where Confucius the philosopher walked. But China does not fall. A giant joke has been played on the pride of all the nations ancient and modern. China does not fall! Missionaries, soldiers, vulgarians, Christian thieves, Rotarians, John Hay and William McKinley hypocrites loot the temples. China does not fall! This is one of Lindsay's noblest efforts, wide visioned, and in places highly lyrical.

One may consult any history of the United States, even Wilson's *History of the American People;* but he will not find the spirit and the fact of the emergence and career of Bryan reported. Lindsay's poem "Bryan, Bryan, Bryan, Bryan" tells his distinctively American story from background to the epilogue. Lindsay's cultural environment, which bred in him a love of Andrew Jackson, gave him understanding of the agrarian battle of Bryan, the second in America within seventy-five years. The first was victorious, for Jackson at least; the second was disastrous to the cause, and to Bryan as its champion as well. In 1896 the frontier was Nebraska, not Tennessee; but once again the farmer, the anti-monopolist, the anti-corporation man, the country made war against the stock gambler and corporation lawyer, against the law-privileged banker, against the selfish city, against "the dour and the old." There are millions of people now, in New England and in New York, who have never been west of the Hudson River, and that was the case in 1896. They know nothing of America as a land, or as a people outside of Boston and Manhattan Island; and they care nothing about either. How could such people understand what principles and interests the West was defending under Bryan and against Mark Hanna and McKinley, and the banks and corporations which had stolen the people's sovereignty to make money, and were pouring that money into the offices of newspapers and magazines, and into the pockets of preachers and orators in order to terrify wavering souls, and confound the mind of the nation? What did New York and Boston and the East care if the farmers of Nebraska and Kansas could not sell their hard-raised corn, but used it in the cold winter for fuel against the icy blasts of Medicine Hat? What time had elegance and class for thought of children born at midnight "in the sod huts of lost hope," what time and what mood for such reflections when sailing the Mediterranean in luxury purchased from the dividends of watered stock and the usufruct of tariff-boosted products? The West was being devoured, by the "Atlantic Coast," by the "giant spider's nest." And then came Bryan.

He came, as Lindsay sang in this poem, as a prophet and a bard, as a prairie avenger, a mountain lion, a gigantic troubadour speaking like a siege gun. Lindsay, then in his seventeenth year, witnessed that marvellous feat of physical strength, of amiable, smiling, satirical, oratorical, courageous, invincible crusading all over the country, in which Bryan travelled 20,000 miles and spoke to hundreds of thousands of people, with no radio, no magnifiers, with no

newspapers to help him, with no other speakers of moment
to help him, with no money to pay even legitimate expenses,
with nothing but himself, his youth, his charm, his matchless skill of meeting hecklers and managing hostile audiences.
Lindsay saw all this. He heard the echo of Bryan's voice
when he appealed to New England through the spirit of
Emerson, for to an audience there Bryan spoke those verses
of Emerson:

> "I will have never a noble,
> No lineage counted great;
> Fishers and choppers and ploughmen
> Shall constitute a state."

He heard Bryan call to the country by the authority of
Jefferson, and in the name of great poets and thinkers, and
founders of free states. Nothing availed; for Tubal Cain,
the great-grandson of Cain, the murderer, was plotting the
downfall of Bryan and the cause he led. Tubal Cain an
"instructor of every artificer in brass and iron," Tubal Cain
in the person of Mark Hanna, and in the name of all those
who exploit and do not work, was gathering money and
paying it out to cunning liars and eloquent betrayers for
the work of lying the sod huts and the wasted farms into the
slavery where they belonged. Jubal, the half-brother of
Tubal Cain, Jubal the father of all such as handle the
harp and the organ, was destined to fiddle on street corners
for pennies, and to walk through Kansas trading rhymes
for bread and preaching the Gospel of Beauty. And so
as this remarkable poem tells the story Tubal Cain Hanna
came to the rescue, seeing the whole East down like a
smashed fence under the blows of Bryan. Hanna requisi-
tioned the roller-top desks, the bucket shops, the banks
of issue which had sprung up like weeds on the grave of
Andrew Jackson, the misers' cellars; and with all this levied
tribute he started forth to beat the "cheap skate," the

"blatherskite," the "deacon desperado." And so came defeat of the wheat, and victory of the letter-files; and defeat of the groves of Colorado, the bluebells of the Rockies, of the blue bonnets of Texas, defeat of the Mississippi by the Hudson, and of the Pacific by the Atlantic. Woodrow Wilson, the man whom Bryan made President sixteen years later, stayed prudently under cover while Bryan battled alone; he held aloof when Bryan in 1900 fought against the imperialization of the Republic. And Bryan, stung by the aspersions of that bitter campaign, started out to prove that he too could make money, but make it honestly. He deserted his alpaca coat, left his farm in Nebraska and gathered in money by lecturing, and travelled over a world which meant little to him after he saw it. His wealth went to a family that would have been better off without it. The defeat of the bluebells and the aspen groves was not the worst feature of that catastrophe which began in 1896. The worst was Bryan's self-defeat accomplished by lecturing for money, and embarking in theology which he did not understand, and in science which was a closed book to him. Lindsay wrote the Bryan poem in 1919, while Bryan went down to a grotesque finish six years later.

But in 1919 Lindsay could well ask where that Bryan was, that heaven-born Bryan, that Homer Bryan; and he could answer that he had gone to join the shadows with Altgeld the Eagle, who was an eagle indeed, and who had died in 1902 with one claw stretched forth to fight back the enemies who had shot his heart full of arrows. Altgeld was like Chang of "The Chinese Nightingale": he knew that love and creation were eternal, that out of tragedy and disaster the drama of life turns fair and bright. When a hundred years have gone by, and men shall want to get the spirit and the meaning, the color and the drama of Bryan's campaign of 1896, of Bryanism in general, they will turn to no history, at least to no history yet written, but to this remarkable poem of Lindsay's whose concluding stanzas are moving and lyrical with the full power and magic of Lindsay's incomparable genius.

We have seen from the diaries of Lindsay the genesis of the poem called "The Santa Fé Trail." For many miles Lindsay walked beside it in 1912. On that tramp he learned the name of the marvellous songster, the Rachel Jane, from the old Negro with whom he broke bread by the way. In this poem the Rachel Jane is singing, as the Chinese nightingale did, love and life, eternal youth, love and truth and glory. But the freight train goes by loaded with wheat, loaded with machinery. Then the motorists go by, who are hunting the places that they understand in the great search for delight. They are the resorts of San Francisco, the bathing and resting places by the Pacific. But Lindsay himself is a traveller; he too has a quest. He is following the Gleam, the mystery of life. The United States may go by; the horns of the cars may rip and rack, quack and clack, he sits on a stone by the Trail and hears the voice of the wheat ridge, and the tall corn, and the little souls of the grass. He listens to the tales of the cottonwood trees, and to the windmills creaking far away over the wells; and to the Rachel Jane singing love and glory, stars and rain. His breast with vision is satisfied. Lindsay called this poem a humoresque; and so it is with its fancies and its caprices. It is like many of his poems and strophes, a scherzo.

Unique and wonderful as this poem is, it is not equal to the scherzo entitled "The Booker Washington Trilogy," which is a miracle almost from first to last. Its first part, treating of Simon Legree, has all the abandon that Goethe might have put into it in defiance of the academicians of his time. Legree had "eyes like dirt"——could anything be more graphic? He had cheeks "fish belly white," but so had the cheeks of old man Finn, the father of Huckleberry. Legree had made it hard for the Negro; but they had their revenge through John Brown, whose name gives the title to the second part of this poem, in which Lindsay in many senses reached the highest point that his wings ever carried him to. He did here in his own way what Shakespeare did in

"Hark, hark, the lark at heaven's gate sings,"

And what Keats did in the often-referred-to lines concerning magic casements. Such miracles of song come forth like a perfect intaglio which somehow has been enclosed from prehistoric times in a great boulder, but falls out to the hand that can split the rock and release the work of art. In reading this poem one tries to bring up from his memory the gospel song, the evangelical rhythm which inspired it, and gave to it the key which it bears. This one tries to do as well with the third part of this poem, which deals with King Solomon and the Queen of Sheba. It is in vain that one does so. Lindsay has accomplished some form of transsubstantiation of those old rhythms, those old evangelical runes; and their exact identity has been lost in the necromancy of his genius. When Lindsay became a professional lecturer he attained an excellence in that rôle as high as James Whitcomb Riley before him, although with a very different manner of histrionism. As we have said, he made a sort of poem game or drama of King Solomon and the Queen of Sheba, in which those characters spoke the respective lines belonging to them, as indicated in the poem, while the audience under the previous instruction of Lindsay gave back the interpolated antiphones. The effect was charming, and humorous also, to the last degree. But to read this incomparable poem to oneself is to get the spiritual wonder with which it is impregnated.

In this connection brief reference must be made to the poem "How Samson Bore Away the Gates of Gaza," in which Lindsay employed spondees and anapests with marked effect; but the poem called "The Congo" is Beethoven jazz with the greatest success. The Negroes are to have their place in the City of the Perfect. For arresting imagery one may look to the third part of this poem, where the apostles are pictured in mail of bright white steel. They sit and watch the jungle fall from its vine snares, cleared away by pioneer angels. They see this with watch-fire eyes.

"The Golden Whales of California" classifies with Lindsay's social reform poems. It has wonderful imagery, fresh as dew; but like the poems on Mark Twain, where Lindsay called to his country to "Behold a Republic," it does not evolve to complete success. The same may be said of "Our Mother Pocahontas"; but here Lindsay on his own ground took up the Whitman campaign. He would renounce all Saxon blood, and look to tomorrow's hopes with their April floods bringing new life.

Lindsay's devotion to Andrew Jackson made him the son of the Jeffersonian Whitman. Grandfather and Grandmother Frazee, the one born in 1824 and the other in 1827, lived during the fame and the roaring talk of Jackson, who did not die until 1847, and whose name was one to conjure with to the last. Whether these grandparents talked to Lindsay of the glory and the wonder of Jackson, as grandparents were wont to do to descendants of the same generation as Lindsay, no less Lindsay got the miraculous story somewhere in his youth. Perhaps it came to him from his father, or from his Grandfather Lindsay, the old blind rebel of Kentucky. But Jackson somehow preoccupied Lindsay's imagination, second only to Johnny Appleseed. He wrote his first poem about Jackson in 1918, during the Great War. What Lindsay saw, but would not confess, except by indirection, was that the election of Lincoln and the rejection of Douglas was essentially a choosing by a dominant minority of the Nation of Hamilton and a repudiation of Jefferson. That was the first time that America lost her

predestined vision and missed the chance to remain what
she had been formed to be, and might well have been. The
second time that America went blind was when she embarked
upon colonialism, and the third was when she entered the
World War. If the labor of Whitman, trying to make an
American culture and to sing it, must fail; and the work
of Lindsay who in the same spirit strove to advance the
cause of Jefferson's republic, must also fail, then there can
be no America such as the dream of the founders of America
cherished. This double failure means that America has departed so far from her original path, that she can never be
sung except as a Lost Atlantis, a realm of perished dreams.
It means that America, having abandoned liberty, having
taken into herself all strange stocks, and wandered after the
ambition of empires, will play the part of the Hellenistic
cities which in every sphere of song and statecraft, of art
and laws fell below the glory of vanished Athens.

"Old, Old, Old, Old Andrew Jackson" is written with a
feeling, a pride and a hope, with tones of remembrance and
praise, and in that pathos which comes to the heart medi-
ating upon the strong man who came into life, performed
his part, and entered the silence; it is written with every
device of music suited to the subject, which shall bring the
tears for things afar and forgotten, noble and heroic, to
the eyes of America forever. One might say that it is equal
to anything of Whitman's, or superior to anything of Whitman's. Nothing much can be made sure by such judgments.
The best thing to do is to go to the poem itself, and enjoy
it to the full for what it is of original eloquence. But this
can be said: it is not a carrying out of the Whitman methods, for it is specific, concrete in its characterization of
America; and the more so because it celebrates an American hero who tried to remake America in the image of its
first makers. Only the rich want Jackson's name to grow
dim, sings Lindsay. And for himself he must ask a boy

who has faded away, he must ask his young heart to speak of Jackson with all the pride that he deserves. And as Lindsay began each strophe with the words, "I will speak of your deeds, Andrew Jackson," so he says that he will do this when he takes the road again. "Oh, the long, dusty highway, oh the rain, oh the sunburnt men." This is the repetend of the poem which gives it enchantment, a sense of being haunted by past days, and by the wandering spirit of Lindsay himself. It is a more significant poem than "By Blue Ontario's Shore," and equally critical of the trend of America. Lindsay directed this poem to be read aloud in the way one would read a political speech, as perhaps he read or recited it at Spokane at Jefferson's Birthday Dinner, April 15, 1925. Rather it should be gravely intoned as from the tragic lips of the Cumæan Sibyl when prophesying concerning Æneas. It is not an oration, but a vast elegy, an epic-threnody to be sung in the forsaken gardens trodden to ruin by the soldiers of merchants and usurers.

Finally we must refer to "The Virginians Are Coming Again," to be found in the volume, *Every Soul Is a Circus*. He inserted a long preface in this volume, recapitulating his art theories, his theories of the dancing of poetry, and the reciting of poetry. It is true, as pointed out by Havelock Ellis, that "the joyous beat of the feet of children, the cosmic play of philosophers' thoughts rise and fall according to the same laws of rhythm." And Ellis calls attention to the doctrine of Schiller of the play impulse as the basis of artistic creation " 'as if' as the kernel of æsthetic practice and contemplation." Truly all of his day's poetry, æsthetic, moral, is but an evolution of Santa Claus, Christmas, and games. So much is brought forward here by way of authority for Lindsay's insistent recurrence to the matter of poem games, and the reciting of poetry as the chief, if not the only way to appreciate it. Having done so, we shall leave many to believe that poetry is philosophy, that it is wis-

dom, that only in its oratorical or dramatic forms, or certain
of its lyrical forms can it collaborate with acting, mim-
icry, or declamation. Poetry becomes childish verse when
it celebrates fairies, baubles, popcorn, and Santa Claus for
their own sake. It is sublime and profound when it makes
baubles of kingdoms, philosophies, love, gold, and fame. It
is then Shakespeare, Homer, Goethe.

"The Virginians Are Coming Again" ranks with the best
that Lindsay did, not so much in virtue of its harmonics, its
artistry, as for its purposes, its vision. It was written, Lindsay noted, as a summary to *The Litany of Washington
Street;* but it is much more than that. It prays for the
downfall of the economic régime which came into power
through the Civil War, and which that war of intention both
in origin and prosecution put into power. It longs for Robert E. Lee to gallop again to the sea in a fury of men. It
means that all of Lindsay's heart at last was south of Mason
and Dixon's line, and that his attachment to Lincoln was
sentimental, and a survival of the Santa Claus mythology
of boyhood.

We may give a passing glance at the poem of this volume
entitled "The Song of My Fiftieth Birthday," only to say
that it is but an imitation of himself. The fresh, vigorous
manner of his characteristic best poems is gone. He only
imitates it here. Unlike Milton, who wrote *The Paradise Re-
gained* and *Samson Agonistes* when he was sixty; and
Browning, who wrote "The Ring and the Book" when he
was fifty-six, and Goethe, who finished "Faust" at eighty-
three, Lindsay was a poet whose work was done at fifty. He
had made all the use of his great material gathering that
his powers were capable of; and for the two years that remained he was fated to watch the shadows creep down the
wall, and to lament his youth which had passed more swiftly
than he could realize. He left a small sheaf of poems which
will be issued posthumously, which were like the gleanings

from a rich harvest field. They were written during his Gulf Park days, to be noticed later, and while he tramped through Glacier Park with Stephen Graham in 1921. One of these poems, however, has a flickering of the imagination that was setting. It is called "The Tall Fifth Monarchy Man," and celebrates Milton with solemn music, with moving dignity. The gallop and the shouts of the great poems have subsided in favor of a twilight interior where Lucifer's enemy and God's holy scholar is playing the organ, while Oliver Cromwell stands by and has to be informed who the musician is. Both in conception and execution the poem is remarkable, it is unique in the old Lindsayian sense. He also left "The Ezekiel Chant," and "Mentor Graham, School Teacher One Hundred Years Ago." The former he privately printed, after having it published in *The Hiram Bulletin* of Hiram College in 1930. The latter was Lindsay's last published poem. It appeared in *The Illinois State Journal* of November 8, 1931. For the rest, his posthumous poems were addressed to the young woman who stirred his imagination at Gulf Park in 1923 and 1924, and are of trifling interest.

A word about Milton and Poe from Lindsay's diaries will show how his devotions ranged and even varied. In 1921 he noted, "A Springfield with 1000 Poes rather than 1000 Whitmans! Poe was after all the final impulse of my life. Poe is the final word, the really creative personality, the jewel case of new radium. The civilization he implies was a circle of Whitmans and Jeffersons on the outer edge, and are only of Whitman and Jefferson beneath it." We are not concerned with the absurdity of this specimen in criticism, and self-understanding, but only with the manner in which his mind worked and the place at which it arrived. But in 1924 he noted in his diary: "It was Milton made me a poet and blessed me and cursed me at nine years of age." Considering Lindsay's many references to Eve and Lucifer in his poems, and that he spent the last summer of his life in a studious reading of *Paradise Lost,* and also that his last considerable poem was on Milton, one may say that if Poe influenced his metrics, Milton sustained his vision and his moral fervor.

CHAPTER XVIII

WITH Lindsay's fame, which came in 1913, the life ended which he had led and from which he had struggled to escape, and so much wounded himself in the attempt. He had, in consequence, something to occupy his energies beside introspection and planning, though he never ceased to do either. By no means is this the case unfortunately. But he became a platform celebrity as well as a famous poet; and instead of hearing the windmills afar as he tramped by the Santa Fé Trail, he heard the clicking of Pullman wheels; instead of livery stables and sheds for a place to sleep he had hotel rooms amid clatter and racket in the cities over America; instead of sleeping like a stone after a day of walking in the open air, he often tossed with his head full of blood and his heart beating with the excitement of an evening of reciting; instead of the song of the Rachel Jane he had the giggling and the iterant questions of the club woman. All this until his nerves ran blood. His last diaries are full of irritable and querulous exclamations. "I have been high-browed to death. . . . I have heard enough tall talk to build ten thousand towers of Babel." Everywhere he went he was asked the same set of questions until all his patience broke down. "I hunger and thirst for a new set of questions." Lindsay had dignity, but he was also democratic of manner, and he was accessible. But on the lecture circuit handshaking, autographing, and some dining out were inevitable. The statesman longs and works to become president. When he reaches that position he is hunted to death by those who want to gaze at him, even if they have no political favor to ask. Lindsay dreamed of impressing his vision, his personality, on his city, on America. It is a species of megalomania to cherish such an am-

bition with the passion and preoccupation with which he did
so. But when he stepped to a place of power where he could
measurably influence the culture of his time he found that
the fatigues and vexations of such a herculean task robbed
him of peace, of strength at last, and of power to write more
poems. Like his mother, however, he lived by forensic excitement, by agitation, and by reform programs, by the
activity of that egotism which he confessed he had, and
which is a distinctive trait of the Frazee psychology. At
bottom it is a kind of Puritan tampering with life, a kind
of fidgety dabbling with the universe, in order that life may
be made over in the image of the desire and the dissatisfaction of one feeble human mind. All this may be but an excess of thyroid. At any rate, it is the basic chemical in the
mind which makes tyrannicides, revolutionists, zealots, re-
formers, and the founders of religions.

All the while such enthusiasts never stop to consider how
many of their fellows would really like a city or the world
made over as such dreams, if realized, would make them. Let
us suppose that Springfield or America could be re-archi-
tectured in the manner described in *The Golden Book of
Springfield*, who would want to live in either? Lindsay got
into the very life that he had sworn he would never live.
He ceased to live for the sake of living, for his thoughts,
his perceptions, as Thoreau lived. No business man slaved
to his desk was more chained down than Lindsay as he
travelled all over America time and again, reciting "The
Congo," and other poems, until he could say that more than
a million people had heard him. He did this for nothing
except for the means of life, and for the sustenance that it
gave to his inordinate desire for applause and appreciation,
without which he was miserable. He could study an Egyptian grammar in order to draw hieroglyphics; he failed to
take to heart what Emerson said that "The strength of the
Egyptians is to sit still." The touring cars went clacking

and quacking in mad haste to get somewhere, and Lindsay could sing the folly of such empty activity, but he himself came to hastening from the Atlantic to the Pacific as a member of the American mass that is never still. He could even observe that in all the cities of America there is nothing but streets for the hurrying multitudes, and not a chair on the sidewalk, nor a place to sit down and enjoy life, not even in the parks. But, noting this fact, so significant of American psychology, he too ran on, and found no rest except in the beds of hotels where he recuperated for the next ordeal of chanting and handshaking. All this was to stave off poverty, to live. And yet poverty overtook him at the last. His helmet was not the tin pan of Johnny Appleseed, but a cluster of flies about his bleeding forehead. Would he have written more and better poems if he had sat down, if he had rested, if he had lived for the sake of life itself? Perhaps not; and so we shall refrain from wishing that we might have re-made him.

In 1920 Lindsay made his first real national tour of the country as a platform poet. In this year he had published *The Golden Whales of California, and Other Rhymes in the American Language*, which was severely ridiculed. For that matter, *The Chinese Nightingale and Other Poems*, published in 1917, had been sharply attacked by one of the New York minor poets who published his animadversions in *The Chicago Daily News*, a medium that had a great circulation in Springfield. Thus Lindsay was put to the test which all poets and writers must meet. He was compelled to write poems, and if possible, in his best manner, and to keep his spirit clear and his nerves fresh to write them; but to do this in the presence of dispraise and ridicule. Criticism did Lindsay no good whatever, for his mind was not of the analytical cast that could take instruction. He sang naturally or not at all. Criticism only made him self-conscious. He was generous about attacks made upon himself, and unresentful. He tried to take them in good part and profit by them. It was impossible. Their effect was only to lower the sales of his books, and to infect him with discouragement. Thus, at this time when he was just about forty years of age, the shadows began to drop about him from every side; and he began to see himself as a jazz poet, a kind of clown, whose vogue was passing and had even passed. All this despite his enormous egotism and resolution to persist to the end.

However, in 1920 a happy experience came to him, and one which greatly extended his fame and gave him courage. On August 14 he sailed with his mother for England, where he was hospitably received in London and at Oxford and Cambridge, where he recited to the astonishment of the British, whose wonder had been stretched about as far as it could go by the colloquialisms of "The Everlasting Mercy." Lindsay was cordially entertained by John Masefield and other notables. On one occasion he received a guinea for a recital; for the rest he exchanged rhymes for tea and cakes. The English notables come to America and take in large sums of money with which to support themselves when they return to England for the composition of more poetry or fiction. They make excellent contracts and refuse to walk to the lecture platform until their honorariums are safely tucked in their pockets; America is their golden goose yielding rich feathers, and an object of satire when plucked and denuded. Lindsay, forever the pilgrim boy, "lame but hunting the shrine," received praise and hospitality in England and seemed content with them as compensation. He returned to Springfield in November, where the glamour of English recognition, still clinging to him, caused him to be received by his home town with acclaim. It now looked as if after long years, after the days of War Bulletins and their disturbing effect upon his standing in the community, he had captured his people, and could abide in their midst as an honored citizen, a treasured possession. It was not to be so. A banquet was given him and his mother, at which, according to the report of one who was present, Lindsay betrayed a pride in his English conquest which seemed invidious to the Springfield assembly. According to the same witness, Mrs. Lindsay measurably mollified the resentment of the audience by a charming talk worthy a finished politician in a tight place. But all independent of this banquet and this episode it was not possible in the nature of things for Springfield to take Lindsay to its arms. Disasters and sorrows now followed which sent Lindsay away again on the long, long road, not walking, but travelling in Pullmans. For the most part this was true, though in 1921 he took a tramp with Stephen Graham through Glacier Park, out of which came the book, *Going to the Sun*, published in 1923.

For a time now he was occupied with his book *The Art of the Moving Picture*, published in 1922. In this year, Lindsay's mother died, which was the disruption of his whole universe. Even a wholly masculine man will feel that the death of his mother severs a spiritual umbilical cord, and sets him apart to live an independent existence, where he must sustain himself the best he can. And Lindsay, who never grew up, whose mother had been his mentorial stay when he disliked and feared her, and his nourishment, his bosom of rest when he loved her, was struck down into confusion and darkness when this tragedy befell him. In the year after his mother died he suffered a complete nervous and physical breakdown from which he never wholly recovered.

Fast following upon this came the legal and business matters of settling her estate. Philistine Springfield now saw its opportunity to get rid of Lindsay. He loved the old residence where he was born and had grown up. He had chosen Springfield for his own for life. To send him into exile unfriendly people in Springfield fomented an artificial disagreement between Lindsay and his sisters, one of whom then lived in China, and one in Cleveland, by which Lindsay lost the occupancy of the house. Thus moved out of his ancestral abode, it was turned into a boarding-house. The old heirlooms were packed in the closets, the miniatures of the Nicholases and the Vachels were locked away, and what Lindsay called "the fat, rich, illiterate, climacteric women of Springfield" had an enormous satisfaction in this circumstance, and in keeping well-disposed heirs on the warpath by a crossfire of "financial advice." Such are his own words. He dreamed that a Springfield university would have put these marplots right, and grieved that it was not yet established. Thus, with his father dying in 1918, and his mother in 1922, and with the loss of this beloved house, his city passed from his hand too, the city of his special choice and illimitable dreams. His world collapsed in ruins all at one fell swoop. His woe had come from those who hated poetry and the whole poetry movement, with a deadly hatred, as Lindsay declared, and who with Lindsay's departure believed that the future of Springfield was in their hands. After Lindsay was gone and was thus out of their way they could, without the offense of his presence, show Springfield visitors the room in which Lindsay was born, and the room where he wrote and drew, which contained furniture made by Lindsay with his own hands when he was a boy of thirteen. "All the fat females who are so lustful of useless power, who brought this about, not one of them willingly opened a book in her life." So wrote Lindsay to me from Spokane in 1927. In this letter Lindsay said that he had not had a five-year uphill fight for nothing, but that he was settled happily in Spokane, with an entirely new start that he would not give up for the world. Yet in about two years after he was back in Springfield, for to quote the letter again, "I am not going to be robbed of Central Illinois by anyone, however deft and powerful they may be. The word Springfield is written in letters of Utopian gold, is going into every paper and book I write till I die. It will be the mystic city of America. Think of all those people in Springfield pawing my things over, and showing them to visitors, as though I were the 'dear departed.' They ran me out to do it, but I will make Springfield a beautiful city yet."

What should Lindsay do now, thus practically run out of Springfield? He thought of going back to the Chicago Art Institute, and there enrolling for another year by way of escape. In moments of flush blood he confessed that he was vain, egotistical, and conceited as a turkey cock. "Just plain, colloquial conceit is the word that describes me. Egoism, egotism and megalomania are entirely too lofty." But nursing his critical wounds, he descended to vast humilities. "I do not want to be asking for the humblest place as a poet. The only words that ever cheer me up are bard, ballad singer, troubadour." At this time he was also planning, theorizing, and dreaming as of old. In his eighty-fifth year he wanted to be a senator, well known for his drawings. He even thought of running for Congress at this time. Again he looked forward to his one hundredth and one hundred and fifth year when he would be producing drawings based on Chinese script and Egyptian hieroglyphics. In point of fact, he ended all dreams and plans by going to Gulfport in the spring of 1923, where he became a sort of resident poet at Gulf Park College. Here he stayed through that spring and the school year of 1923–24, leaving there for Spokane in June. It was not a happy experience.

Lindsay's love-life has been more or less indicated as this study has proceeded. The truth is that his days were a battle between his sworn and innate chastity, and his intense æstheticism in regard to women. In 1904 he became greatly attached to a Springfield woman, and an engagement followed which lasted for several years. The romance began while he was at Hiram. He was really in love with this woman's sister, but she had married another and Lindsay transferred his affections quite completely. When he was unable to make an income sufficient to base a marriage upon he asked to be released from this engagement; and so before he was thirty he experienced what was an inevitable and painful disappointment. He dreamed of love all his life, and his poems are full of it, and all the while he was very proud of the fact that he was a virgin, and was not ashamed to boast of it. As a little boy his father had terrified him of venereal disease, and this fear coupled with religious scruples kept him on the lonely path, where he was miserable enough, even to nervous disturbances and physical ills which were traceable to an abstention so prolonged and so unnatural.

On the other hand Lindsay never had any great temptations to lapses. He was not attractive to women, both because of his austerities and principles, and because his manner was self-consciously histrionic, and lacked the simplicity which guarantees comradeship and understanding. When he went to Gulf Park he was but in his forty-fourth year, which is to say he was at an age when many men are youths in body, and men in minds; and for this double power are irresistible magnets to women of understanding and appreciation. Lindsay had celebrity, which was impressive enough, and perhaps in places like Gulf Park was of an awe-inspiring sort. But though he here fell desperately in love with an admirable girl in her early twenties it was not returned; though his love was honored by scrupulous honesty, by no coquetry, by the most straightforward words from the first that she felt no emotion for him upon which a marriage could be possible. Lindsay was hurt; but the matter is less important than other things which bear upon his tragedy and the contributions to it which just now were multiplying.

The malapert intermeddling of one of Lindsay's relatives
may be noticed, not because it produced a misunderstanding
which ruptured this romance; for there was no romance in
the real sense; but because in Lindsay's state of health and
mind this blow from the side and from a quarter where he
had the right to expect good will and good judgment in his
behalf was humiliating to the last degree, and helped to
stagger his insecure state of mind. Lindsay at times thought
that but for this busybody he would have won this woman,
but in his clearer moments he knew better than that. Once
before, if not twice before, Lindsay had loved, only to lose
the woman to another man, and he had survived serenely.
For to the credit of Lindsay it should be said that despite
his training and his heredity, and his intense prepossessions,
he could say farewell without bitterness, and keep the memory of lost ones in a sweetness of reflection. What is more
important is that he overcame many weaknesses to become
a sweet singer, and in many particulars a sane singer, keeping by the exercise of some overmind a control over his towering imagination, which always threatened his thinking and
the clearness of his vision. Lindsay was alone in Gulf Park, a
wanderer on the face of the earth, a lame boy compelled to
play the part of a man when he couldn't; and he was an
ill man. He would have been greatly fortuned if at his time
he could have found peace and support in marriage. But
that he did not does not seem to be the most poisoned tip
of the arrow which had entered him deeply, and which he
could not withdraw. That was the growing sense that he
could less frequently transcend himself, as he had done in
"The Santa Fé Trail" and "The Chinese Nightingale";
that his material came plastic to his hands less powerfully
than formerly. These feelings were likely to create the
dreadful fear that he could do no more, or would soon be
able to do no more. And as people sometimes in a mortal
illness complain that not enough is being done for them, that

something ought to be done and could be done to restore
them, so Lindsay was now inclined to blame this or the other
one for the falling off of his muse, for the state of his mind,
as to which last item he was in the right in part. But at
no time did he commit the injustice toward the young woman of Gulf Park by saying that she was unfair. He recognized that she honored his affection, and that her attitude
was dictated by the most delicate good will and kindness of
heart. And accordingly he kept her memory in affectionate
regard to the last. The crisis at Gulf Park was more at-
tributable to a complication there with the school authorities
than by this unfortunate love affair, depressing as that was
to Lindsay's spirits.

He felt that if there was not a thwarting of his plans at
Gulf Park there was a lack of interest in his work. He had
not gone there to be a routine teacher, or to mark time in a
recitation room. He felt isolated, and as he declared had
no ally in the Seven Arts. To the extent that there was any
interest in what he did, it was because of curiosity in him as
a novelty, a literary figure. There was no interest in his
books. *The Handy Guide for Beggars* did not impress the
students, except as a ballyhoo, not as a veritable creed. He
said that one year of isolation there was enough; for he belonged to nothing there, and was welcome in no group outside the school, if he advocated a single idea in any of his ten
books. The situation at the college at last became impossible,
and the accumulated mass of despondency and depression
over the failure of his work forced him to leave. Dancers
experimented over America with his poems—not Gulf Park!
Dramatists dramatized his stories, and movie-people read his
books, but not Gulf Park, not a soul from New Orleans to
Mobile! His book on the movie had won the great praise of
Gordon Craig. But no Gulf Park girl had ever read it, or
applied it to a single film, though the girls were all marched
to the movie every Monday morning. This indictment of

Gulf Park is taken from one of his letters, in which he declared that in Spokane he had found the hearty co-operation of Percy Grainger. He had been consulted on pageants, he was introduced to dancers who danced his poems. In Gulf Park the board of trustees was openly hostile to a library; and indifferent to himself as a writer of books. In a word Lindsay was hurt. Life in Gulf Park had been suffocation. We quote in terms from the letter to one of the officials of the school: "While I was at Gulf Park I was making the best effort I could to be loyal to my life in the school, and in the country in which it was located. Consequently I buried as deeply in me as I could all that was untoward, and refused to acknowledge it to myself as far as possible. I paid the penalty for it further on. Under other skies, and with contrasting surroundings all that was buried came to the surface of memory with redoubled force, and I had to reckon with it." The whole story is that Lindsay was an artist, and could not live where there was no aliment for his artistic life. His vanity always had to be fed; but a fairer way to state this circumstance is that here at his school Lindsay was spiritually starving to death, at the very time that his creative energy cried for expression. Do not poets live on love and fame? Hence it happened that Lindsay, who went to Spokane in June and who expected to return to Gulf Park College in the fall, stayed on in Spokane, and made it his residence until 1929.

He established himself in a hotel, where his rooms became the literary center of the Northwest, as one writer has extravagantly phrased it. They were certainly the center of Spokane, and the Mecca of travellers who knew of Lindsay's celebrity. He began to write again, and to appear in schools and colleges to chant his songs. He had found his life again. Here he was refreshed with the companionship of Percy Grainger. Spokane and his experiences there furnished him many themes and inspirations. He played poem games with

Stoddard King, a columnist of Spokane, and he was forgetting his troubles and his disappointments. Elizabeth Conner, whom he had seen at Mills College when she was a little girl, was there. She was herself a talented writer, variously trained to be the wife of a poet; and he married her on May 19, 1925. Their honeymoon, spent in Glacier Park, has been mentioned.

But Spokane was not a Utopia after all. A letter by Lindsay tells the story. "The attitude of the Spokane Gentry," he wrote, "who are all millionaires, or pretend to be, is that if I be a good boy all my days, maybe I can be a columnist on the evening paper, or maybe a special writer on the morning paper in the far, far future. They have not the remotest notion they are insolent. If to cure this evil I modestly submit a clipping from London or New York it is dropped into the waste basket, and I am patronized some more, and told to write like Eddie Guest, and that I am too high-brow, and nobody in the whole world understands my exceedingly high-brow poems, and if I am to have a local standing among these millionaires, who consider Eddie Guest a book worm, I am to stop eccentricities, change my church, my party, my clothes, my wife, my opinions on golf, and write up the president of the National Greeters' Association as he passes through town. I have received this point-blank order in so many ways it actually amounts to insolence. It comes from millionaires who have been above the law till they have become senile. The idea that Elizabeth and I are two bronchos that will not be broken is utterly anathema to them. They know how many children we should have, and that I should quit writing poetry. They are 'favorably surprised,' and make a special case of it, whenever I am proved to have done well. This town invited me here as its guest after the death of my father and mother, and while the Springfield estate was being settled up. Then yesterday I had a long 'friendly talk' from one of the inviters. In substance it was that I was a paying guest, and was to pay through the nose before I left town, and pay from the day I landed here. This though I was teased nine months, absolutely besieged to come. My crimes are that I have refused to be socially a lounge lizard, and absolutely at the disposal of people worth over a million dollars, and have refused to treat with contempt people whose fortunes are below that figure. Then I have been as frank as this letter, but I was born that way. . . . Then I wrote a poem on Andrew Jackson when I was ordered to write one on William Waldorf Astor. Then another crime was I went on writing the same kind of poetry I wrote before I came here, and expected people to read it. Then another crime was I did not write like Eddie Guest. I was thoroughly skinned by my great and hospitable host yesterday, this marvelous Lorenzo, through a messenger and subordinate, because my work was too 'high-brow.' A man forty-eight years old is to be drummed out of town because he will not write poetry for the kind that never read a line of poetry in their lives. I am an old fashioned democrat, a Jeffersonian, Al Smith democrat, a Wilson democrat. I have been ordered to turn Tory Republican or leave town. I have been ordered to join the Episcopal Church, or remain ostracised by all the millionaires who own the town and that church. Meanwhile these fake debts do keep me down." Did Dante have a much worse lot?

"I think," he went on, "they were looking for a poet something like Robert Herrick, in character and writing, and a little like Alexander Pope, with the manners of Beau Brummel, and the prejudices and asinine ideas of Fitz-Greene Halleck. They certainly did not want Vachel Lindsay, and obviously did not open one of his books before he arrived. Now that is all over; I actually have presumed to pick out my own wife, and write poems on subjects I myself select, and have had the nerve to have two babies without consulting anybody but dear Elizabeth, I discover that the hospi-

Vachel Lindsay with Mrs. Lindsay and their children (1929).

tality of this town was bunco from first to last. They hate every fundamental idea for which I stand, and assume if an author is not worth from one to ten million dollars all offers of hospitality are withdrawn, as secured under false pretenses. Hospitality represented some fake on my part. I was actually a poet with the income of a grocer, a baker and a candle-stick maker. There are still rumors going around the town that I am a millionaire who will not pay up; that I am subsidized to advertise a railroad; that my wife and I have started the first papers for divorce, and everything under the shining sun in the way of Jesuitical persecution, while my books have been cut dead, and there is not a soul converted to what I stand for but my wife. I am certainly a citizen of Springfield, Illinois, and will be till I die. I want to get back there as soon as possible, to my birthplace with my wife and children, and stay there forever. De La Mare's Listener represents exactly the way I feel about the old place Springfield, Illinois. If you are to lecture about me I want you to know the bottom of my heart, and not to skim the surface. I hope you will go on saying I am a citizen of Springfield, Illinois, for that is the real truth. A trust company holds the house at present, and lets school teachers room there who are glad to show any time the place where I used to write. Since I am the only son, and my son is the only son of the only son, and one sister lives in Italy, and the other in Cleveland, it seems to me I have the right to go back where I belong and write in the old home where I did the most and best writing. I see no reason why I should be banished like Dante, and heckled by strangers. They heckle me and then say, 'Isn't it sad?' These are the things that keep me from being the singer that I once was. I want to sing and I want a place to sing. Why should the room where I once wrote be exhibited as a commercial curiosity, while I have to fight for the chance to live there? It is like cutting off the leg of a perfectly well man, and then exhibiting it in alcohol in a museum. They all expect me to be as good a lawyer as Elihu Root, and as good a poet as Homer 24 hours of the day; or else to take the consequences. And how they love to break me, and then try to pity me."

And so in the spring of 1929 Lindsay with his family moved back to Springfield and abandoned the Utopia of Spokane. During his years of residence there he was lecturing over the country as before, in order to support himself and family. He was nearing fifty years of age and needed honor, peace, obedience, troops of friends. He had none of them. His mind was like a piece of exposed radium, it was rapidly dissipating itself. The electric currents of his highly charged nature were producing an accelerated electrolysis. His diaries and letters show this very clearly. A time or two while sojourning thus in Spokane, and on lecture tours he had passed through Springfield, looking longingly at the capitol, the familiar houses, of which he wrote feelingly to his wife, saying, however, that he would not go back to Springfield until he could take the town like a conqueror. On these occasions he did not get off the train, but contented himself with gazing at the passing scene from the car window. Sorrow was tearing from his lyre the string which was worthy the strain.

Illinois, like the other States, is devoured and always has been devoured, by bureaucrats, by the parasites known as officeholders and politicians, by poseurs and patriots, by war men howling for preparedness, by all sorts of Cagliostros of good and bad causes. In Chicago alone there were firemen's pension funds to support men who were engaged in their active years in putting out fires. In this civilization, who had regard for the man like Lindsay, who spent all his life fighting the fires of lust and hate and greed? There were municipal employees' annuities to feed those who carried precincts and wards as local captains in order to get a job at the city hall, and who got it, and then fed at the public trough for years, and then retired on this form of gratuity. There were park employees' annuities, and policemen's annuities, and annuities for employees of the public library, for those who kept books in order on the shelf, Lindsay's included; but how absurd to give anything to Lindsay, who wrote the books! Let him lecture. If his books didn't sell something must have been wrong with the books; and this is a world where only the fit deserve to survive. Lastly, there were teachers' pension and retirement funds. Was Lindsay a teacher? Did he deserve to retire, to have tranquillity and leisure? Illinois has given purses to the widows of dead governors, and governors at that who betrayed the State. Lindsay was greater than any governor, or any man that Illinois has produced, and in addition he spent himself trying to enrich the life of Illinois and to make it civilized. Illinois would have honored itself by granting a pension to Lindsay for life, and by that token signalized his return. In that way Lindsay would have come back to his native State as a conqueror. Instead he entered the city only to start forth again to lecture until he died. One hundred and fifty dollars a month from a State whose wealth was more than twenty-two billions of dollars in 1929 would have relieved Lindsay's distress; and it would have spoken volumes for the civilization of Illinois. Springfield was then full of millionaires, not to mention Chicago, some of whom had made their money by exploiting and stealing the resources of the State; and others by operating mills of hate and false reports, ignorance, and calumny. They had thriven on the fame that Lindsay had brought to Illinois, while ignoring him, or libelling him. Money is all, practically and in the Marxian sense. Resolutions of respect, speeches, prayers, editorials, and even funeral wreaths are much cheaper than pensions, and make so much more noise!

During these years of lecturing while Lindsay abode in Spokane his letters written to his wife tragically tell the story of the impact which anxiety, fatigue, and the failure of his books were making upon his vitality and his mind. He was a centrifugal nature, expansive and discursive, and therefore lyrical. As he went on, and the centrifugal forces in him increased under a relaxed check, they became wild flames at times, flames of spurts and flares; they ceased frequently to be the steady fire of the crucible. For this reason his habitual ideas, like Mystic Springfield, cathedrals, the bringing in of a new era for America, all the Lindsay preoccupations became less like the speculations of Swedenborg, and more like the Cumorah visions of Mahomet or Joseph Smith. Again he wrote letters of great beauty, and of clearest reason, letters as well which spoke his magnanimity, and the purity of his heart.

In April of 1926 he was on the train near Detroit, and thus wrote to his wife: "I am in sight of a new nationalism in poetry, possibly best voiced from the Spokane region after we have really made friends with some injuns. I see this whole land as a unit. I have traveled over it so much, and a thousand songs and drawings have almost reached the surface about it. There is something in me that is patriotic, I just can't help it, and I see the whole land as a unit from the very beginning. Patriotism like love is a most imperfect passion, and surely I have it, with all its imperfections. The fact that it is generally tied up with war has almost spoiled it for me, but just the same I have seen this land as a whole, and as a peaceful splendor, and it really means a very great deal to me. I seem to have a kind of heartache for every State in the Union, no matter how silly that may seem. I love the United States, however strange that may be. And in spite of all the struggle of this tour I love the land I have passed over, and the land I have looked upon. Every morning from the train has been lovely, and every evening has been lovely. Spring will not be all gone when I get to Spokane. We will love the earth."

In this month of April he had paid a visit to New York, and called at the Players Club where I saw him, and for the last time. His voice boomed and his laugh rolled and soared as of old. He seemed to me a vigorous man. I procured for him a guest card for which he was profusely grateful. He wrote to his wife about this courtesy, saying that "it is just wonderful." Despite Lindsay's contacts with the world, and his acquired social understanding he remained in some particulars a villager to the end, lacking that valuation of things which a citizen of the world possesses. On this occasion I proposed him for membership to the club, which he was inordinately desirous of joining. The same evening he was induced by some of the really distinguished members of the club, who gathered about him, to read some poems from the proof sheets of a forthcoming book which he had with him. He did so, but in the excitement of the moment forgot that he was in a club where members were reading, writing letters, and resting. An old member of the club, a sort of Warwick of its affairs, and a former magazine editor, took great exception to this reading, and threatened to prevent Lindsay's election to membership. But the matter passed off agreeably, and Lindsay was admitted. Whether Lindsay knew about the attitude of this member I do not know. But I saw when talking with Lindsay that his heart was hurt by the circumstances into which his career had come. He lamented that he was no longer received in New York as formerly. Once he had to bar his room door at the hotel, once he had to hire some one to answer the telephone for him; once he had to refuse himself to newspaper reporters, and to select his dining-out invitations, refusing many of them. Now he could come to New York and no one noticed him. The explanation was that he was no longer a curiosity; New York had seen him often, and heard him often. But Lindsay, who could not live without affection or homage, could not understand this change, at least he could not bear it with equanimity. So it was that he wrote his wife from New York in this April, "I am no longer fashionable in New York, and have been shown it very plainly, especially this last time."

A description of Lindsay as he looked in the flesh at the Players on this occasion will preserve a picture of the man. He was not changed from his former self, as I had seen him in Chicago from 1914 to 1920, as I had seen him in Springfield during those years. He stood perhaps 5 feet 9 inches, and seemed to weigh about 150 or 160 pounds. His hair was sandy brown, his eyes gray to yellowish to bluish, his nose large and fleshy, his brow retreating, and with a Neanderthal ridge over the eyes. His jaws swept and curved from the ear to the chin, which was rather pointed and stuck forward with a certain self-assertion. His mouth was ample, with the upper lip protruding beyond the lower. Its gully, or groove from the nose down was deep and conspicuous. When he talked the corners of his mouth had a tendency to cling together, which gave a sort of lisp to his enunciation. One can notice this lisp in the Victrola records made of his poems in the fall of 1931. The whole contour of his head and face was of a rhythm which swept back like a leaning zero. He looked at times very much like a Pierrot, like a clown in serious mood, with the paint washed from his face, with his manner changed to that of the average gentleman. This leaning sweep of his head was accentuated by his posture when facing one in conversation. Then his head seemed thrown back; his eyes had a way of squinting elephantine fashion, as if he was not sure of the tenor of what was being said to him, whether it was quite friendly, or half satirical; or as if he were trying to follow studiously the words addressed to him. All these mannerisms combined as ensemble had the appearance to some people of vanity and self-sufficiency of which he was not really guilty in any objectionable sense. But he was vain, and he was proud of his suc-

Photograph by Herbert Georg Studio.

Vachel Lindsay reciting his poems (1928).

cesses, when not cut into humilities by indifference or ridicule; and he could not abstain entirely from carrying his platform presence and manner into the moments of private converse. In a word he had ways which displeased many people, and interfered with his acceptance. On this day at the Players when I last saw him he said farewell to me when departing with his old smile; but I could see that his mood was overcast, that he was unhappy. I stood watching his figure as he walked toward Fourth Avenue. He rolled from side to side like an old pedestrian, like a tired man; he was casting his head up right and left, as if looking at the tall buildings, as if possibly talking to himself. And so he passed from my view forever.

His letters to his wife during this month of April betray a circular psychology which passed from hope to discouragement, from happiness to melancholy. One time he was lamenting his decline in New York; another time he was feeling the queer strength which he had experienced between the time of the *War Bulletins* and the time he wrote the Booth poem. Then he would write, "I have to grow up and be a statesman. I just can't be a boy any longer, so you must make a statesman out of me." Again he would be asking, "How do men develop when they are at my age, when they begin to have careers as governors, senators, and the like? So I want to be a political fact." He felt somehow that the Jews were throttling his career, and devouring, past restoration, the America that he loved. He wrote: "This month's *Century Magazine* confirms my statement that the Jews are in absolute and triumphant control of New York City. We did a very strategic thing when we identified ourselves with the far Northwest."

Though he now feared New York, though he had been greatly damaged by the iota-subscripts of the reviewing world, he was still carrying on a correspondence with many of them, as he had done for years. He was still mentioning them in his prefaces as he had put them as dramatis personæ in *The Golden Book of Springfield*. It is inconceivable that he did not recognize the enmity at heart of these ephemerides. One cannot escape the conclusion that he was feeding the hands that bit him, with the hope that food would make them cease to bite him. All this was no less than obsequious gestures, one feels sure, and makes a false note in Lindsay's character. To be wise as a serpent and harmless as a dove may take the form of biting if you can, but if struck on the head to mourn like the dove and to hang the wounded head.

His letters of this period are characterized by a degenerating handwriting, which is sometimes so large in its rolling Spencerian curves that one of his written pages looks almost like a poster; again he used some kind of a stub pen or brush which made his script look as if made with a Chinese writing-stick. He took up with cigarette smoking, and at last smoked to excess, as he drank coffee to excess. Then he changed his mind on prohibition. In January of 1926 he wrote his wife, "the dry issue is a private and personal question." So had his unfriends said in Springfield and the surrounding country when he was preaching prohibition and chastity in the name of Sir Galahad. Let all Utopians of the future who want to build Magical Springfields have a care if they know enough to do such great work. After countless prayers to Lord Christ, and many poems to him, Lindsay could at forty-seven years of age write this in his diary: "I prefer the American flag to the cross. I have been a wildly patriotic American, yet a near pacifist, and the inner conflict can go on no longer." In this year of 1926 he made but $1500 after a hard lecture tour; and so he lamented that no publisher believed in him, or would let him make the fortune of the publisher and himself. In point of fact his books had been badly managed. Business skill and attention would have made them immensely successful, immensely profitable both to him and the publisher.

As of old he was still busied with self-analyzing, and thinking back to the days of his precocity at six years of age; and hence every influence of that far time from his grandfather demanded that he be restored, at this age of forty-seven, to some Olympian aspect. He was having dizzy spells when on the platform. He thought they were the result of cutting his nerves into three pieces to win first honors in creative work in speaking, writing, and drawing, and that he had rhythmic exhaustion. In fact he had had a heart-attack when suffering from influenza just before he went to Gulfport; and he had had another shortly after his marriage. He was now surely running to the end, whatever his dreams for the time when he would be eighty-five and one hundred and five.

From the record given in this book of the Frazee and the Lindsay families, and of the influence of Lindsay's father and mother upon him for good or for ill, judgment can well pass on the part of all who read it. Whether his father and mother did enough for him, or did the right thing by him, may be a matter of opinion justifying a difference according to the quality of different minds. What Lindsay himself thought of his father and mother cannot fail to be valuable. In a letter to his wife dated in January, 1929, a few months before he returned to Springfield to live, he unburdened his mind of the following: "It is the Lindsay half of me that is iron and clay, and writes *The Tramp's Excuse.* 'Old Doc' Lindsay has retired for repairs this Spring. What is left is a stringy cartoon of Ma hanging on like grim death to the main chance. . . . You never need thank her for anything, she thanked herself with such amplitude, and never hid her light under a bushel. But you can thank her flesh, if not her, if I get home and am able to rally. No Lindsay could hold out. When they bent they broke . . . all you can love in me from bridegroom to poet is Lindsay. And you will have to admit the Lindsays have so many private local fights on hand they leave you peace. . . . The more I think about the Lindsays the more mysterious they get. They are really phosphorescence that keeps people wondering and asking, 'Where did it come from?' If you want a picturesque time in Springfield make people talk about the 'Old Doc,' and forget his self-important wife. My mother's soul must guard me till I am a mile from Spokane. Then we shall be bowed out of the Pullman, and I will pray to the soul of the Old Cinnamon Bear, whose heart was tender as any woman's, Vachel Thomas Lindsay. He only could make me into a bridegroom fit for you, and what pride he would take in making his son a man."

Whether at Gulfport or Spokane, whether at New York or on the tramp, Lindsay dwelt forever in cuckoo cloudland, and so far as he could fortify himself against the realities of life with moons and mists, and the playthings of childhood he could dream magical cities and plan great campaigns for the reclamation of his country. He never really grew up. The curled darling became a man of great emotional strength; but the memory of himself as the apple of his mother's eye, as the child wonder of the grammar school, produced a sort of Narcissism, not very marked, and not at all offensive, but still definite and recognizable. He was not exactly stunted, but rather he reached a full maturity while remaining in many ways a child. His analyses and summations were logical enough when he saw that every soul is a circus; but who beside Lindsay would have reduced man's nature and the philosophy of human existence to the tropes of the sawdust ring, to clowns, horses, tinsel, tights, balloons, and popcorn? Jesus, with him, after all, was a sort of Santa Claus grown up and made suitable for adult wonder and devotion. He coupled angels and clowns in his imaginings; Christmas trees abounded everywhere in his poems; and when he dreamed of heaven it was of a celestial circus. In one poem entitled "The Celestial Circus," to be

Vachel Lindsay in his later period.

found in his *Collected Poems,* he saw himself dancing with some beloved one, where he would whirl her over his head when the trumpets of God spoke the millennial word. These two would howl praises to God, they would ride in the joy of God, on circus horses of pure white; and they would leap from the horses' backs, making Saturn and his triple rings their tinsel circus. Were the sublime aspirations of the human heart ever more reduced to the proportions, the color, and the childish wonder of silver tinsel, of baubles, and trinkets? All his sense of magic, of Poe as a magician, had its roots in these delights of Christmas morning, in these days under the white top. The imagery of the Old Testament and of Revelation exactly suited a creativeness so primitive and oriental, though in his thinking moments he could speak of the prophetical writings as ravings.

An imagination so powerful, so all compact, was susceptible to constant deception. It is not wonderful that he discovered that Spokane was not the place for him to abide. He needed, in his own language, "an old battered, scratched violin called Springfield for my most modern and ultra tunes." Nay, he needed a house with a few rooms, and an old chair in which to sit contentedly by the hour; and a vegetable garden in which to work several hours every day. He needed plenty of sleep, and simple food taken regularly; he needed above all a contented spirit. These he might have found anywhere, if he had known how to find them. Looking at his lecture receipts, lessening as they were, they would have sufficed by a simplification of living, by the philsopher's spare economies. He was not extravagant, he was not a high-liver; but he could have reduced his expenses so that they would have been well within his income, and an income besides made by easy travels and neighborhood lectures. These things were the scratched and battered violin that he needed. For above all peace was the indispensable condition of writing poetry; it was the only cure of his perturbed muse, which was forever elevated and cast down, made feverish and cooled off by the applause of audiences, and the lack of it. His mother's passion for public speaking, for organizing societies, for reclaiming a naughty world, for building the moralities of the community, for changing the world over, was the fatal defect in Lindsay's organization, which carried him down at last, after preventing him from going forward. Because he lacked the vigorous intellect of Mencken, and his courageous, humorous, invincible sagacity; because he lacked the penetration of Lewis and his gifted warriorship, he could record of himself that those two men were forever in his thoughts. They were what he wished to be for the purposes of song.

Though he wanted Springfield as an old scratched battered violin, when he got ready to go thither he wrote to an editor there, "So once when we are emphatically in Springfield we will hide till we have to travel, but distinct notice to the public that we have arrived is a very great practical favor and will make the re-conquest of the State of Illinois emphatically easier." That is, there should be a blare of trumpets to the coming of the conquering hero, entering for the re-conquest of a city never conquered. But no sooner was he back in the old Lindsay residence, which he had reclaimed by submitting to an onerous contract, which he could not fulfill easily, than he was planning to leave Springfield "for long periods without any sense of having deserted our post." And again, he was planning work to be carried out "with complete energy and precision" to force on America, "(1) a complete new conception of music; (2) a complete new conception of Americanism; (3) a complete set of religious ideas; (4) a complete set of new ideas of design." He hoped to surpass William Morris as an artist, after a quarter of a century of making drawings that were utterly bad.

Springfield gave Lindsay a cordial welcome, and he set-

tled down in the old house to what he believed would be
a long life, in spite of heart disease, and diabetes. He started
forth again on the lecture tours, and when absent continued
the writing of interminable letters to his wife. He went to
places of lost happiness, and increased his misery by behold-
ing the old faces no more, and the old days vanished. He
wrote his wife in February, 1931: "What I am really hungry for is my youth that will never return." He was tired
of wearing on his brow the idle mask of author great or
mean. A growing family increased his expenses. He was
consumed with hurt pride, and tortured with neglected egoism, and he was sweating his brains over stunts to pay rent
and taxes on the old Lindsay house. The battered, scratched
violin was too much for him. Fatigue had entered into him
so deeply that no sleep but that of death could rest him.
The picture taken of him when he arrived in Springfield is
of the face of a man smoothed round by middle-aged fat,
and the emery wheels of pitiless fate. Senility had already
taken him. Like Grover Cleveland he was mortified by the
youth of his wife, and the unfitting age of himself; and with
Christian generosity he declared that he would step aside in
order that she might enjoy her youth, and have love when
and where she craved it.

In the summer of 1931 he rested near Hazelhurst, Wisconsin, where he sojourned incognito, without telephone,
newspapers, or companions. He wrote his wife: "My head
is clear as a bell for reading. It's my poor heart that needs
the harness. There is no vacation for my heart. Always it
will tear me cruelly for you. And I know you need kindness
and wise co-operation from me. Desperate love does not
help." He asked her to practise the piano so that she could
play for him during the ensuing winter. By that music he
hoped to drive the "clickety Pullman and the jazz" from
his "tortured heart."

Where now was religion? Tears and confusion, travel and

fatigue, harsh contacts in the lecture field, the discipline of marriage had killed the mystic in him, except in rare moments like the flowering of Ezekiel. He wanted union with the godhead, and next to that with his dream America; and any other form of marriage was really an impertinence, a sacrilege, an impossibility, and a source of disillusionment, conflict, pain, disaster and death. In his marriage he was in exactly the mood that Shelley came to be in with Mary Godwin. "After the slumber of the year the woodland violets reappear, but never life and love." But unlike Shelley his attitude toward sex was complicated by a poor sex education, by his fear and hatred and love and dependence on his mother, by a morbid fear of old age and frantic hunger for youth, which began in the Gulf Park period, by too long waiting for a normal sex life, by the unhappiness of his own parents together, by a Tolstoyian conviction that sex was debasing, by his aversion to reality, by his desire for a patriarchal position without its responsibility, and above all by the tragic loneliness which no one could get through to give him solace. His dream of marriage and love was one of pure beauty, freedom, naturalness and innocence, plus a constant tension of ecstasy which flesh and blood are not made to endure, plus a complete refuge and protection in love, as if he would find with a wife what he had in the womb before he was born; plus a complete emotional and spiritual interchange by which lovers may be reborn in each other's image. Added to all this was a pronounced case of virgin fixation, of Mariolatry, of which his letters to his wife are full, telling of dreams that he had of the Virgin Mary, and asking her somehow to dream the same dream.

He would have been happier as a celibate; but after forty he could not stand the loneliness, not like Thoreau. And after long abstention from a normal sexuality he reached the point where some sort of companionship and attempt at care and the satisfaction of desire had become imperative. He arrived acutely at this pass while at Gulf Park College when about forty-four. The unhappy love interest there set him forward to find a happy one. Elizabeth Conner made him a wife as much adapted to his needs as he could have found in the world, one feels sure of this upon consideration of her personality and his. But he was a man whom religion did not suffice, and whom love and marriage left thirsty for the music that is divine.

He was his mother's son, born with the prophet's caul over his face. But deep down his mother's memory could do nothing for him in these days of desperation. In a late letter to his wife Lindsay mentioned that his sister had asked him to dedicate a book to the memory of his mother. His comment was that he was to do this "in spite of the fact that my mother fought me like a wild-cat every poem I wrote till she found Oxford listening to me. My mother had great qualities, and I tried to do them justice in 'Adventures While Singing these Songs,' which covered the ground till I was 7 or 8; but whatever I owe my mother or father, I certainly do not owe them the dedication of a single line I ever wrote. 'The Hearth Eternal' is an idealized picture of her."

There was hence no comfort to him in the memory of his mother. Her opposition to his verse was the bite of a serpent. The wound was not noticeable, may indeed have seemed to have healed in the days when acclaim surrounded him at every step he took over America. When there was silence and even jeers for his work, and when as the result of all the disasters and reverses which have been chronicled in these pages he became morbidly acute to the behavior of his fellows, and even believed at times that he was the object of a concerted enmity, he could not take his eyes from the place where his mother had bitten him in youth. He studied it, and somehow it seemed to him to account for the falling of his days. He saw that after all the wound had never healed, that on the contrary it had festered; and what was worse it could never heal as the days grew more pitiless toward him. All these things had got inside his most vital nature, like a demoniac possession; and what was worst of all he could not deny that they were part of himself, and that they could not be exorcised. Yet he was carrying in his pocket for years a sheet of paper on which his mother had written Browning's lines:

> "Grow old along with me.
> The best is yet to be,
> The last of life for which the first was made."

And he carried this sheet of paper to the day of his death, trying to believe that the best was yet to be. It was impossible for him to do this. Neither a moral will long exercised, a self-control and a submergence of congenital weaknesses out of which his hopeful, inspiring poems had been written; neither this nor a deep religious faith, a passionate vision of God, and a lifelong love of Christ, could save him from the blackness of despair that settled down about him. Instead of believing that he had great years ahead, being at this time just turned fifty-two years of age, he grieved with heart-sickening emotion at his early youth now no more. He was given to tears at times, saying that he was an old man. He had come to a pass where human comfort could not touch him; for he believed that he could write no more; and that belief robbed him of what power remained to him.

One feels sure that if Susan Wilcox, his teacher, drew his longest affection, Sara Teasdale was his life's most inspiring, most satisfying friend. They were still in his life as he was walking in the desert where the carrion birds were wheeling around the glistening bones of Christ, half buried in the sand. Miss Teasdale had come into public notice about the time that Lindsay did, when as a contributor to Reedy's *Mirror*, her delicate poems were among the first written by a woman to distinguish the new poetry in America. Lindsay had dedicated *The Chinese Nightingale and Other Poems* to her; he had dedicated his *Collected Poems* to her; and in the dedication of his posthumous poems he referred to her as that "golden queen for whom I wrote the best songs of my days." "Her hand was on my head and on my heart," are the words, "and we were no more than one breath apart the day we wrote the best songs of my days." But no hand on his head could save him from the shadows that now fell around him. The wounded deer must seek the herb no more in which its heart-cure lies. He could not find in friends a mitigation to his pain; and he dared not try.

On November 30, 1931, Lindsay gave a lecture at the First Christian Church of Springfield. He had returned exhausted in the late fall from a lecture tour which was marked by a distressing discourtesy to him in Washington. For some reason, for something that he said, for something in his manner, the audience to the extent of about 200 persons walked from the auditorium. An orator, an actor must have the support of his audience. A poet still more requires this support, because his recital is not only dependent upon it, but his writing, for which the sustained mood created by appreciation and applause keeps him in singing strength. With all that we have recounted, this Washington episode was deep in Lindsay's mortification; and he was a man in fast failing health. When therefore the chance came to appear before an audience of his beloved Springfield he was heartened. When he found the audience large and cordial, and the applause enthusiastic as he ended, he turned to a friend saying: "I feel that at last I have won Springfield." But this great consummation contained no heart-cure of moment. It was too late.

Ill and exhausted, with only $76 in his pocket as the profit of a grilling lecture experience, and with $4000 in debts for living expenses for his wife and little children and for himself, there was no place for him to turn for solace.

[359]

He was in the fatal trap, the door had sprung to and fastened itself, and there was nothing for him to do but to wait for the end. The wait was not long, it was but a week, but the torture of that week defies words.

He was up and down in bed, at times too weak to go about safely. He was having auditory hallucinations. He thought he heard voices on the porch plotting his death and the death of his wife, and blackmail. His wife could not assure him that he had been merely dreaming. After he took her word that it was all a dream he would recur to the wild belief that enemies were about the house seeking his death. He was taking bromides and luminal, but sleep fled him.

The afternoon before he died he went with his wife to the Abraham Lincoln Hotel to have tea with a group of friends. On this occasion he was at his best, in high spirits and full of humorous words. After the tea Mrs. Lindsay parted from him to do an errand, which was in fact to consult the physician about him. Lindsay went home. The doctor told her that his way of passing from melancholy to high spirits was an ominous sign. He had previously said that it might be well for her safety and that of the children to separate herself from Lindsay. However, she returned to the house to find that he had gone to bed, having become too weak to sit up. She prepared to bring his dinner to him on a tray; but he insisted on coming down to the dining-room. At dinner he fell into pitiful tears, saying that he was an old man, and that his life and work were finished. After dinner Mrs. Lindsay got him upstairs again, and then she descended to the living-room to read. He had asked her to leave him, he wanted to be alone.

In about half an hour he came downstairs full of energy and fury about every real or imagined wrong that had ever been done him; he stormed with accusations against Mrs. Lindsay for the injury she had done him in her double rôle of tyrant-mother, and scarlet woman who had taken his virginity. He wanted to get away from her and the children, and so announced himself. He wanted to go back to Hiram College, there to begin over the dreams of twenty-one, and to write more magical songs. His wife told him that she would not stand in his way, that she was only concerned for his care and support if he left her. Lindsay replied to this that He who watches over the sparrows would take thought for him. This frightful frenzy, these whirling words lasted for three hours; then he was exhausted, and in the wrath of an angry ghost he stalked upstairs. Mrs. Lindsay after a time followed him, and found him pretending to read.

She closed her eyes, finally, though not in sleep. Then Lindsay arose and descended to the lower floor again. Mrs. Lindsay in anxiety for him followed him. She found him in the dining-room putting up the family pictures, those of Mrs. Lindsay and the children, those he carried with him on his lecture tours. He looked calm and peaceful now, and when she asked him if he were all right, he replied, "Yes, dear, I'm quite all right. I'll be up in a moment."

Mrs. Lindsay went back to bed, and fell into sleep. In about fifteen minutes she was awakened by sounds of something crashing downstairs. And then she heard footsteps heavy and fast, and then the sound of Lindsay coming upstairs on his hands and knees. Mrs. Lindsay rushed out to get him, fearing that he was making for the room where the children were asleep. By this time, Lindsay was running through the upstairs hall, with his hands up, looking white and scared. As Mrs. Lindsay screamed he fell. When he was put in bed he asked for water, saying, "I took lysol." A doctor was quickly summoned, but when he arrived Lindsay had ceased to breathe. His last words were, "They tried to get me; I got them first." It was December 5, 1931, at one o'clock in the morning.

When Mrs. Lindsay went downstairs she found her picture and those of the children propped around the table centerpiece with two lighted candles burning before them. In the bathroom she found a tea-glass stained with lysol, and a large empty bottle of lysol. On the floor was a pillow from the library, and a picture of Mrs. Lindsay at seventeen propped over the little blue coat of Susan, his little daughter.

His funeral was as distinguished as sorrow could make it, and desire to erase past neglect could contrive. The City Council of Springfield, and the Legislature of Illinois passed resolutions of respect, and sermons and orations filled Springfield at the churches and in the schools, to the accompaniment of many tributes from the American press far and near. He was buried not far from the tomb of Lincoln, and committed to the centuries, as his idol had been sixty-seven years before.

CHAPTER XIX

Of those who figured in what has been termed the Poetry Revival of 1914 Lindsay was the first to become famous. E. A. Robinson belonged to an older generation than Lindsay's, and was ten years his senior. He had published *The Torrent and the Night Before* in 1896, and *The Children of the Night* in 1897. He was included by Stedman in his *American Anthology* published in 1900, and mentioned in Stedman's biographical note as a poet with an individual cast. Robinson republished his *Children of the Night* in 1905, and a new poem entitled *Captain Craig* in 1902, and *The Town Down the River* in 1910. By these books he had attained a local name bounded for the most part by New York City, though he was known to careful readers of verse in some Eastern cities and in Chicago, who had come within the radius of his personal influence and faithful friends. But Robinson had found the struggle a hard one, and that the public was indifferent to poetry and to his work. President Roosevelt had admired his poetry and had generously given him a position of support. But whether Robinson grew discouraged or not, it is true that he turned to prose plays for six years after the publication of *The Town Down the River*, and did not take up poetry again until he published *The Man Against the Sky* in 1916, which was three years after Lindsay stormed the country with his Booth poem and his book with that poem as the title piece. The revival of poetry which began to manifest itself with the emergence of Lindsay revived Robinson. As to Frost and Robinson, they followed after Lindsay. Frost first published his *A Boy's Will* in England, where he lived from 1913 to 1915, and his reputation was late and grew slowly. *The Spoon River*

Anthology was published serially in 1914, after Lindsay's name was beginning to be known far and near; and did not appear in book form until the spring of 1915. Sandburg's first book, *Chicago Poems*, was published in 1916, though his poem on Chicago was something of a sensation in 1914.

Lindsay excited a marked interest in England before there was even cultivated admiration for the work of Robinson and Frost. The English are so thoroughly aware of their own genius in literature, together with the nature of that genius and its expressions, that they are quick to see when a writer attains to their own manner of excellence and speaks in their tradition. Because of this acuteness of faculty they are sensitive to an originality which departs from their spirit and their formulas. They perceived that Whitman was a new note. Swinburne and many other leading minds of England accepted Whitman as something original and without precedent, and as an authentic spokesman of America. Likewise they saw Lindsay riding a real Pegasus, an animal that went of itself, and that pranced not along the racetracks of England, but over the plains of America, over the Appalachians and the Great Divide. So keen an observer as G. K. Chesterton called Lindsay the most national poet, and the one with the most normal energy of literary genius since Walt Whitman. He quoted in characterization of America's formal poets and of Lindsay the verse of Roy Campbell:

> "You praise the firm restraint with which they write,
> I'm with you there, of course;
> They use the snaffle and the curb all right,
> But where's the blooming horse?"

The almost unfailing critical acumen of Ludwig Lewisohn hit the mark when he said that Lindsay's poetry was the purest in America since Poe.

Lindsay went wide of the mark so frequently when exercising what critical faculty he had that his pat judgments, which are infrequent, attract attention. Thus he was on right ground when he wrote, "The new poetry movement is a Western movement, and the East and England have tried in vain to drag us in chariot wheels. The one degree Amy Lowell boasts, she received in Texas at an assembly of the new poets." In saying this he may have had in mind the uncritical inclusiveness of the Monroe-Henderson *Anthology of the New Poetry*, which took between its covers seventeen foreigners: Thomas Hardy, for example, who was nearly an octogenarian in 1917, the date of the publication of that book. Also Rabindranath Tagore, an Indian and an old writer by that time, and of no moment to American readers who were familiar with the Upanishads and the Bhaghavad Gita, was classed with the new movement by including several of his poems. In addition to these names English writers were represented who were clearly of the quality of many American ephemerides. This catholicity made the book more interesting perhaps, at least for the hour, as it made it more saleable among those who wanted to educate themselves, by one book, in the facts and work of an entire phenomenon; but such an aggregation made the book something different and beyond the import of its title.

Though Lindsay fought with desperation against the forces that choked his utterance, he could not prevent the partial occultation that came upon him about 1920, and very definitely when Robinson published *Tristram* in 1928, which by the aid of book clubs, and the tactics of careful management on the part of his publishers, by a concerted effort of New York City, was given a synthetic success. The Union which was forged in fire and blood by the Civil War is not a Union of sovereign States, united for international ends and separated as to local interests and cultures; but it is a Union under a materialistic tyranny, with no culture either national or State. This materialistic domination, this rule of commerce and money has its spiritual plane of operation. Centralization in government has placed all political power in Washington, and all money power in New York. With money power have come all the organs of expression that are of moment in America, which have drawn to their side all the book reviewers, who are really the barkers at the side-shows of Vanity Fair, paid to cry up and cry down attractions. Many of these writers are syndicated; so that the review of a book appearing originally in some New York publication shows up in a few days in Denver, in Omaha, in Portland, Salt Lake City, Los Angeles, and even Chicago. Chicago has never had a magazine, a literary supplement to direct and to encourage interest and taste in literature. The result is that what New York says about a book is imposed upon Chicago, and over the country goes the judgment of the financial capital of America 3000 miles from one of its most populous States and a thousand from its center of population. The voice of America west of the Hudson is only the ululation of an echo. It is possible for some one who has only travelled in the Mississippi Valley to write a story of the Mississippi River, and to have the writing so coached and advertised and hailed in New York that Missouri and Illinois will take up the cry, and drown their own first-hand knowledge of their own country. As there are no sovereign States, there is no independent judgment.

It was therefore a misfortune of great magnitude that William Marion Reedy died in 1920. He was the only mind in the West at the time, the only one that had been there for untold years who had the scholarship and the independence of mind and the vision to see the country as a whole and to know what a book meant, and where it was to be placed. Had Reedy lived he would have prevented, very probably, the strangulation of Lindsay, even after Lindsay had swallowed many grape seeds and was strangling himself. Under nearly all conditions of vulgarization such is

the power of thought that a judgment that goes straight
to the mark and tells the exact truth cannot be turned
aside, but will have its effect. Such were the judgments of
Reedy, who was listened to by the reviewers of New York.
They could not mould public opinion wholly unaffected by
his thinking. His death left no one to protect the country
against a lopsided development. Many sentries sprang up
to guard the tents of the West; but most of them were
blind. Those who could see had such small voices that their
cries of alarm and of praise could not be heard. H. L.
Mencken, though suspicious of poetry as an art, was friendly
to phases of the poetry movement, especially where it spoke
for liberty of thought and life. Though of the East he saw
the West, or to be more accurate, he saw merit in spite of
the fact that it was from the West. The other editors
trembled excitedly while the storm was at its height, and
published a few poems of the new poets. They did not follow the example of their English idols which make poetry
in large measure a magazine feature. The whole result was
that simultaneously with the falling off of Lindsay, and the
rise of the Eastern poets, Robinson and Frost, the magazines slipped back to their former attitude toward poetry,
which was that of the days of Gilder and his like. They
returned to sonnets written by the secretary of the editor,
or by favored hostesses where the editor was dined. Having
resisted the poetry movement and found support for their
stand in the sophistical and cold-blooded preachments of
neo-humanists, poetry became fancy-work and embroidery
again. It went back to the English tradition of Browning
and Tennyson. Literary Tammany, with all the rest that
happened, took control of poetical America. That is, this
Tammany captured the political machine of poetry; but
like the political machine could not elect its candidates.

The motley stocks and alien breeds which have taken
America cannot be America until there is an America to

mould them into Americans. And where is that America? Lindsay might sing himself hoarse of the old courthouse America, the old-horse-and-buggy America, the America of the Santa Fé Trail, of Boone, Johnny Appleseed, even of Andrew Jackson. After all, was *that* America? the East could ask, if it deigned to be interested. After all, did the East, did these alien stocks want that to be America? This was what Lindsay was up against. In this connection mention must be made of the Jews who are enormously numerous, powerful and influential. Jews are not Americans in the sense that Jews are English or French, according to habitat. The American spirit is not strong enough and of deep enough flavor to flavor them. On the contrary, they dominate the spirit of the old courthouse and the like. They do not understand it or want it. They regard it as hostile to their regimentations. What they call the pioneers are objects of aversion to them, just because the pioneers were of a different life from that which they can live and understand; just because the pioneers, who were agrarians, are a standing reproach to the artificialities and machinations of the cities, where they rule; and just because the spirit of the pioneers, despite its Bible culture, is an obstacle to a Hebraization of America. Finally what did the Jews care for Lindsay's idolatry of Lincoln? They cared little or nothing for it; because they admired Lincoln as an apostle of Hebraic-Puritanism, as a builder of a centralization in which all the brains and nerves of the land were collected in the East, in one spot in fact, where they could be used and managed; while Lindsay's idolatry of Lincoln was based upon the misconception that Lincoln was of the pioneer spirit. Lindsay despised the greedy and ignorant parasitism upon the republic and its traditions which thrives in money centers over America. To the demands of this power which said to him you must make money, you must commercialize your art, you must let us make you a freak

[368]

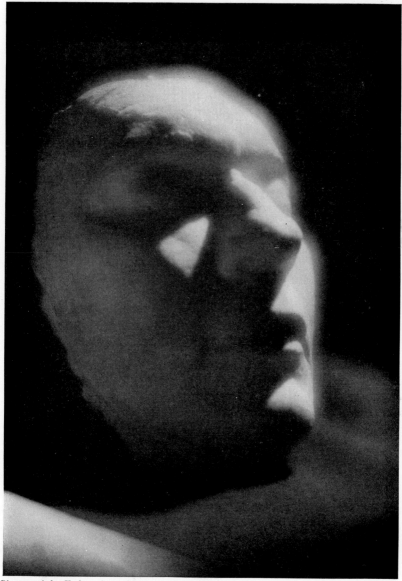

Death-mask of Vachel Lindsay.

and exhibit you for money, and if you don't we will send you to the poorhouse, he had answered that he would go to the poorhouse before submitting to these impositions. He even had to sit by and see anthologists who had used his poems rolling in money, while he was almost in want; but he stood fast. He was so saturated with American fair play that he never indulged a social or race prejudice as such; but he knew that to dislike being eaten alive was not to indulge any such prejudice.

Lindsay saw that material prosperity was beating down the hope of youth, something that Altgeld saw and expressed. Lindsay knew that the defeat of Bryan was a defeat of the wheat. Many of his purest songs radiate from economic centers like this. When he wanted to make Magical Springfield he had in mind the Athens of old, just as Alcott cherished that dream with respect to Concord. Channing said many years before Lindsay was born, "The true sovereigns of a country are those who dominate its mind, and we cannot consent to lodge this superiority in the hands of strangers. . . . A foreign literature will always be foreign. It has sprung from the soul of another people, which however like, is still not our own soul. A country like an individual has dignity and power only in proportion as it is self-formed."

It is absurd to say that men like Lindsay cannot be cherished, protected and preserved. There are ways in plenty. They did not condemn him to hemlock, but they doomed him by failing to protest against his doom, by failing to give him help out of their useless abundance. They could have consulted and decided upon some way to give him bread, and let him do his work for his city and the country, taking from that work what was good, and throwing the rubbish away.

But it was not his own city, it was not his own State that let him wear himself to death; nor was it even the America that we have been describing. He was at last as a creative artist in the hands of vast forces, some of which had been set in motion by the spirits he most admired and with whom he was closest in blood. It was men like Alcott, Thoreau, Channing, and Theodore Parker who did the most to destroy that Virginia which was Lindsay's deepest love, and the subject of his last great poem. It was these men who gave honor to the materialistic movement which imperialized America; it was these men who unmenacingly disguised with their moral character the campaign of money Hamiltonians, which overthrew Jefferson in the realm of practical affairs. That having come to pass, every other plutocratic device and trick followed. With the vulgarization of the American mind, resulting from cupidity, came the 2,000,000-subscriber magazine, proving by its popularity that there are not more than 200,000 enlightened people in the United States. These readers of such publications are part of the contingent who tortured Lindsay in Spokane. These publications and their readers give no support to poetry or to any art, or to any work of genuine merit. They may read Lewis and Dreiser and Mencken, falling in line to do so out of a mob psychology. But in the language of Nietzsche, "mercantile morality is nothing but a refinement of piratical morality, buying in the cheapest market, and selling in the dearest." These are the forces that demonstrate the proposition of Proudhon that property is robbery, and that for the reason that property is mostly obtained by the boldest kind of robbery. The rule of such people, and such a civilization was hard enough for Lindsay; but this peaceful man, and lover of the whole world in the name of Tolstoy, had to live in a time when internationalism was preached by New York, before America as a nation had anything to give as a nation. He had to live in a land already internationalized by the unassimilated breeds of many lands, and really by the dominance of Old World cultures, but made incoherent and without a natural spirit by such mixtures. How could the old courthouse America cope with such vast forces as these?

"There are two Americas," wrote Will Durant. "European America is chiefly the Eastern States, where the older stocks look up respectfully to foreign aristocracies, and more recent immigrants look back with a certain nostalgia to the culture and traditions of their native lands. In this European America there is an active conflict between the Anglo-Saxon soul, sober and genteel, and the restless and innovating spirit of newer peoples. The English code of thought and manners must eventually succumb to the continental cultures that encompass and inundate it; but for the present that British mood dominates the literature, though no longer the morals, of the American East. Our standard of art and taste in the Atlantic States is English, our literary heritage is English, and our philosophy when we have time for any is in the line of English thought."

All this is immensely true and well said. Lindsay, with all his other difficulties, inward and outward, had to stand against the enormous power behind this cultural condition. Not being Eastern American he made in fact only a slight impact upon it; and after the first excitement about his poetry subsided he was treated with supercilious indifference, and the field which he had broken and harrowed and sowed was taken and reaped by pro-English artists. He found that there was no union of spirit and mind in America; and that his own West cared more for the East than it did for the West, and cared more for Eastern poets than for him who had striven to give Springfield and Illinois a soul. They preferred the Arthurian legends to those of Johnny Appleseed and Andrew Jackson. A union implies a homogeneous sentiment and vision without reference to breeds or localities, East or West. America has not such a union, and may never have it, though many Lindsays

arise. America is politically sectional, it is sectional in matters of literature. And plutocracy is the basis of both sec-
tionalisms. There is as much sectional bitterness today as
there was in the days of a free North and a slave South,
for the reason that slavery was not the cause of the old
sectionalism, but money and political ambition were the
causes, which the war so far from wiping away exacerbated
and increased. Today the America of the million-circulation
magazines is fighting the America of the enlightened minority; the America of the Republican party is fighting
the America of what is left of the Jeffersonian Democratic
party; the America of the various churches is fighting within
itself; the America of New York, if it can be called such,
is fighting the America of the West, and the West is fighting New York. Side by side with these warfares is the fight
of the different schools of literature. And the total result
is that the American mind is not yet made.

The period of Longfellow was one of wine that had fer-
mented and settled into its characteristic flavor and body,
even if the product was second rate. But today the American mind is in another ferment, and is not made. For this
reason it is not established in a definite American character. It is touched with irrationality, corresponding to the
bubbling and the popping of mashed grapes in a jar. It is
vacillating without well-grounded principles of any sort,
without the integrity of a matured substance cleared of all
alien and inharmonious stuff. It is like the English mind
during the Wars of the Roses, in respect to its tumult and
its incoherence. Our political leaders prove these things,
and some of our best writers are proofs of them. Their
vision and imagination are defective and half born. Lindsay
himself suffered from this defective imagination and vision.
The physical and spiritual plasm of America are both in
the making. Lindsay with his excellent thyroid and his
pituitary instability was a budding outgrowth of this life

stream. His education and environment did the rest to make him what he was. But if there is no real America how can we ever win it? Leaving undiscussed now the method it may be said that when America ceases to be many things, and so ends its life of being nothing, and when it becomes one thing, and by that becoming is a union of peoples fused and homogeneous, Lindsay's poems will live to address it, even though the America of the old courthouse passes completely away. It is a good deal to say of any poet that he is for all time. But in that comparative sense in which Herrick and Donne, for example, are for all time, Lindsay too will last. The fact that America is young, that Lindsay lived in the first century of the Nation's career, and interpreted in his peculiar way one of its most luxuriant stages, will fix his historical permanence.

But finally he did sing of an America, real and imaginary, historical and fantastic, worshipping and skylarking, toiling, building, and at games and trade. He was the voice of that mythical America of Colonial heroisms and splendors, which is the imaginative setting of Washington and Jefferson, and of horse-riding and fox-hunting Virginia. The travels of Ulysses over the ancient Greek world, encountering giants, lotos-eaters, enchantresses, and marvels of earth and air, are scarcely more varied and charming, more resplendent and magical than the vision which Lindsay recorded of America. He was the celebrant in free and sinuous measures of Daniel Boone, Johnny Appleseed, and the pioneers of the Appalachians. He sang Andrew Jackson, one of America's priceless possessions, into a new fame which is bound to mount higher as a matter of heroic lore as America recedes from the days of men in jeans who fought for a principle, and having won the fight celebrated the victory in dance on the hills, where they poured libations of cider to the spirits of great emancipations from city gods. Lindsay was the bard of the Indian, and the best that we have had; and he chanted the covered wagons, the long trails to California, the tragic transformations of the war between the States, and the ruin of Virginia and its pastoral culture. Lindsay was the comic muse of the Negro, of the amorphous and awkward-footed days of 1889, which soon turned to the agrarian revolt under Bryan. He saw America, and rightly enough, as baseball all through long summer days of white clouds and blue skies. He saw it as the prize ring of John L. Sullivan, as the white tops of the American circus, the only circus of magic in the world. He saw America as movie queens, as transcontinental motoring, and as a race of youthful, dancing sweethearts, crying out the joys of new freedoms as they swarmed over a terrain of mountains, plains and forestry; or swam along the golden coasts of California, radiant in the ecstasies of music and passion. These were the young who inspired his heart, and then broke it when he was no longer young, but still continued to see them pouring ever fresh into new life, while he longed to sing them as he did at first. All this was Lindsay's America. It was a democracy of youth and happiness, strength and hope. It was America at play, highhearted, free, and just, with all wrongs ended in the name of Jefferson, and the great heroes like Milton, men of vision and music. This motley America, so noisy, so irrational, and so confused, was well reflected by Lindsay's mind, whose nature partook of the things his imagination pictured for it. He was in truth the lame boy, whose fairy was "the shoes of song, the wings of rhyme." How little of the scholar he was, the man of conscious artistry, the precious jeweler of verse! How much the man who believed, who loved, who felt, whose character and moral fervor were his style, that style in truth which cannot be learned, but is bestowed at birth by the good fairy, even upon lame boys! His style was his love of America, and this was his wonderland too. But above that were his dreams about America and his city. And at last only "the ships of love" could take him back to peace after his hopes passed with the dying away of his youth. How American he was in one of the most definite senses in which that characterization can be used! The land he sang can be lost, because in so many fundamental, even phenomenal senses, it never existed. But the song he sang, and by which he created a land and a State, belongs at least to the history of literature.

THE END

INDEX

INDEX

INDEX

INDEX